INET 10⁰⁰
1ST Edition

GIVING CANADA A LITERARY HISTORY

GIVING CANADA
A LITERARY HISTORY

A Memoir by Carl F. Klinck

Edited with an Introduction by Sandra Djwa

CARLETON UNIVERSITY PRESS
FOR THE
UNIVERSITY OF WESTERN ONTARIO
1991

Copyright © 1991 Sandra Djwa and the Estate of Carl Klinck

ALL RIGHTS RESERVED
The use of any part of this publication reproduced, transmittted in any form or by any means, electronic, mechanical photocopying, recording, or otherwise, or stored in a retrieval system, without the prior consent of the publisher is an infringement of the copyright law

Canadian Cataloguing in Publication Data
Klinck, Carl F., 1908-1990
Giving Canada a literary history

Includes bibliographical references and index.
ISBN 0-88629-162-3

1. Klinck, Carl F., 1908-1990. 2. Canadian literature (English)--History and criticism. 3. Literary historians--Canada--Biography. I. Djwa, Sandra, 1939- II. Title

PS8025   C810.9'00092   C91-090486-3

Printed in Canada

CONTENTS

Acknowledgements		vii
Introduction		ix
1	Early Years: 1908-28	1
2	Columbia and Toronto	11
3	Waterloo and Europe	21
4	Wilfred Campbell	29
5	Laying the Foundations	43
6	Research into the Literature of the Canadas	59
7	*Canadian Anthology*	87
8	*Literary History of Canada*	103
9	Canadian Writers and the New Canadian Library	141
10	Later Research	163
11	The 1970s and Retirement	197
Afterword		211
Bibliography		213
Index		217

Acknowledgements

I wish to thank John E. Brent, through whose generous support this book is published by Carleton University Press for the University of Western Ontario. This record of Carl Klinck's scholarship was brought to publication through the kind offices of Alan Somerset, Chair of the Department of English at Western. Above all, I would like to thank Margaret Klinck for her continued encouragement .

A number of Carl Klinck's friends and associates have helped with the developing of this manuscript; notably Wilda Graber who assisted with tape-recording sessions, Pauline Campbell of London, Ontario, who prepared the first type-script, Jean Wilson of the University of British Columbia Press who copy-edited the manuscript in an earlier form, Jane Fredeman of Simon Fraser's Continuing Studies who copy-edited the final manuscript, and Marilyn Flitton, who prepared the index.

Beth Watters and William F.E. Morley read the final manuscript and provided helpful and informed comments. I am especially grateful to John Lutman, Head of Special Collections of The D.B. Weldon Library at Western, through whose efforts we secured uncatalogued copies of letters for proofreading. This manuscript could not have been published without his assistance.

I would also like to thank Gail Bertrand, Marie Stephen, and Helen Takala who checked references, and Anita Mahoney and Ian Munro who typed the final version of the text.

Further editorial work on this manuscript was supported by the Simon Fraser University President's Grant Fund.

Introduction

Carl Frederick Klinck was born on 24 March 1908, in Elmira, Ontario. The Klincks had come from the Palatinate in the 1820s and settled in Canada West, now Ontario. As the second son of dedicated Lutherans who combined piety with good works, Klinck was both energetic and bookish. He soon displayed independence of mind—at first by reading selected books prohibited at the local library (brought home by a tolerant father) and, later, in his twenties, by absorbing some of the anti-clericalism of one of his professors while still retaining a strong religious sensibility. He finished high school at Waterloo College School in 1923-24, and when Waterloo, now Sir Wilfrid Laurier, affiliated with the University of Western Ontario, he stayed on to complete a B.A. in 1928.

His mother, who loved poetry and music, had wanted her son to become a Lutheran pastor or, failing that, at least a missionary. But his missionary work was to take other forms. As he recalls: "When one day in the library, I was writing an essay on Shelley I forgot lunch until I realized it was 4:00 p.m. Then I knew I had to study more English poetry."[1] This young man made a bargain with his parents; he would take a year of theology in 1927-28 at Waterloo Lutheran Evangelical Seminary if they would provide a year's graduate study in English **or history.** When he was halfway through his year of theology, the English instructor at Waterloo College resigned, and a position was offered to Klinck with the stipulation that he obtain his Master's degree in English.

He was directed to the Department of English and Comparative Literature at Columbia University, New York, which he attended in the spring and summer of 1928 and again in the summer of 1929.

There he had the good fortune to be taught by Pelham Edgar, then a visiting professor from the University of Toronto. Edgar helped him to find a "Canadian subject" for his M.A. thesis and introduced him to Lorne Pierce, to E.J. Pratt, and to Charles G.D. Roberts, thus bringing a young provincial from the periphery to the centre of the Canadian literary establishment. In the following pages, in Chapter Two, we catch a glimpse of the graduate student in 1929, visiting Roberts as he began research on his M.A. thesis. As he stood outside the poet's apartment on **Sherbourne Street** in Toronto, he was prepared to be overwhelmed by "greatness." Nonetheless, he wrote down every detail for posterity, including the fact that the sixty-nine-year-old Roberts was still sufficiently agile to scratch a match on the sole of his shoe. Klinck never lost this capacity for observation, his joy in "sleuthing," and his belief that one had to go to the literary "source," whether it was Roberts's apartment or Samuel Hull Wilcocke's prison or Sara Jeanette Duncan's grave.

II

It is difficult for us to visualize what a leap of faith was required to become a student of Canadian literature in 1929. There was no Canadian literature as we know it today. Literature consisted of English literature—the greats of Wordsworth and Tennyson and Arnold. North American literature, chiefly Emerson, Longfellow, and Whitman, was just emerging and Canadian literature was seen as a minor branch of American (H. L. Mencken refers to "our Haliburton" in the pages of the *American Mercury*). For Klinck, the Canadian canon in the twenties consisted chiefly of the Confederation poets with the addition of the moderns, E.J. Pratt and Wilson MacDonald; prose was a lesser field with Thomas Haliburton, Thomas Kirby, and Stephen Leacock.

There were few scholarly tools. The resources at his disposal included a few anthologies, a few books of criticism, and a few biographies. For texts there were Campbell's *Oxford Book of Canadian Verse* (1916-18) and Garvin's *Canadian Poets* (1926). In criticism there was Lorne Pierce's *An Outline of Canadian Literature*(1927) (which Pierce later asked Klinck to update), J.D. Logan and G.D. French's *Highways of Canadian Literature* (1924), Archibald MacMechan's *Headwaters of Canadian Literature* (1924), and Lionel Stevenson's *Appraisals of Canadian Literature* (1926). But there was no comprehensive bibliography of writing in Canada, no representative anthology of poetry and prose for college students, no reprint editions of classic texts, and, above all, no literary history. Thus there was no historical overview of the subject, little reliable periodization, and no easily consulted index of persons, titles, and dates.

That Canadian literature is now an established discipline reflects developments in the field and the fact that many of these deficiencies were remedied by Carl Klinck. It is not generally known that it was Klinck who persuaded the Committee on Commonwealth Studies, an offshoot of the Humanities Research Council of Canada, then chaired by A.S.P. Woodhouse, that what was needed for the study of Canadian literature was a comprehensive bibliography on the lines of the two-volume bio-bibliography on Australian literature then just published. Woodhouse set his student Reginald Watters the task just as he had earlier directed E.K. Brown to write *On Canadian Poetry* (1943). The book became Watters's *Check List of Canadian Literature and Background Materials 1628-1960* (1959). Klinck and Watters jointly edited *Canadian Anthology* (1955), the first text of poetry and prose to establish a canon for the university teaching of Canadian literature. Klinck supported the development of the New Canadian Library Series in paperback and edited and wrote introductions to five classics. Singlehandedly, he set in motion the working committee that established the *Literary History of Canada* (1965).

Most importantly, as a working biographer and critic, Klinck helped show younger scholars of the 1970s and 1980s what might be done with their literary heritage. In a career that spanned four decades he published 22 books, beginning with his doctoral dissertation, *William Wilfred Campbell: A Study in Late Provincial Victorianism*, 1943, and followed by *Edwin J. Pratt: The Man and His Poetry*, 1947 (co-authored with Henry W. Wells), *Canadian Anthology*, 1955 (co-edited with R.E. Watters), *William "Tiger" Dunlop: "Blackwoodian Backwoodsman,"* 1958, *Tecumseh: Fact and Fiction in Early Records*, 1961, *Canadian Writers / Ecrivains Canadien*, 1964 (co-edited with Guy Sylvestre and Brandon Conron), *The Journal of Major John Norton*, 1970 (edited with introductions and notes by Carl F. Klinck and James J. Talman), and a biography, *Robert W. Service*, 1976.

To read through *Giving Canada a Literary History*, especially the chapters which detail his struggles to write a thesis on a Canadian topic, to research a book on a Confederation poet, to prepare an anthology for class use, and, finally, to bring together a team to write a literary history of Canada is to recognize not only that Klinck was a literary pioneer but also that the task he undertook was enormous. His own projects are a history of the development of Canadian literature since 1924. That he is now recognized as Canada's foremost literary historian is because his studies in bibliography, biography, and textual criticism established the norms for the study of Canadian literature in a comparative, historical, and cultural context. In recognition of these accomplishments he was elected a member of the Royal Society of Canada in 1961, made an Officer of the Order of Canada in 1973, and awarded the Lorne Pierce Medal for his contributions to Canadian literature in 1978.

Years earlier Pierce had told a much younger Klinck that some day he would receive this award. As this remark implies, Klinck was a bridge between the older generation in Canadian letters, in particular, Roberts, Pierce, Edgar, and Pratt, and the younger poets and critics of the 1930s and 1940s, A.J.M. Smith, Northrop Frye, Roy Daniells, Reg Watters, and Desmond Pacey. Both groups were Klinck's near contemporaries, and they appear in the following pages because all shared his determination to "give Canada a literary history." In one sense his reminiscences are addressed to these colleagues who shared his literary struggles, his high aims, and, more often than not, his modest self-effacing tone, a tone that we should not mistake for any lack of awareness about the significance of his endeavours.

However, there is another sense in which his comments are meant to be overheard by a still younger generation—the bright young "sleuthers" whom he addresses at several points in the narrative. It is with this audience in mind that he documents the process of literary discovery, pointing out biographical or critical facts that he might have missed, candidly admitting his successes and failures. He wants to establish this next generation on the right track, "digging," as he says in his favourite phrase, "for the facts" of Canadian literary history.

To his successors he leaves a carton of papers on Wilcocke, editor of *The Scribbler*; the titles of a number of manuscripts that have been lost over the years, including the Mohawk translation of "The Lady of the Lake"; and some intriguing puzzles to be solved. Was it Edmund Ward, Sir Frances Forbes, or John Lambert who hid behind the pseudonym Jeremy Cockloft the Elder when he published *Cursory Observations Made in Quebec Province of Lower Canada, in the year*

1811? Above all, he leaves this memoir, a record of his quest for the texts, personalities, and contexts of a Canadian literature.

III

For Lorne Pierce the nationalist desire to support a Canadian literature (and so advance the cause of a Canadian nation) was a defensible scholarly pursuit. Klinck's generation found it more difficult to yoke together nationalism and literature. Although many felt a strong sense of the new Canadian nationality in the early twenties, post-war revisionism soon brought this sentiment into disrepute as the cause of World War I. To complicate matters, nationalism was associated with chauvinism by the *avant garde*, as in F.R. Scott's satire, "The Canadian Authors Meet" (1927). Unfortunately for the cause of a Canadian literature, Canadian nationalism became suspect just as the discipline was developing. To be sure, many of the younger critics retained a vestigal nationalism, rather like an appendix, but it was severely conditioned by the fact that all had received graduate training outside the country. Many, like Smith, brought international standards of literary taste to a national literature still in the process of development.

Because Canadian literature was not yet established, scholars between 1930 and 1965 combined the serious study of one of the major branches of English literature on the right hand with a general interest in Canadian literature on the left. Smith, for example, studied the seventeenth-century Anglican poets, Daniells took Milton as his subject, and Watters surveyed American literature. Klinck was unique in that he began the study of Canadian literature with his M.A. and persisted to the Ph.D. "without surrendering to 'American,' " despite strong pressure from his supervisor. He was convinced that Canada had a literature worthy of study. Unlike the work of his contemporaries, all of his scholarship was devoted to the study of Canadian literature albeit within the comparative context of English and American literature.

Klinck was also unusual in that he began his graduate studies as an outsider to the Canadian literary and cultural establishment. Most of the younger critics had taken their undergraduate training at the University of Toronto where they had been influenced by one or more influential professors, notably Pelham Edgar, head of English at Victoria College, and A.S.P. Woodhouse, head of English at University College. Edgar had taught Pierce, Pratt, and Frye;

Woodhouse taught Frye, Daniells, and Watters. Then too, unlike his contemporaries, Klinck was not English or Scottish; he was not a Methodist like Pierce, an Anglican like F.R. Scott, or a Presbyterian like Robertson Davies. German in origin, an Evangelical Lutheran in religion, and a graduate of the little-known Waterloo College, he was sensitive to these differences.

As a beginning graduate student he was, he says, "conscious of a lack of sophistication, [my] rather small stature 5'7, 146 pounds, irritated by the arrogance of my inferiors in intelligence and learning, I was modestly stubborn about facts and contemptuous of unsupported absurdity." Nonetheless, he had a good sense of his own worth and capacities; in time, he developed what he considered an appropriate persona. He wished "to have the sophistication of a professional teacher and critic who could handle literary jargon so smoothly and (apparently) so learnedly. [But] being a small college man, I settled for a simpler unaffected diction which relied on demonstration, quotation, and examples."[2] His gentle and mild demeanour and his courtesy and flexibility masked, but did not disguise, great integrity and determination.

His literary memoirs are given in a biographical frame because, as he writes elsewhere, autobiography provides "a humanization of the process of discovery. For me the opening [of] doors of high literary consequence to Canada, seeking for understanding while I was something of a rebel against [the] established literary authority of my time, is the very centre of my story."[3]

IV

Klinck became the principal architect of the new, systematic, historically based scholarship that emerged in Canada in the early sixties. He was well equipped for the task for although he shared the nationalist impulse documented in the *Canadian Forum* debates of the twenties, the desire to prove the existence of a Canadian literature, this zeal was tempered by critical caution. As a graduate of Columbia with extensive training in Comparative Literature, he had acquired the new tools of historical literary scholarship. He was a student of Henry Wells, a fine comparativist, and of Ralph Leslie Rusk, the bibliographer whose text, *Literature in the Middle Western Frontier* (1925), helped to chart the emerging discipline of American literature.

Klinck's M.A. thesis at Columbia was entitled "Formative Influences on the '1860 Group' of Poets." He says in the preface that he wanted to find "the facts" regarding "the formative influences" upon the poetry of what we now know of as the Confederation group. Klinck found nature to be of the greatest influence, and in some of the poems he discovered "a real Canadian spirit, different from the spirit of any other land."[4] He finished his thesis promptly in 1929, but there was a ten-year hiatus betweeen his M.A. degree and the completion of his Ph.D. During these depression years he continued to teach full-time at Waterloo College and learned the fundamental tools of literary history, especially archival research. When he married Margaret Witzel in 1934, he gained a supportive and intelligent colleague as well as a wife. In 1937, supported by a windfall of salary payments delayed by the depression, they began a series of literary expeditions that took both of them across the Atlantic several dozen times to study the English and European contexts of Canadian writing.

During the thirties Klinck was also writing his doctoral dissertation. He wished to write on William Wilfred Campbell alone, but his Ph.D. supervisor, Professor Rusk, wanted the dissertation to cover all *belles lettres* in the post-Confederation period. This Klinck refused to do. He felt that the area was largely uncharted and that the study of one representative figure in depth would be of greater value. He recalls, Rusk's "attitude to anything but American—and my stubbornness in this matter—caused a delay in completion of my thesis until the end of the decade, when I was rescued by Professors Henry Wells and Emery Neff, who 'found' my proposals to belong to 'late Victorian.' " This late Victorian designation was appropriate as it was the Victorian aspects of Campbell's poetry—the late romantic lyricism, the love of nature, and the crisis of belief—that most appealed to Klinck. His dissertation, *William Wilfred Campbell: A Study in Late Provincial Victorianism*, was published in 1943 through Pierce at Ryerson Press.

It was also during these years when Klinck began his mission to refute Roy Palmer Baker. A Harvard graduate, Baker had published a doctoral thesis *A History of English Canadian Literature to Confederation* (1921) in which he referred to "the intellectual sterility of Ontario."[5] This he attributed to the quality of Ontario's pioneers. For Klinck, the grandson of immigrants who had settled Canada West, this phrase rankled: he determined to prove Baker wrong. His first call for literary "fact-finding" was a talk, "Salvaging Our Literary Past," given to members of the Ontario Library Association in 1943.

> You will feel the glow of pioneering....You will do something even more significant in helping to discover the meaning of "Canadianism."...Consider...what is unique about Canada? What distinguishes Canadianism from any other sort of national "-ism"? In short, who are we? What are we?...Our national soul is hidden within us, in what we are, in our expression of ourselves, in our literature.[6]

As he recalls, Baker's "aspersion to Ontario bothered me for many years and caused me to collect evidence to the contrary. In fact, it gave me a program: finding, sorting, and presenting the real bulk of the early literature, not only of Ontario, but of the English in Quebec." One could argue that much of Klinck's academic work—his studies of John Richardson, John Norton, John Galt, and William Dunlop, and his edition of *Belinda*—developed from this beloved geography. Especially in the *Literary History of Canada*, he reserved Ontario for himself: "I have chosen the least explored and most controversial field—the pre-Confederation literature of Ontario and Quebec—also the field of greatest opportunities. I wish to recreate a picture of our basic literary activity."

His next sustained academic work was *Edwin J. Pratt: The Man and His Poetry*, which he wrote in collaboration with Henry W. Wells. Klinck wrote a biographical essay relating Pratt to his Elizabethan predecessors in Newfoundland and charted the development of his poetry from an early romanticism to a later modernism. This book established Klinck as a critic and laid the foundations for his academic future. In 1947 when he resigned from Waterloo College on a question of principle—he could not reconcile an overly fundamental Lutheranism with his vision of a liberal Christian education—he was promptly hired by Arthur Jewitt, the head of the English Department at the University of Western Ontario who knew his book on Pratt. In the following year Klinck became a Full Professor and Chairman of the English Department, a post he was to retain until 1955.

It was at the University of Western Ontario that Klinck was to undertake his most important work in Canadian literature. Between 1947 and his retirement in 1973 he instituted courses, built up the library, and, most importantly, taught several generations of scholars and writers, including Carl Ballstadt, Mary Markham Brown, Paul

Fleck, William French, Donald Hair, Mary Lu MacDonald, Louis MacKendrick, Hugo MacPherson, Kathleen O'Donnell, and Douglas Spettigue, as well as creative writers such as George Bowering, Don Gutteridge, and Alice Munro. Klinck established Western as a centre for the study of Canadian literature, a tradition continued by the publication of *Canadian Poetry* edited by D.M.R. Bentley of the English Department and by the recent appointment of Frank Davey to the Carl F. Klinck Chair in Canadian literature.

He also began to push back the historical period for writing in what is now Canada. By the mid-1940s Canadian scholars had available for classroom teaching Smith's *The Book of Canadian Poetry* (1943), which demonstrated the existence of a native tradition in poetry dating back to the eighteenth century. But there was no companion text for prose and no combined anthology for teaching the subject as a whole. With Reginald Watters Klinck developed *Canadian Anthology* (1955), a text that also began in the eighteenth century and made it possible to teach Canadian literature from what were then seen as the beginnings.

Some thirty years earlier, Smith had written "Wanted—Canadian Criticism," for the *Canadian Forum* (1928), which called for a "critic-militant"[7] to improve the state of Canadian literature. But, as is self-evident, a genuine criticism requires a firm basis in a developed literature, and painstaking research as well as critical fire. Neither the literature nor the criticism had been established by mid-century. In 1955 when Klinck and Watters were editing *Canadian Anthology*, Watters could still say of Canadian literature: "when the scholarly foundations are still weak or even wholly lacking the only kind of literary judgements possible are impressionistic 'appreciations' or superficial 'evaluative criticism.' " Klinck's Chapter 7, a record of the editing of *Canadian Anthology* sets out the situation in Canadian letters in the mid-1950s and suggests that we have undervalued the importance of Watters as critic and editor. Watters compiled the first extensive bibliography of Canadian literature, made the initial contacts for *Canadian Anthology*, suggested a literary history, and, but for an accident of timing (he was invited to Australia when the editorial committee required an editor), would have been the first editor of *Canadian Literature*.

Klinck's next foray into criticism was *William "Tiger" Dunlop: "Blackwoodian Backwoodsman"*; this was a collection of essays by and about Dunlop, published in 1958. He was attracted to Dunlop because his story showed in detail "how the life and letters of the old world came into the new: the personal experience of transplanting culture, which formal history cannot bring to life, finds imagery and expression in Dunlop, man and writer."[8] In 1961, Klinck published a second edited book, *Tecumseh: Fact and Fiction in Early Records*. As an editor he resisted the temptation to offer his own critical appraisal of Tecumseh but instead collected the principal documents relating to Tecumseh and the War of 1812 in order that students might draw their own conclusions.

During these years, Klinck honed his scholarly skills, continued his forays in research, and enjoyed a happy personal life. His wife Margaret, who continued to accompany him on forays in search of Major John Norton, Sara Jeanette Duncan, and Robert Service, became a contributing colleague in his work. He was increasingly proud of his son David, who studied both English and history and later kept the Klinck name prominent in western Ontario by becoming head of the Department of History at the University of Windsor.

V

From the mid-1950s to the mid-1960s, Klinck was absorbed in planning his most important book, the *Literary History of Canada*. As he recounts, this project began one morning in 1956 after a meeting of the English Institute at Columbia addressed by Northrop Frye on "Lexis and Melos." Frye's paper prompted Klinck to ask, "Do you think that we could have a literary history of our own?" Several events had led to this question. *A Literary History of the United States*, edited by Spiller, Thorp, *et al.*, had been published by 1948. Secondly, Watters's essential bibliographic inventory of Canadian literature was then underway.

As Klinck knew, once a bibliography was underway, a literary history could follow. The problem was one of literary standards. He recalls that he said to Frye: "Can Canadian literature could be tested against international standards? Norrie replied, in effect, 'Of course, why not?' He added, 'First of all, there must be a great deal of research in basic facts.' This was precisely what I wanted to hear." Klinck needed Frye's theoretical advice and his academic prestige. In his first letter enlisting Frye's support on 20 November 1956 he was quite frank about his aims, "I turn to you in the hope that you can see in it a service to Canada which only you can perform."

It is difficult to determine whether Klinck's primary concern with evaluation influenced the content of the paper Frye was then beginning to write, "Preface to an Uncollected Anthology" (1957). In this essay Frye addresses the problem of value as it relates to Canadian literature, remarking that the Canadian literary critic takes up an uneasy position between the social scientist who has no questions of value to consider and the ordinary literary critic who considers nothing else. He also characterizes Canada as an "environment" that presented particular problems for the creative imagination. After an early 1960s meeting of the *Literary History* committee Klinck appropriated the latter term for his own use, interpreting "environment" as the place in which nationalities mingled and literary events occurred. Thus he was able to use both of Frye's formulations when establishing the contexts for the *Literary History of Canada*.

Some thirty years later, recollecting their first meeting at the English Institute, Frye characterized Klinck in the following manner:

> Yes. Well, at that time of course, I took to him so strongly—I thought here's a man who really cares about his subject. And after all that posturing and general nonsense that goes on at conferences and English Institutes and things, it was a very refreshing change to have him get so intense and white-eyed and his nose turning pink and so on. He was talking about the possibility of doing something about Canadian literature and I thought, "This guy has the guts to carry through what he starts." I've never lost that kind of affection and respect for him. Again, he cultivates a mask—he gave the impression of being much more innocuous than, in fact, he was. I knew that there was quite a strong will under there. That's why I was quite happy about joining his committee and then having him direct things.[9]

Klinck did direct the *Literary History of Canada* with a firm hand. In Chapter Eight he gives a sense of the individuals, the process, and the problems involved. Throughout his academic life he had taken pleasure in being "something of a rebel" in his determination to explore Canadian literature rather than the greener pastures of English and American literature. Often, and sometimes at his own university, he was obliged to respond to allegations that Canadian literature was not a viable subject. He knew that a great deal of "digging" in the early historical periods would have to be done before such arguments could be countered. His rationale was blunt: "If we do not launch out from a studied knowledge of ourselves and our own ways, no one else will."

Because writing in what is now Canada covered a vast field stretching back to the seventeenth century and because the method had been successfully employed by the American scholars who had produced the *Literary History of the United States*, he advocated the group method of research. The "historical spade-work" had to be done by a number of people "so that maximum results may be obtained in our generation."[10] Moreover, what he wanted was not a history of literature but rather a literary history. Literary history as he defined it was a history of "human experience as literary works have expressed it."[11] Finally, he refused to establish a formula for individual chapters and insisted that when contributors did basic research, the book would take its own shape.

Throughout the decade in which the *Literary History* developed Klinck fielded very stiff criticism, some of which is reflected in this memoir. There were criticisms from Donald Creighton, who felt that a literary history must be written by one man to ensure unity; there was pressure from George Brown and Marsh Jeanneret, editor of the University of Toronto Press, to include Quebec literature, and there were letters from Roy Daniells who preferred literary value judgements to what he described as the "historico-informative concept." Throughout this controversy Klinck stuck both to his principles and his courtesy: yes, he was sure that his correspondents knew far better than he; yes, he was convinced that their comments were motivated by a desire to improve the manuscript; but no, he did not think he could change his views. He believed that the team method of scholarly investigation was essential for Canadian literature at that time. With the benefit of hindsight, we applaud his prescience. Indeed, if there is any danger in English Canadian literary studies at the present, it is perhaps that criticism has leapt from the 1920s concern with historical inventory to the frequently anti-historical bias of the 1980s without having first completed the task which Klinck initiated.

In the spring of 1965, with the task behind him and the *Literary History of Canada* just published, Klinck took a rare moment for summary and modest self-congratulation when describing the project to a group of graduate students at the University of Leeds. The book had taken seven years, occupied the spare time of thirty-five editors and contributors, and resulted in 900 tightly-packed pages: "One is left with a dangerous sense of achievement—the feeling that there must xxi—Introduction

have been something worth writing about."[12] Klinck saw a second edition of the *Literary History of Canada* through the press in 1976 and had the great pleasure in 1990 of seeing the third edition, edited by William H. New, dedicated to him.

His great achievements in literary and cultural history are perhaps best summarized by Klinck himself in a letter to Dr. Edward Hall, President of Western, in which he attempted to set out a rationale for his own research and for Canadian literature.

> The basic fact is that Canadians have been writing for nearly two hundred years, and that the tools for systematic study of the subject are still incomplete. I have tried to be one of the pioneers....But I should rather put it this way. If one could think back upon Canadian <u>history</u> as a subject without status, without trained personnel, and without tools for research, one could see the position of Canadian <u>literature</u> at the end of the last war. Since then I have attempted to give leadership in establishing library holdings; an anthology (from which I receive no royalties); a consequent increase in such courses in other universities (over twenty of them now); connections with other commonwealth literatures; graduate courses in the subject; and finally a <u>Literary History of Canada</u>. The new areas to which critics believe I am pointing the way are Anglo-British literary relations; pre-Confederation literary activities; clues to social and intellectual history resulting from literary interpretation; and, in general, systematic study of our own literature because it means something seriously to Canadians. In short, I wish to perform a patriotic duty of which I believe I am capable, as a teacher and literary historian—happily, in this university, as both at once—for the good of a cause and the good of my students.[13]

A few years before his death on 22 October 1990, Carl Klinck wrote a few bibliographical notes to supplement this memoir. One of his comments included the following speculation: "The life of a scholar is a good life, if he can flourish in opportune times. What would have happened over the years if I had been born a decade earlier?"[14] The question is an apt one. If he had been born in 1898 he might have been a late Victorian like his good friends and mentors, Pierce and Pratt. Because his scholarly career began in the twenties, he returned to Canada from graduate study in the United States equipped with the new modernist historical criticism. A man of vision and dedication, he was the right man in the right place at the right time: one equipped by character, by circumstances, and by training to change the direction of Canadian literary scholarship.

VI

The idea of writing a book describing his scholary activities came about in the late-1970s as the result of a visit to Carl Klinck at his home in London, Ontario. He had retired from active teaching, had undergone a series of operations, and had no literary projects at hand. As there was no written account of how the *Literary History of Canada* came into being, and as questions of his family background and his past life were very much in his mind, I urged him to sit down with a tape-recorder to make a general record of these important years that could later be fleshed out with reference to his papers. The project began with Carl Klinck recording some biographical information, which he sent to me for typing and which I returned to him with further questions.

As it was apparent that he would need assistance if he were to continue with his work, in 1979-80 we drafted an application to the SSHRC requesting funds for a tape-recorder and a typist. When the project was approved, we listed a number of literary topics and grouped them under decades. He then began to record sketches of his research on specific authors with reference to his papers. Very early in the project he found that he needed the stimulus of a listener. Wilda Graber, a former student and a family friend who had long believed that he should undertake his memoirs, came to listen and ask questions as he spoke on various topics during taping sessions. The tapes were then typed by a former secretary at Western, Pauline Campbell, and together we assembled chapters into a rough draft manuscript.

This manuscript was then twice reordered after further discussion between Carl Klinck and myself. As we soon discovered, the problem with oral discourse is that it is both choppy and repetitive. Even when chapters are delineated by topic and decade, the same individuals, books, and snippets of literary history recur. Moreover, literary conversation produces a very different text from the written account.

He once remarked ruefully of the finished manuscript that it was not "vintage Klinck." He was also concerned that the first three chapters were overly biographical in nature and asked that these be abbreviated. Finally, there were subjects he did not feel comfortable addressing personally—his differences of opinion regarding the nature of *Literary History*, for example. To remedy these problems he proposed that I edit and rewrite the text in whole or in part as required, and to assist me with this task he prepared some biographical notes.

I have edited substantially and revised the text as a whole for chronological consistency, for unity, and for repetition. The first three chapters have been abbreviated. The manuscript has also been revised for clarity, and where possible dates, titles, and citations have been corrected. Several years ago when I was considering the nature of the editing process I discussed the text with Northrop Frye, who commented of the original manuscript that it was "fundamentally a catching of Carl's own tone...that proverbially mild and gentle tone, and it seems to me that if you dug into archives and did a kind of history of what exactly was going on behind the scenes it would be an excellent study in its own right, but it would have an almost schizophrenic relationship to Carl's memoirs."[15]

Consequently, I have refrained from substantial interpolation because doing so would conflict with the real purpose of the book, which is the gathering together of Klinck's own comments on Canadian literature in his own voice, both as a record of his progress in the field and as a guide to younger scholars. Instead, I have revised and edited and provided a context for his work in Canadian literature through this Introduction.

The final assembly of the manuscript took place shortly after Carl Klinck's death in October, 1990. His papers had already been deposited at the University of Western Ontario, but he had removed the letters he quoted from while he was dictating his reminicences, and not all of them were returned to their proper location. Through the heroic efforts of John Lutman, Head of Special Collections at The D.B. Weldon Library, at the University of Western Ontario, the majority were retrieved and made available to us for checking.

Sandra Djwa
Simon Fraser University

NOTES

1. Biographical Notes, "Waterloo College 1924-27," p. 7.
2. Biographical Notes, "The Crucial Decision," p. 4.
3. Biographical Notes, "For Consideration," p. 2.
4. Carl F. Klinck, "Formative Influences upon the '1860 Group' of Canadian Poets," M.A. Thesis, 1 November 1929, pp. 128-9.
5. Ray Palmer Baker, *A History of English-Canadian Literature to the Confederation: Its Relation to the Literature of Great Britain and the United States* (Cambridge: Harvard University Press, 1921), p. 22.
6. "Salvaging Our Literary Past," *Ontario Library Review* (August 1943), p. 341.
7. A.J.M. Smith, "Wanted—Canadian Criticism," *The Canadian Forum* (May 1928), p. 601.
8. Carl F. Klinck, ed. *William "Tiger" Dunlop: "Blackwoodian Backwoodsman"* (Toronto: The Ryerson Press, 1958), p. ix.
9. Discussion with Northrop Frye, 9 September 1988.
10. Carl F. Klinck to Northrop Frye, 20 November 1956, p. 1.
11. Robert E. Spiller to Carl F. Klinck, 11 February 1958, p. 2.
12. Carl F. Klinck. Notes for a lecture delivered to the English Graduate Seminar of Commonwealth Students at the University of Leeds, 3 March 1965, p. 3.
13. Carl F. Klinck to Edward Hall, May 12, 1960, p. 1.
14. Biographical Notes, "Growing up, British Canadian in War-Time in a Village in South Western Ontario, 1908-22," p. 23.
15. Discussion with Frye, 1988.

CHAPTER ONE

Early Years: 1908-29

I was born on 24 March 1908, the second son of John and Anna Klinck, in Elmira, a farming centre in Waterloo County in southwestern Ontario. The village was surrounded by farms founded by people of Dutch Mennonite, western German, Alsatian, and Scottish stock. About two thousand people lived in Elmira, where there were a few large houses, many substantial middle-sized ones, and many more smaller ones on the sidestreets, a half-dozen churches, several blocks of stores along Arthur Street, two railway stations, and several large factories producing furniture and shoes.

Our house was a tall white-brick one, situated at 91 Arthur Street, away from the business section and opposite a well-kept park where there were trees and a bandstand. We were not recent immigrants. Nicholas Klinck, my great-grandfather, and Adam, my grandfather, then about twenty years of age, had left the Palatinate (western Bavaria) in the early 1850s to settle in Elmira. My maternal grandfather had also come from southern Germany, and my paternal grandmother and her family had left northern Germany and settled in Bruce County, Ontario, in the early 1860s. All these families were in Canada West before Confederation and belonged to a kind of establishment when new groups of immigrants arrived after the First World War. My father was born in 1874 on his father's farm near Elmira; my mother was born on a farm seventy-five miles north of Elmira, in Carrick Township.

My father had been pressed into the pattern of immigrants. His father, who had come to Canada as a carpenter, had become a farmer. For young men of the next generation a move was difficult, especially if they were members of large families. Although he wanted to go to university, there was no money for him to pursue a professional career. He escaped the farm to a clerk's job in hardware stores in Nebraska and Hanover (both Ontario towns). In 1904, after his marriage, he returned to Elmira to start a hardware store, Klinck and Ahrens.

He preferred practical matters to office work, and he was very successful in winning customers by his integrity, good judgment, skill in mechanical procedures, and unusual ability in effecting repairs. The Mennonite people especially appreciated him and brought their problems to him. The poor of the village found in him a friend and blessed him for his practical help and generosity. I was always impressed by the gentleness of my tall, strong father. Not quite six feet in height, he was muscular rather than stout; his arms and hands were powerful. His face was composed rather than expressive. He liked hard facts and reasonable conclusions. He never judged my actions, proposals, or desires without listening to explanations.

He was always willing to work. For example, he helped to build St. James Lutheran Church and, also, as secretary of the high school board, the central building that still stands. Unwilling to be a mere overseer of construction, he gave physical assistance when it was needed. For these services he neither desired nor obtained credit. Election to official positions never interested him. My father's long hours at work limited his time at home. In those days store hours in Elmira were subject to customers' whims, and opening in the evening was not unusual. On Saturday nights even people who lingered until near midnight received attention.

My mother had little social life, for she had no desire to join the "society" of the village. What she dreamt of having was the home life of the vivacious and musically inclined brothers and sisters that she had known in her youth; relatives and associates of my father's did not provide an adequate substitute. She did what she could to brighten her home, with a garden and flowers outdoors and books and a piano in the living room, and nursed her dreams with indomitable courage. When I was old enough, I was sent to a lady with pudgy hands to take piano lessons—with few artistic results. She was as emotional as my father was composed. I remember her tears and laughter and, above all, her open affection for us. I think I owe my sensitivity to her. She adored my father and centred her life in him and her children. But she felt that it was her duty to make out of me, a bookworm, a suitable candidate for the ministry or for missionary work in foreign fields.

She could be resolute. If she gave way to sympathy as the higher good, she kept her convictions and trotted them out on later occasions.

I began my schooling at the public school at the far end of town, no doubt led through the streets at first by Jack, my older brother. Our teachers were Scots, and I remember enough of the First World War to realize that the Canadian-British influence was strong and that we were small flag-wavers. My brother and I and our friends played "soldiers" with wooden guns of our own manufacture; we longed for uniforms.

Claims of German ancestry were unpopular in Ontario; during the war it would have been useless to argue that neither our parents nor our Canadian ancestors had personal knowledge of the Germany of Bismarck or the kaiser. At school we sang hymns of the British Empire, but at church there was not the same patriotic fervour, for the pastors in our Lutheran congregation evidently had been imported from the neutral United States or from Germany. They were tenaciously foreign and opposed to services in English. Projects such as Saturday classes in German script and vocabulary were imposed on my brother, myself, and some of our friends. When my father and some others demanded services in English, the pastor made a few feeble efforts to deliver English sermons. My parents sympathized with me in the rebellion I stirred up at home and allowed me to drop the Saturday classes and the Sunday School. Our family then attended services in churches of other denominations in the village. Finally, as I grew older, we drove to Kitchener to attend the First English Lutheran Church.

I now think of my encounter with German as an asset. I never became bilingual, but I later became interested in comparative literature and I always remembered many rhythms from Luther's translation of the German Bible. More importantly, my faith remained grounded in Lutheranism, a liturgical form of worship similar to the Anglican, to which I have now been attached for many years. I was never Calvinistic, evangelistic, separatist, or prohibitionist.

I still recall the pleasure of making my first letters on a slate and on paper; and under the care of my mother, I soon learned to read. When I tired of Peter Rabbit and his friends, I read on through boy scout fiction to adventures in the Canadian West as they appeared in the romances of Ralph Connor, James Oliver Curwood, and others, such as Zane Grey. As I became a reader, learning from newspapers, magazines, and books was part of my family life. During the war there were many pictures and stories of Canadian and British soldiers. We often had copies of the *London Illustrated* and the *National Geographic* as well as, occasionally, *Boy's Own* and similar juvenile literature. I learned to be critical by comparing this material with the dull Sunday School handouts that were still lying around the house.

I was happy with my schoolmates, but by my early teens, I began to have independent opinions and I took sides readily. I recognized the tolerance of my parents, who must have wondered why I was so different from my brother Jack. I was less handsome and amenable; in fact, small, shy, rather stubborn, alert but bookish. They were strict in ways that mattered but inclined to respect individuality. My mother, who was a keen reader, found me interested in her scrapbook of sentimental poems. My father, a member of the local library board, occasionally brought home books that had been challenged as unfit for readers; he was merely amused when I read through his collection.

It was to my mother that I owed my childhood vacations. In particular I remember going with her on nostalgic visits to her parents in Elmwood, a hamlet and railway stopping point where my brother and I studied locomotives, trainmen, and freight cars. Grandfather's pony was also an attraction. In my teens mother arranged summer weeks at Sauble Beach on Lake Huron. Soon I also pursued my love of fresh air and exercise at YMCA camps near Kitchener and, very happily, at a leaders' camp on Beausoleil Island in Georgian Bay.

I passed the high school entrance examinations with honours when I was twelve. The next year I entered the pre-secondary program being initiated in Elmira in anticipation of the founding of a high school in the village. After two years there, I enrolled in Waterloo College School, where one heavy year could suffice to qualify for university entrance. This school was a preparatory institution established by the Evangelical Lutheran Seminary, and it was housed on the seminary campus at Waterloo. I began as a day student in 1922. In my time at the school, the College affiliated with the University of Western Ontario, and I registered for the college/university courses, giving up my application for Honours English and Philosophy at Victoria College in Toronto.

I was able to take part in the life and work at Waterloo and, during good weather, to commute to and from Elmira, sometimes by bicycle. In the winter, I lived in Kitchener with my grandparents or my aunt and uncle. My principal extracurricular activity—other than sports—was editorial work on the new college paper, *The College Cord,* where

I learned about some aspects of journalism the hard way. I had excellent courses in political science and on Canadian history, but I cared little about current politics. My contact with natural sciences came chiefly in the chemistry lab, where as demonstrator I played assistant policeman over dangerous experimenters. In deference to my parents' wishes that I should educate myself for the ministry, I also enrolled in theological options permitted for the degree, Church history to 1500 and New Testament Greek.

In the summer of 1927 I received my B.A. from the University of Western Ontario. Then I bargained with my parents, offering to take one more year of theology if I could thereafter do some postgraduate study in English or history. Consequently, in the autumn of 1927, I registered in the Evangelical Lutheran Seminary at Waterloo, taking Hebrew, New Testament exegesis, liturgics, an introductory course to the Old Testament, Church history, homiletics, and dogmatics.

Anything prosaically literal or dogmatic alienated me, but I enjoyed the chapel services, the rhythms of the Bible, and Greek. What I found most fascinating were textbooks with footnotes and scholarly documentation. These belonged to a world of moral responsibility and knowledge also to be found in secular disciplines, not only in theology. I soon began to question whatever was pontificated and developed a certain self-respect in searching for certified proof.

An opportunity I could not refuse broke up these arrangements at mid-term. The Reverend Nils Willison, an inspiring teacher of English literature, decided to leave the College, and a replacement was required. I was offered the position with the rank of instructor for 1928-29, provided that I would spend the first term of 1928 and the summer session at a graduate school.

Most graduates of my generation who wished to study for advanced degrees in English literature enrolled at major universities in England or the United States. A Ph.D. was offered at the University of Toronto, but the English department there accepted very few candidates without the entrance requirements of a B.A. Honours degree and a Toronto M.A.

My parents temporarily waived their preference for theological studies and generously provided money to support me at Columbia University in New York City. Dean Alex O. Potter of Waterloo College, who had suggested my applying to Columbia, also nominated me for residence at International House there. I was then nineteen years of age, and on my arrival in February 1928 I knew no one in New York.

My world was opening up. I was thrilled by my journey through New York State and along the beautiful Hudson River to the great city, where the George Washington Bridge had not yet been built. The train journey there on the New York Central always fascinated me. I would leave at night and at 6:00 a.m. I would wake up, watch the dawn, and enjoy the hills and mountains on the west side of the Hudson. It was in this summer that I had a closer look at West Point, on its magnificent heights, during an excursion. We were told then that a highway being built nearby had disturbed the organ in the chapel: opposition was aroused and the road was rerouted.

I settled into a private room at International House, scarcely aware of the enjoyment soon to be offered me in informal conversations with graduate students at dinner or in the elegant common room. The six hundred residents were drawn, as a matter of policy, from as many as seventy-five or eighty countries. International House was on Riverside Drive, near Grant's Tomb and across a park from the Riverside Church, where Harry Emerson Fosdick preached. The church like the residence was a benefaction of Mr. and Mrs. John D. Rockefeller. In both institutions idealism and practicality flourished. I lived at International House, not only in the spring and summer of 1928, but also in the summer of 1929, for all of 1930-31, throughout the 1930s whenever I had interviews with professors regarding my thesis, and in the autumn of 1941 when I read for my general orals.

I did miss the chapel services at Waterloo, but I often made up for them by listening to the brilliant and humane Canon Raymond C. Knox at noon in the Columbia chapel. Fosdick, of course, was a revelation to me: he was a great preacher who had been driven out of a neighbouring Baptist church because of his liberalism. I also had models of Christian charity in the Reverend Dr. Frederick J. Oberlander and his sister. Dr. Oberlander held services in a Lutheran church in Greenwich Village and lived nearby in a house that was one room wide and four stories high. They took me in and taught me by example. One day, Dr. Oberlander shook me out of my complacency by taking me on a visit to the Cancer Hospital on the East River. I have never forgotten that experience of poverty and pain.

In my first term at Columbia (February-May 1928) I had graduate courses filling in periods of English literature I had missed, and my parochialism was replaced by a new internationalism as I was treated to lectures by some of the best teachers to be found anywhere. Chaucer was taught by a visiting professor from Holland, Adrian J. Barnouw. He led his class in *enjoying* Chaucer. We studied Shakespeare under another visiting professor, René Feuillerat, of the University of Rennes.

Columbia excelled in teaching English and comparative literature in those years. It also excelled in the number of its distinguished professors. Two of these conducted classes I attended in my first half year. Ernest Hunter Wright was in many ways the most logical and informative lecturer I was ever to know; he taught eighteenth-century English literature. He would come into the room, go straight to the blackboard, and write down a date; 1798, for example, promised discussion of the French Revolution and Wordsworth's *Lyrical Ballads*. The impressionistic treatment of my college classes faded before his authoritative facts and logic. Harry Morgan Ayres' rewarding and delightful sixteenth-century course provided a different kind of experience, reflecting his life interests in language and literature. My fifth course in the 1928 winter session was given by Frank A. Patterson, a Milton scholar.

My personal horizons widened under this thorough review of English literature, my social life with men and women of many lands, ready access to great library collections and the life of the streets, restaurants, and institutions of New York in a time of affluence and gaiety when Broadway was Broadway, great musicians gave recitals, and Babe Ruth was slamming homers. New York, of course, also had many notable visitors. I heard such speakers as Brandon Matthews, a Columbia writer and critic; Admiral Richard Byrd, who had been to the South Pole; and Amelia Earhart, who was to disappear in 1937 on her airplane journey around the world with Frederick J. Noonan.

I was, indeed, in danger of seeing too much of New York's glitter. The first thing I had done when I arrived was to get tickets for Sergei Rachmaninoff's 22 April 1928 concert in Carnegie Hall. I also heard Jascha Heifetz and Fritz Kreisler, and I made early attempts to get tickets to the Metropolitan. I was successful in seeing a special performance in French of *Faust*, *Andre Chenier*, and Edward Johnson's farewell *Carmen*. Other entertainments in the 1928 spring session were lectures by Irish patriots A.E. (George W. Russell) and Lord Dunsany and by Sir Wilfred T. Grenfell on the far North (with motion pictures). Bow-legged, funny Sir Harry Lauder, the Scottish baritone, gave one of his farewell performances.

There were also sports at an intercollegiate indoor track meet in the 168th St. armouries and hockey at Madison Square Gardens, against the Montreal Maroons. Nor did I neglect the theatres or film. Al Jolson's *The Jazz Singer* may have been one of the first movies with "Vitaphone Accompaniment." I saw it at the Roxy Theater, where the whole elaborate prologue was completely "Roxy"—the disappearing grand organ, the jazz band, the chorus, the ballet corps, and the Roxyettes. During the summer session of 1928, I attended musical and dramatic productions mainly in university circles, such as the New York String Quartet and the Washington Square College Players in *Candida* and *Enter Madame*.

Summer was baseball season. I saw my favourite team, the New York Yankees, beat Chicago in the American League. The Yankee line-up was famous for home-run hitters: they performed well for me. During the summer of 1928 I also took advantage of the excursions to Oyster Bay, Washington, and the Washington Irving region, and I also went to Atlantic City, where I had my first happy experience of being up-ended by huge rollers.

I also attended lectures five days a week from 8:30 until 1:30 and read in the library. Since I was to begin teaching at Waterloo College in the autumn of 1928, it was also thought advisable that I should be exposed to some courses in the College of Education, an institution whose graduates (especially its Ph.D.'s in English) found no praise in the University's Department of English. This was a time of great controversy when Edward Lee Thorndike and John Dewey were prophets of a new psychology of teaching. Well armed with prejudices, I decided to know the worst by applying for a course given at the College by one of their bright young professors. Fortunately, I was denied this experience by being far down the list of applicants. Instead, I entered a course taught by one of the old guard, William C. Bagley. He did not man any barricades against the radicals but instead quietly got down to the practice of teaching. His philosophy of teaching spoke for itself. It was good for me in my bewilderment about standing before a class.

In this summer I had my first course in comparative literature, conducted by Frank W. Chandler, Dean of the College of Liberal Arts of Cincinnati, and a prominent authority on the new dramatic literature, its varieties, techniques, aims, and problems, beginning with the later plays of Ibsen and incorporating the art and thought of many other writers for the stage—Scandinavian, German, French, Russian,

Italian, Spanish, and British. Chandler was a pioneer in putting all this together, and for many years his were the standard works on contemporary drama.

My third course was given by Charles Sears Baldwin, Professor of Rhetoric and Composition at Barnard, where he had taught for thirty years. Few teachers have made such a remarkable change in my writing habits. He made the teaching of composition something of value to reasonable people and helped me see that the paragraph was the unit of expression, but that exposition and argument required paragraphs of a type different from the "paragraphs" of description or narration. Unity begins with the reader in mind, and the following paragraphs are arranged, not so much by logic as by what is needed step-by-step to lead the reader to the desired conclusion. Baldwin's book, *Composition, Oral and Written* (1909), became a kind of Bible for me.

I returned to Waterloo in August 1928. In this 1928-29 term, I was the only instructor in English. I had to teach the first-year survey, composition, public speaking, nineteenth century and modern, and even more courses. I managed to keep ahead of my students by hard work and conventional material, except in composition. For composition I triumphantly produced Baldwin to explain expository paragraphing. I insisted upon the use of details, especially images in narrative and description, and advocated the use of supportive detail in argument and exposition. Perhaps I helped along a few writers of fiction by repeating occasionally, "If you want to tell a lie, tell it in detail and it will be believed." I used examples and probably encouraged a number of liars.

In July 1929, Waterloo College acquired a new dean, Willis C. Froats, M.A., whose reputation for efficiency had preceded him. He gave me an "almost final" statement regarding my courses for 1929-30 at $1,700 per annum. By his reckoning that meant sixteen hours of classroom performance! It also meant that I had adopted a secular profession. My mother revised her dreams for my future: the more learned I became, the better missionary I eventually would be.

CHAPTER TWO

Columbia and Toronto

In July 1929 I returned to New York for my second summer session. As always there was lots of music. I heard the Juilliard String Quartet and the Philharmonic Symphony Orchestra, and on Broadway I saw Eddie Cantor's *Whoopee* and Earl Carroll's *Sketch Book* and *Show Girl* at the Ziegfield, with Ruby Keeler, Al Jolson, Lou Clayton, Eddie Jackson, and Jimmy Durante. Once more I watched the Yankees play.

At Columbia I had three courses but only two professors—Hoxie N. Fairchild, lecturing on the Romantic period, and Pelham Edgar, a visiting professor from the University of Toronto, on the later 18th C. and on the Victorian period. Fairchild was soon to become famous for *The Noble Savage* (1928), his book about the cult of the Indian in romantic literature. Fairchild was one of those lecturers whose classrooms were always full of students, both enrolled and visiting. His subject was of great interest to me because Indian history—as much as I could find—was basic to Canadian history and literature.

Pelham Edgar also gave me advice about my M.A. thesis. I wanted a Canadian subject, preferably on the "Canadian," or "Confederation," group of poets. It was great good luck to have a Canadian scholar, highly regarded by his American colleagues and his students, make my project seem at least plausible. In time I had Edgar's prestige on my side, both in Columbia's Department of English and later at the University of Toronto, where a graduate of the small college at Waterloo could not on his own expect even limited acceptance. Edgar was achieving international importance as an authority on the novel. His book, *Henry James, Man and Author,* had been published in 1927, and it was followed by *The Art of the Novel* in 1933.

Fortunately for me his interests were wide and included "Canadian": he had, for example, written a chapter on Canada for the *Cambridge History of English Literature*. Pelham Edgar had been Professor of French at Victoria College in Toronto until 1912, when he became head of the Department of English. As such he belonged to the academic elite of the University of Toronto. He specialized in the literature of England, but he had good friends and colleagues like E.J. "Ned" Pratt who were both professors and creative writers.

Edgar was a man of distinction; he appeared aloof and perhaps austere, but he was actually most friendly. His father was Sir James David Edgar, one of the "twelve apostles" of the "Canada First" group. Edgar senior was Speaker of the House of Commons from 1896 to 1899. He published some patriotic verses in *This Canada of Ours and Other Poems* (1893) and wrote a book of poems, *The White Stone Canoe: A Legend of the Ottawas* (1885).

When I obtained approval for a thesis on "Formative Influences upon the '1860 Group' of Canadian Poets," I began my sleuthing as a researcher and was caught up in the prevailing trend in comparative criticism, the unproductive search for "influences." It often meant that, since Canadians were borrowers, the critical game was to find out what and where they had "lifted" material.

I had little to work with in the way of systematic treatments of Canadian literature. I soon found out there were few helpful books. Lorne Pierce's *An Outline of Canadian Literature* (1927) was the best reference then available, and I should have called the "Group" by his title, the "Canadian School of Poets." John W. Garvin's *Canadian Poets* (1926) revealed a desire to make the poets known through selections of their poems, portraits, and biographical sketches. It could be used by schoolteachers, especially those who had no other way of giving classroom poems background context. Lionel Stevenson's *Appraisals of Canadian Literature* (1926) was admirable, but it was not widely used. Archibald MacMechan's *Headwaters of Canadian Literature* (1924) also contained useful material.

There were a few biographies, such as James Cappon's *Charles G.D. Roberts and the Influences of His Time* (1905), Odell Shepard's *Bliss Carman* (1923), and the gossipy *The Book of Roberts* (1923) by the poet's son, Lloyd Roberts. I found H.D.C. Lee's *Bliss Carman: A Study in Canadian Poetry*, a thesis for the University of Rennes (1913), neglected by Canadians, but excellent, but Norman Guthrie's *Poetry of Archibald Lampman* (1927) was of little use. In July 1929, I received an important letter from Charles G.D. Roberts, probably through Lorne Pierce or Pelham Edgar as an intermediary. Roberts replied to a query regarding "influences":

> For my part, the influences that drove me to creative expression were, at least, four-fold. My father, a keen and understanding lover of poetry, and of all beauty, filled me with his own enthusiasm from earliest childhood. Then, the poets, whom he early taught me to love—Spenser, Milton, Shelley, Keats, Emerson, Tennyson, Poe. (Browning and Wordsworth, Arnold and Swinburne came later).
>
> [B]oth Carman and myself were profoundly influenced by our study of Latin and Greek, of Greek particularly. We both soaked in the Greek poets. Third, love of country,—in a way, in the broadest sense, the beginnings of the national consciousness in the young Confederation of Canada—born when I was seven years old.
>
> To my father also I owe this impulse,—for he had the vision of what Canada should and might become,—he filled me with that vision, till I burned to express Canada.
>
> Fourth,—the beauty and picturesqueness and freshness of the landscapes that surrounded my early years thrilled and inspired me.
>
> In regard to my colleagues of the Group of 1860—all junior (?) to me,—I should say that they were moulded primarily by the Canadian life and landscape, and secondarily by the great masters of English literature whom they studied; and less consciously than myself by the vision of Canada as a new and inspiring political entity. Of course the stirring of the new life in Canada reacted upon them powerfully,—but more or less subconsciously, it seems to me!

This was a ready made outline for my thesis.

I have also preserved a note written in 1929 after meeting with Edgar, Pratt, and Roberts:

> Literary people, real live ones at least, had never played a big part in my life before that morning in 1929. Those who wrote books dwelt on the mountain-tops, it seemed; and I

was surely of the valleys. But here, in Victoria College, this morning I was suddenly plunged into the midst of the Canadian 'literati.'

There was Dr. Pelham Edgar talking to me as if he had plenty of time and Canadians were not eager to listen to his critical estimates of her literary works. There, in the phone-booth, was Dr. E.J. Pratt, whose "The Roosevelt and Antinoe" was soon to appear....And Dr. Edgar was about to make an appointment for me with Charles G.D. Roberts, the Father of Canadian Poetry....

For all that, I felt suddenly very shy when I stood before the door of Roberts' suite in the Ernscliffe Apts. at the corner of Wellesley and Sherbourne Sts. In fact I was prepared to be struck dumb by the sight of greatness. On the contrary, I received a very humane and cordial welcome in the refined and polished manner which I have since found to be habitual with him.

His sixty-nine years seemed to weigh very lightly upon him. True enough, there was his hair, grey though abundant, and something about the lines of the face and mouth that belied the youth of his bearing and manners. And yet this man will never be old, I am sure. His grace of carriage and energy of movement are those of a man twenty-five years younger. Justly proud, as he is, of his fine physique, he is not really a tall or a large man, just of moderate height and of a well-knit frame. Perhaps the most significant thing about his face is the keenness of expression betokening keenness of intellect as well, and the eyes, the eyes of a young man and a poet.

My first impression was the quick realization that I was in the presence of a gentlemen of the older polished school who had at the same time the gift of lasting youth. He wears eyeglasses with a long black cord and they seem to fit with the real distinction of the man. When he lights a match for his cigarette, he scratches it on the sole of his shoe held out before him—not a mean trick of agility....

But I had to take in all this at a glance, because he soon had me talking and feeling at home. I was soon seated in a chair and in the midst of talk about literary matters. He would not sit down. It is useless to wait for him to do so.

He stood up for the whole two hours of my visit. There is nothing old about him. Nothing was left undone to make me comfortable. Cigarettes and wine were produced—I refused the cigarettes.

Bliss Carman had died not so long before. My host was full of the subject. I believe he loved Carman like a brother. Carman had many times come to this very apartment. What conversations they must have had, these two great literary giants of Canada, these two who in so many ways made Canadian literature? I managed to get him talking about days long ago, when Carman used to visit in the land of Evangeline, and when the two of them absorbed the beauties of nature and radiated poetry. But this is many years ago, and it required tactful questions and moments of silent thought on my host's part to recall much of this in detail. Then he spoke of the days in Toronto, of Lampman and of Campbell and others. In answer to questions of mine, he said that there never was any definite school created by the Group of the Sixties to produce Canadian poetry. They just worked side by side, under common inspiration.

He insists very strongly upon the Canadianism of his work. From his father he had caught a great Canadian vision which was to voice itself in his great patriotic poems. He felt himself to be thoroughly and consciously Canadian throughout his work from beginning to end. In his Toronto days, he said, he was connected with the "Canada First" Movement.

We spoke of Logan's book, "Highways of Canadian Literature." I remember mentioning Logan's dispute about Roberts' claim to be in a real sense a Canadian poet. The fervor of the poet substantiated my own impression that Logan was wrong. Then: [we spoke] of Cappon's book on Roberts himself. Roberts believes Cappon to be a very excellent and capable man and critic with regard to poetry, apparently of the less subtle kind. But he was very sceptical as to Cappon's ability to do justice to Carman. Cappon had shown him a sample of the way he intended to go about criticism of Carman by interpreting for Roberts a certain bit of Carman's verse as the essence of Carman's work. (I wish I could now remember the poem). Roberts said that Cappon either had not read all of Carman or had entirely misunderstood him. But to go back to the book on Roberts.

"Cappon has missed the very thing that lies at the heart of what my poetry really is," the poet said.

As tactfully as possible I asked what this was that Cappon had missed, in effect.

"The cosmic sense," was his thought-provoking reply (I thought of...["Kinship"] and of "Resurrection").

We spoke of Wilson MacDonald. Roberts' tribute to him was from the heart.

"He has the lyric cry," he said. "In getting the lyrical line none of us can equal him. But what he does lack is," and here he touched his forehead, "the fundamental brainwork. Now Carman, he was not only an artist but he was a deep thinker as well."

It was difficult to get him to speak of anyone but Carman.

From what Roberts said, it was quite apparent that Wilson MacDonald had never been exactly a favorite friend of Carman. It is true that, one evening when Roberts was out of the city, Carman did spend his time with MacDonald, but they were little more than cordial.

The books in his room were not really numerous, but I would have given much to have even one of them. Perhaps I could have had one for the asking. He told me that his books lent to friends scarcely ever returned. He was very proud of some books by his son and by his brother Theodore Good[ridge] Roberts. The latter, he believed, had written the best memorial poem on Carman. He spoke in glowing terms of the work of Francis Sherman, and showed me a book of his (now very rare). Perhaps Sherman was one of the greatest poetic spirits Canada had produced, he thought.

When I could no longer decently keep him from lunch any longer, I rose to go. He accompanied me to the door, gave me my hat and coat, inquired as to whether I had been carrying a walking stick, opened the door for me, all the while inviting me to come and see him again.

He was kind enough to say that I was a good interviewer. "Not everyone can get me to talk as you have done," he said. Surely the fates were kind to me that morning. At least I "once saw Shelley plain."

However, I was not happy with my completed thesis; it was sketchy, and my style was abominable. Nonetheless, Pelham Edgar, wrote reassuringly on 27 January 1930: "There is material for a full dissertation, and it is rather an advantage than otherwise that some of the group are still living. You might extend your title and call it: 'The Beginnings of Canadian Poetry, with special emphasis on the Group of the Sixties.' Have you seen Roberts's reminiscential article on Carman in the January Dalhousie Review? It is subtle and sound."

My second year of teaching at Waterloo College (1929-30) consisted mainly of hard work, but there were compensations. For example, in the spring of 1930, Roberts visited the College to give a recital, after which there was a reception at the home of Dr. and Mrs. A.J. McGanity (the birthplace of Wilfred Campbell, near the corner of the then Yonge Street and Duke Street in Kitchener).

Despite the Great Depression, which had just begun, fate handed me two delightful surprises that were to affect the rest of my life. I had begun to be depressed, fearing that I might be a junior instructor in a small college forever. Therefore, I took the risk of asking for leave in 1930-31 to study at Columbia and was pleased both to be granted leave and to be assured, upon my return, of a promotion to professor and a salary of $2,000 ($2,200 if I came back with a Ph.D.). My father was generous, ready to supply money, so I began to make plans.

My second surprise came in my Sunday School class of senior high school girls at St. Mark's. I was immediately attracted to one of them, a lovely brown-eyed, brown-haired girl named Margaret. I found her alluring whether she was in repose or warmly smiling. I could not have found words to describe her in my trance-like state; in fact, I could scarcely find words in order to conduct the lesson. After a few days, I remembered that, when we were younger, I had seen this girl playing baseball with the boys on Francis Street, near my grandparents' home. She must still be a good sport! The next Sunday I held to my intention to ask Margaret to go to the movies, and, happily, she agreed. After that she became my friend, and by the time she went into training to become a registered nurse at Toronto General

Hospital—and I went off to New York for another year of advanced study—she was my fiancée.

I did not invite her to share the life of a clergyman, for I had put that behind me, reluctantly because of my parents, but with no feelings of betrayal. Yet my theological studies had not left me without resources important for my life and career. I had laid a basis not only for a commitment to faith and responsibility, but also for a scholarly approach to knowledge. I was becoming a man by questioning authority and demanding diverse opinions. I had the right to choose for myself, not necessarily for others. I could never have preached, but I hoped to teach literature with joy, enthusiasm, and devotion.

When I registered in the autumn of 1930 at Columbia, I was again filling in gaps in my personal coverage of English and comparative literature. My professors were Harry Morgan Ayres for Anglo-Saxon, George Philip Krapp for the history of language, William Witherle Lawrence for medieval literature, Ralph Leslie Rusk for two courses in American literature, and Ernest Hunter Wright for the "comparative" Romantic movement. At this late point in my training, I had not studied any period before that of Chaucer, and even then no Middle English dialects; that is, I had no training in the history of language or in Anglo-Saxon.

These two essential subjects gave me a bad time in 1930-31. It was probably a mistake to enrol in Professor Krapp's course because it consisted almost entirely of the history of English *sounds*. He was near the end of a distinguished career as a philologist and phonologist. He was thus a very old man, and his voice was weak. Sound changes were inaudible in most of the room; only the eager beavers who sat in the first and second rows could distinguish what he was saying. My only clues came from the symbols he put on the board. Once more I would have to be self-taught.

I therefore bought a book on the history of the English language and a detailed book on the history of English sounds and memorized them. Such blanks in basic explanation had happened to me before—in my math courses at college—with disastrous results. Fred Ahrens, from Elmira, was preparing for a Ph.D. in German and, discovering my weakness, instructed me in linguistic basics with explanations and cross-references to English. Indo-European and early Germanic were useful tools for him; I learned about them very slowly.

In Anglo-Saxon I was very much alone, having never been closer to reading Anglo-Saxon than Tennyson's "The Battle of

Brunanburh." The help I was receiving from Krapp and Ahrens was too late as I was plunged into an *advanced* course in Anglo-Saxon. Ayres, although genial, did not make concessions to beginners. Yet because he was a remarkable talker, it was one of the most "cultural" courses I ever attended. Ayres could talk about anything—and he did talk about almost everything *except* Anglo-Saxon.

In Professor Rusk's courses in American literature I felt at home and eager to learn. He was a fair, but hard, man when I tried to obtain approval for a Ph.D. with a thesis in Canadian without surrendering to "American." American literature itself was still being defended as a post-graduate subject, and Rusk was engaged in upgrading the basic materials. His attitude to anything but American—and my stubbornness in this matter—caused a delay in completion of my thesis until the end of the decade, when I was rescued by Professors Henry Wells and Emery Neff, who found my proposals to belong to "late Victorian" and therefore not in Rusk's field at all.

Although I was still unsure where I stood, someone wisely suggested that I select courses from both English and comparative literature. I had some knowledge of European history, but knew nothing of European literatures. By great fortune, I enrolled for Professor Lawrence's course in comparative medieval literature. Like all the best lecturers at Columbia, Lawrence always found his class filled with people who were registered for it and many who had registered for something else. The course was most orderly; one always knew the topic of the day and the reading one should do before and after the lecture. Lawrence's lectures were sane, evocative, and illuminating—a splendid basis for enjoyment and learning.

I consequently became a life-long buff of medieval literature and art and, in particular, a reader in archaeology and romances about King Arthur and his time. Few professors have influenced me as much as Lawrence did, and it was because of his course that I made an effort to meet the Arthurian authority, Roger Sherman Loomis. The Columbia professors I knew were like that: they were leaders in discovery and thought in and beyond their disciplines.

The lectures of Ernest Hunter Wright, from whom I took a course on comparative literature, were models of clarity, criticism, and good judgment. His book, *The Meaning of Rousseau* (1929), was controversial and bold. Such men as Loomis and Wright preserved Columbia's outstanding tradition in scholarship. In the halls, one could sometimes see one of those who had built the tradition in an earlier day. For example, in addition to the courses for which I was registered, I attended a few lectures on aesthetics by Henry W. Wells, who had written a doctoral thesis on *Poetic Imagery Illustrated from Elizabethan Literature.*

Apart from Columbia, New York itself was very attractive in spite of the Depression. I enjoyed meeting learned and inventive minds, hearing fresh ideas, talks by famous people, watching baseball at Yankee Stadium, going to recitals, Broadway plays, and musicals, visiting luxury liners, and the constant view of the Hudson River. In the winter, there were long hikes along the Palisades with the hardy Scandinavians and skating at downtown rinks. But New York was suffering. I had glimpses of other sides of life on the streets.

At Carnegie Hall there was a memorable reading of poetry by India's Rabindranath Tagore, whose subject was "The Meeting of the East and West." His readings were extraordinary for their rhythmical effect. The translator would tell the audience what a certain poem would "be about," then Tagore read the poem in his own language. The predicted "meaning," I felt, was almost fully carried to me by rhythm alone. I never forgot that. Later I heard Professor Neff demonstrate by using a phonograph that each language has its own characteristic and recognizable rhythms, distinguishable from other languages by rhythm alone while words are not understood. He also demonstrated the special rhythm of Romantic, as distinguished from classical, English verse. I thought then of Tagore, and now I think also of Dylan Thomas.

This was a most enjoyable and educational year, enriched by new and old friendships. I was no longer a transient; I felt that I belonged at International House and at Columbia. And it all had a richer meaning as I was conducting an extensive correspondence with Margaret.

CHAPTER THREE

Waterloo and Europe

In the late spring of 1931, I returned to Elmira. I had completed the minimum residence for the Ph.D. as well as all my language tests except Latin. My summer's task would be reading a book of medieval Latin between periods of leisure and tennis. I had no way of knowing that it would be over a decade before I completed my dissertation.

At Waterloo College I took up the heavy program of teaching Dean Froats had outlined for me; I was well supported by Eleanor Doherty, who had taken my place during my year of absence. Together we improved what Waterloo had to offer its students, and by the beginning of 1932-33 we were offering first-, second-, and some third-year courses in honours that matched courses given for general arts. There were only a handful of students and, therefore, opportunities for intensive study of texts and "refreshers" for the instructor.

I lived in the college dormitory that autumn and winter, but I had many pleasant times at home and much use of the family car. This vehicle was also vital for my courtship, for writing letters to Margaret gave way to long drives to Toronto every two weeks or so until she finished her course early in 1934.

We were married at St. Mark's Lutheran Church in Kitchener on 27 February 1934, the coldest day of the year and the coldest night in which to leave for our honeymoon. We stopped off in Chatham that night and went on to Detroit the next day by train. I had taught classes the wedding day morning, so we had only one weekend of honeymoon leisure. Things were like that in the Depression days.

We had rented an apartment at 143 Albert Street, near the College. Our parents had given us some good furniture, and soon we bought a second-hand Model A (wire wheels and four-wheel brakes) for $125.00. Two weeks after we had settled in, Wilson MacDonald came to the College to recite and sell his books. Our small apartment had one bedroom and one smaller room which was my study. Yet we put MacDonald up for the night after a party with some friends and students. He kept us up until about 1:30 or even later that evening, talking about himself and his achievements—especially about how he was acclaimed in the United States as a great poet. Also he did sleight-of-hand tricks—he told us that he had once done so in Muskoka at a big hotel where Edward, the Prince of Wales, was staying. The prince saw MacDonald from a distance and asked if he would do tricks for him. MacDonald, who had a rather inflated ego, replied, "I am a poet, not a doer of tricks." For a number of years after this, we communicated with him, though he wasn't invited back to the Athenaeum Society. He did turn up from time to time in various high schools. By then he had written what he called songs—they were improved psalms, which he claimed to have done over "properly." The high point of the recital for me was when he said he had improved the King James version of the Bible. He didn't get any laughter at that one, though I thought he should have. "To rid the ancient writings of obscure phrasings was a heartbreaking task," he said in his prospectus. "In Ecclesiasticus 11, v. 5, we read," he said, " 'Many kings have sat down upon the ground;/ and one that was never thought of hath worn the crown.' My metrical version of this is 'Many kings have been commoners/ and many commoners have been kings.' I am enclosing a subscription sheet. Those who will sign this will receive an autographed numbered first edition copy of the book, price $5."

Wilson MacDonald turned up again later in the 1930s with a delightful wife, younger than himself. Despite Roberts' opinion that Wilson MacDonald was inferior to Carman, I must say that I was then enthralled by his lyrical, old-fashioned, melodious verse. One poem I admired greatly was the "Ode on the Death of Bliss Carman":

> The world of beauty is in deep distress
> And sorrow, like a frost, is everywhere
> For one sweet singer had laid down his lyre

Another poem I sometimes recited to my classes—in the manner of Pelham Edgar reciting what one didn't particularly admire but what made one's voice sound good—was MacDonald's poem "Bras d'Or":

> When I saw under the diamond stars
> The jewel heavy Lake Louise,
> I dreamed the last of the avatars
> Had come in the guise of rocks and trees
> And water and sky and fragrant breeze
> And cried "No beauty shall ever again
> Stab me as now with its lovely pain
> But here on a long amazing shore
> The old wound opens afresh once more
> And I laugh and weep by the singing floor
> Of the lovely wild untamable deep
> That men have called Brador."

I knew that this was a live "relic," not in the taste, theme, and music of the Canadian poetry then emerging at McGill (although I did not know of it), but as I was settling in as a literary historian, I could not turn my back on any "artifact" illustrating the "Confederation" period of Canadian poetry. While W.E. Collin of the University of Western Ontario was preparing *The White Savannahs* (1936), which was to introduce the "McGill School" to readers of Canadian literature, I was working on what was to become my book on Wilfred Campbell. My heavy teaching load was not altogether a hindrance because I could draw upon literary knowledge that came to me as I prepared for so many different courses. I worked on Campbell at leisure, without interfering with the private happiness Margaret and I shared, our expanding social life, our church-going, and our yearly holidays on Lake Huron beaches.

The Athenaeum Society later did have one other very interesting, but also very dificult, writer, Frederick Philip Grove. He and his wife came up from Simcoe, where he was teaching at a private school. He was tall, austere, perhaps not unfriendly but certainly not outgoing, hard to talk to, rather stiff in what he had to say. However, by that time I had met Ned Pratt, who somewhat made up for Grove.

At Waterloo, I could teach anything in the calendar; I particularly enjoyed nineteenth century, modern, and honours courses, taking a rather hard-nosed attitude with regard to Romantic literature, which was giving way to "modern." Modern comparative literature was late in coming to Canada, though it became popular in Europe and the United States in the 1920s. At this time, in 1934-35, Waterloo College was still affiliated with the University of Western Ontario, and I had taught Western's courses, particularly those given by William Tamblyn. Dr. Tamblyn carried on as he had done for years, though other people were teaching in various new fashions. He had not neglected reading recent literature, but he remained a lover of poems in themselves, emphasizing artistic and human experience. I didn't realize this at first because I was fresh from graduate school, but I began to enjoy the courses Tammy gave, especially in "modern" literature. Many of the poets were Georgians, such as Rupert Brooke. I have collected Rupert Brooke originals too, of the period 1910-1920, and I went overboard for the Georgians, though I kept teaching other things as well.

At the end of one of Tammy's courses he tacked on "Canadian writing." There were very few anthologies and not much that we could use. Not until the 1940s did we have more than a handful of reference books. We found our Canadian poets in that big book with the honorific headings, the Logan and French *Highways of Canadian Literature* (1924), and J.W. Garvin's collection of *Canadian Poets* (1926). As for fiction, we read William Kirby's *The Golden Dog* (1877), the novels of Ralph Connor, and Gilbert Parker's *Pierre and His People* (1892). In Tammy's course we mainly used *Canadian Poets*. The University of Western Ontario, as early as 1930, had some Canadian reading in its curriculum, but it did not yet offer a course labelled "Canadian literature." The University of New Brunswick did have a half-course and so laid claim to being the first to teach the subject.

It was then mid-Depression. Our apartment cost forty dollars a month, plus five dollars for the garage. This was a modest price for a good place to live, but the College was not always able to meet its salary payroll. The workload increased, but the money did not; there were promises rather than monthly cheques. Somehow we got along, and suddenly one great day the balance was paid. As a kind of celebration Margaret and I decided to take a trip abroad, to visit her relatives in England, see the Scotland of Wilfred Campbell's dreams, find my grandparents' homeland in Germany, and explore the Latin Quarter in Paris.

On 2 July 1937, we sailed for England on the *Empress of Australia*, out of Quebec. It was a rough trip on this converted

German ship, but I felt jubilant on my first view of the English coast. At Southampton, where Margaret's relatives lived, we spent a few days viewing a city that would soon be destroyed in the war. With the help of Margaret's uncle we bought an old Austin 7 for £16 and drove 3,000 miles exploring England, my first glimpse of what was to become my literary laboratory.

We visited cousins in London and on 31 July set out for the continent on the boat train to the Hook of Holland. After Amsterdam, we took a train through industrial Germany to Düsseldorf and Cologne, boarded a Rhine steamer to enjoy the scenery down to Mainz, then went on to Frankfurt and Heidelberg. On 22 August, we took a slow branch-line train through Mannheim, Ludwigshafen, and Kaiserslautern, to Homburg in the Saar.

We were going through beautiful country, the evergreen hills and valleys of the Hartz foothills. But we were also aware that we were in the Nazi domain; the army was much in evidence, and the easy-going southern Germans were well advised to watch their speech. At Kaiserslautern we saw barracks and steel foundries. At the hotel in Homburg, where we stayed overnight, we were watched and heard through a microphone on our dinner table. We were either over, or not far from, the fabled Siegfried Line.

While I regretted the grim welcome Germany was giving us, I was delighted, on going up the station stairway, to be greeted by a large advertisement for Cafe Klinck, Bahnhoferstrasse 58. Leaving Margaret at the station, I walked to the café, where there was a real welcome from the proprietor, Karl Klinck, a jolly, keen-eyed, short man about fifty years of age. He spoke no English and I very little German. Perhaps that was just as well, because even discussion of non-Jewish ancestry could have been dangerous. In fact, there was no blood relationship.

The next day, we woke up very early. When I looked out, I saw that it promised to become a fine clear day for tracing the family, at Jaegersburg, Waldmar, Schoenenberg, and other of my ancestors' villages. We took a quaint local train for about thirty minutes, first through rolling country, considerable woodland often with wide swaths of open space behind, swaths that probably had been cut for military purposes towards the French border. Few farms were scattered around the countryside, as most people lived in small villages.

We went on to Eljesbach station and soon saw Gries lying on a hill off to our left, far beyond the houses of Sand, Schoenenberg, and the smokestacks of Jaegersburg. At the top of the rise we found a few houses and then walked in to the edge of the town. At the linden tree in the centre of the village, we took the right fork and found the house whose door had "Kristian Klinck" on the portal. We enquired of the women here concerning the Klincks and were told that they knew George Klinck in Elmira. He was from one of the *other* branches of Klincks at home. The present possessor of the house was named Jakob Kristman, and his daughter-in-law was a Klinck too, but of what branch or what relationship to us we could not discover.

This daughter-in-law took us to the burgermeister, who occupied part of the school my grandfather attended. He took an interest in us, looked up his records, found much of interest, and promised us typewritten copies. Old Jakob Kristman came back for lunch, and he identified the site of my great-grandfather Nicholas Klinck's house and the place where my grandfather, Adam, was born on a site on (then) Adolf Hitler Street, where a new house had been erected in 1929. He told me that no old houses existed in the village. The original houses were of wood, and the Klinck house had burned down. Eventually the burgermeister, as promised, gave us official, stamped certificates of the desired information.

We then went on to Schoenenberg, a somewhat larger town, which straggled gradually up a hill to the cemetery and railway stations. The village square boasted a house belonging to a "Metzger Klinck," and we stopped at the shop of a druggist, Albert Klinck, with whom we had afternoon coffee. It seems that the people of these towns intermarried and that the Klincks had married several times into this particular branch. The druggist found an official in the local burgermeister's office to help us. This man spent an hour digging up official records in the old town books dating back to the French Revolution. The early records of our family at Schoenenberg are written in French by officials of the Republic and of Napoleon. We noted everything on record, all of which was remarkably good and fairly complete, providing a permanent contribution to our family's knowledge of its origins.

That evening we returned to Homburg, and after supper we talked to Karl Klinck again, who promised to send us a copy of his family tree and also said that the Klincks were reputed to have been

Huguenots who left Switzerland about 1617 because of religious persecution.

The next day we were on our way to cross the border at Forbach, going toward Metz, and we sighed with great relief when we came to France. From there we went to Paris to the Exposition, where the Russians had built a huge building and the Germans one almost as high, as if they intended to stay in Paris. We went through the Louvre, of course, and stayed at the Cité Universitaire. From Paris we took a train to Dieppe, a channel boat to Newhaven, and another train to Southampton. We left for home on the *Duchess of Richmond*. Landing in Montreal, short of funds, we appealed to Margaret's father by telephone for money to take us back to Kitchener.

So ended what we thought was our "first and last trip abroad." There were some valuable by-products. England became our second home. And I had become an enthusiastic genealogist—a foundation for my future work. I discovered that the Nazis, in their genocidal campaign against the Jews, were also recording the ancestry of other Germans in various places that were available even to foreigners. Requesting such information by mail, I was able before the war to obtain certified transcripts of records of my ancestry dated well before the time of Napoleon's domination of the Palatinate.

This trip had been an education for both of us. It increased our confidence in literary matters, for we had visited many literary shrines. Semi-final writing of my thesis flowed more smoothly during the following years, and this encouraged me to make a new appeal to the Department of English at Columbia in an attempt to secure my Ph.D.

CHAPTER FOUR

Wilfred Campbell

My efforts to settle upon a subject for my Ph.D. thesis had not met with much success. Before I left for New York and Columbia University in 1930, Pelham Edgar had advised me "to deal with genuine formative influences. There is no sense in evaluating what has no value." But it was not him, but rather Ralph Leslie Rusk, the American literature specialist, with whom I had to deal. I explained to Edgar in a letter of 27 October 1930 that Rusk's interest was in literature in the widest sense of almost all published writing as "revealing the social background of the belles lettres of any given time."

Rusk thought I should investigate "almost all sorts of published writings in Canada as background for the poetry of the Group of the 'Sixties.'" He was himself engaged in an effort to survey such background material for literature of the mid-western frontier of the United States. However, I found this proposed enlargement of the study of the Sixties difficult for two reasons: first, because this literary background had scarcely been touched by anyone, my work would be a study of the literature of Canada practically from 1860 on, whereas my primary interest was in verse. Second, as Rusk recognized, there was a scarcity of biographical and documentary material that I could produce. Accordingly, we developed a compromise: I was to work on the life of one representative man of the Sixties, Wilfred Campbell, with "the hope of eventually presenting a more mature book on the Group as a whole." I had known since 1929 what Edgar thought about Campbell as a poet, for I had written down these words: "In conversation with Dr. Pelham Edgar at Victoria College about a week ago about the group of the '60s; he enumerated Carman, Roberts,

Lampman, Duncan Campbell Scott—and perhaps Campbell slips in by the grace of God."

About this time I learned that Wilfred Campbell's son, Major Basil Campbell of Toronto, had made an authoritative collection of his father's papers. I wrote to W.J. Sykes in Ottawa, who had in 1923 published *The Poetical Works of Wilfred Campbell*, with a memoir outlining the poet's career. "Through the kindness of Mr. W.J. Sykes...," I told Professor Edgar, "he [Basil Campbell] has consented to help me in every way in a study of his father's letters and papers." Subject to advice, criticism, or suggestions that Professor Edgar might be willing to make, I had decided to make my thesis a life of Campbell.

Basil Campbell's wish to have the letters and papers published in some way may have taken me to Lorne Pierce of Ryerson Press, whom I had met for the first time in this year. Since Pierce had published his own *Outline of Canadian Literature* it was natural that the Campbell material should be offered to him for the preparation of a book. He might have written a biography if he had had time, but he was overwhelmed by other tasks. He told me that the collection had actually been turned over to Cockburn Kyte, Librarian of Queen's University in Kingston.

One disturbing factor was that Prime Minister William Lyon Mackenzie King, a friend of the poet, had "at one time in contemplation a life of Campbell." I wrote to King and had a prompt reply. King had never found time "to so much as make a beginning" in this project. He wished me success and expressed his own opinion: "Campbell was one of my most intimate friends, and I believe that, at the time of his death, there were few, if any, to whom he was more attached than to myself. We differed in our views on many questions, political issues in particular, but there was a strata of common ground, much beneath all that was controversial, which related to what was most real and profound, where we shared a community of interest and outlook which was very real." King supplied much more information about the poet when he received me in August 1932 at Laurier House. There he also showed me his study, the famous picture of his mother, and rows of his files in the basement. He lent me several Campbell books and asked a secretary to search out Campbell letters in his files.

King was consistent in his respect for Campbell's memory. At Basil Campbell's request, he later read my manuscript, but he did not write an introduction or a preface as I hoped. Perhaps both Basil and

King hesitated to certify the humble conditions of the poet's life in Ottawa, which I felt constrained in all honesty to provide. Or perhaps my demonstration of the poet's imperialism was too rich for a Liberal like King. However, he showed nothing but courtesy to me. In 1946, when I sent him a photograph of a plaque in honour of Campbell to be erected at Kitchener-Waterloo Collegiate, he sent me a long letter of appreciation to be read at the ceremony of Campbell's nature poetry and "the spiritual insight into the mysteries of life."

Another old friend of Campbell was Alexander McNeill, who lived on an estate called "The Corran," near Wiarton. Visiting McNeill to conduct research was like going home, for I had spent summers in Campbell's "Lake Country," especially at nearby Lake Huron. I knew where the Campbell family had lived, at the top of the hill in the town, and I had seen the memorial cairn.

McNeill had been born in Ireland and come to Canada in the 1870s. Someone said that he turned his Canadian home, which was a very large estate, into "a little bit of Ireland," where he raised thoroughbred horses and prize cattle and entertained lavishly. The house was a handsome building with seventeen rooms, situated on the cliff overlooking Colpoys Bay. He had beautiful grape arbours, orchards, and tropical plants. His three Irish setters were named Ulster, Antrim, and Kildare.

McNeill had helped Campbell when the poet, who was living temporarily in Southampton, decided to give up the ministry and wanted to get into the civil service. The way to such appointments was through the influence of members of Parliament, and McNeill enlisted some of his friends in an effort to get a position for Campbell in Ottawa. Success was just at hand when Sir John A. Macdonald died in 1891. In the end, McNeill did get Campbell a modest job, and Campbell was employed in the civil service in various tasks until his retirement.

I visited McNeill twice. Once was in the winter of 1931. The snow was falling softly when I got out of the train. Waiting for me was McNeill's man with a cutter. We drove from the station up the hill, turned right, and followed a lane for a long way, to fences, and went another long way, this time accompanied by some of the Irish setters. Finally we drew up in front of a palatial house, where I was ushered in to meet McNeill. We had a very fine dinner and sat around a roaring fire, the dogs all around us, the old man reminiscing in his big chair, drinking Scotch. He told me, "You're too young" and gave me coffee instead, and then he proceeded to tell me anecdotes about Campbell until he went to bed. I was given a big, well-furnished bedroom, with a fire. In essence, I was back in the nineteenth century, the time of Campbell's youth. I was beginning to get excited about my subject.

In July 1931, I was invited to see McNeill again, during our vacation. He and his family told me stories about Indian lore, Dead Man's Lake, and Dead Man's Point, which Campbell had known in his youth. They also described the waters, shores, and various aspects of the scenery in Campbell's part of the country. On McNeill's side, the Georgian Bay side, the cliffs are very high, but if you go eleven miles west, as Campbell often did, there were sloping, sandy shores.

I was beginning to know Campbell through the people who had known him, the places he had seen, and the movements he had participated in. A very important aspect later in Campbell's life was imperialism. He had been in Ottawa in the 1890s, and I began to appreciate that I would have to get authentic information. For example, because Campbell had studied and preached in New England, I made a trip to Concord and to Cambridge because Campbell had studied there for two years at the Episcopal Theological School. I also went to the French-Canadian town of West Claremont in New Hampshire, where Campbell had his first charge as a clergyman. I interviewed people who had known him, particularly one woman who remembered him as a rector and blushed to tell me of his attractions. I suspect she had liked him very much until he brought a wife back from Canada. In *Snowflakes and Sunbeams* (1888), lyrics of the West Claremont and St. Stephen periods, Campbell appears to have been contented, though he later became a very fiery individual.

Duncan Campbell Scott, whom I interviewed in Ottawa, was distinguished looking, but he was also standoffish. Nevertheless, he treated me very well and drove me all over the city to see and photograph the houses where the Campbells and Lampmans had lived. They never could afford anything like luxury. I was received graciously in Rockcliffe by Campbell's daughter, Faith, who lent me an unpublished biographical sketch she had written about her father. It was particularly valuable concerning Campbell's trips to Scotland.

I did not need an introduction to Campbell's "Lakes of the West." I had felt their charm since boyhood when I had spent two weeks each year at the Midland YMCA Camp on Beausoleil Island, a wonderful spot, lying out from Midland and from Honey Harbour into Georgian Bay. I enjoyed the life there, the waters, and the canoeing trips up into

Muskoka. We saw the steamers and got to know the region in its summer aspect. Wilfred Campbell, I think, liked the Wiarton area best in its winter moods. I had known enough about high water and storms at Sauble Beach to put it all together. At Wiarton there were people who could talk to me about Lovers' Leap—about an Indian girl who in love and desperation, jumped over the cliff into Colpoys Bay. I also learned about the Indians. At Southampton, I had talked to an old doctor whose life had been spent treating the local Indians, just as one of Wilfred Campbell's brothers had been a doctor among them.

I went to Queen's University to see Campbell's letters together with supplementary material. I had some of the letter books sent to Victoria College in Toronto so that I could study and copy them. From the beginning of my study, I knew that I would have to follow up all the clues, to try to do a definitive work. In this process, once in New York I decided to try to find specific periodicals in which Campbell's poems might be found. At the New York Public Library, when the librarians asked me what I wanted and I told them I wanted *whole* years—for example, whole runs for ten years of such and such a journal—they said "Come on in." They took me to the back of the loan desk and brought in several trucks loaded with periodicals. I had no other way of finding these poems. There were scattered references; I couldn't make a clean sweep without going to both American and Canadian periodicals themselves.

The problem of getting all the necessary material in my possession was formidable. For example, there were letter books at Queen's that I copied: I brought them back in handwriting. There were extracts of poems that Campbell had never published. My handwritten notes on Campbell gave me a complete bibliography of Campbell, including reviews and other apparatus. I typed it myself—two-finger stuff—and made copies for Waterloo College Library, Queen's, and myself. Another thing that was difficult then but would be relatively simple now was to get extracts from the literary column to which Campbell contributed "At the Mermaid Inn," published in the Saturday issues of *The Globe* in 1892-93. It had valuable information about Campbell's literary theories and practice.

While I was gathering documents in these early years, Lorne Pierce was also arranging interviews for me. Through him I met M.O. Hammond of *The Globe*, collector of first editions of Carman. In a letter of 1 November 1933, he added information about Campbell's appearance on their first meeting on 20 July 1907: "He is a rather squat figure, with a nervous twitch to his face and blink to his eyes which give individuality, but do not add to his personal charm. He is an unceasing talker and rattles along with a lot of good sense. His talk indicates wide reading and thought combined with acquaintance and sympathy with the world. He is not a mere worldling of to-day, but seems to look at the future with insight or prophecy. His talk reflects the poet and idealist.

Pierce also joined me in an evening visit to T.G. Marquis, literary historian. I had the feeling that Pierce tried to find out what his friends thought of me. I was too unworldly to attempt a show of knowledge; had I done so, I might have lost Pierce forever.

The most interesting of the Campbell correspondence came from the ninth Duke of Argyll, Lord Lorne. He did not raise great hope for Canadian imperialism in Wilfred Campbell. Lorne had learned a good deal about the kind of place that Canada was and about what Canada needed. Campbell had hoped for a position in England, but the duke, who had a tremendous influence on him in many ways, had to tell Campbell that his place really was in Canada. On 25 July 1911, Lorne wrote saying: "The literary area is overstocked here and unless a man has a talent for story-telling he is, in a literary sense, nowhere. In your place, I would not dream of abandoning Canada. As soon as you do so you will desire to be back there. All the world is before one in the New World."

Before my book was finished, I published an article entitled "William Wilfred Campbell: Poet of the Lakes" in a Ryerson periodical, *The Canadian Bookman* (August-September 1939). This was also my personal declaration of the literary program I was setting for myself, although I did not realize then how far it would take me. "His [Campbell's] history will reveal how his people went about the task of making the desert bloom as the rose in a sort of defiant anticipation of the chronic allegation of 'the intellectual sterility of Ontario.' " The author of the statement, Ray Palmer Baker, had graduated from Harvard. His *A History of English-Canadian Literature to the Confederation* (1920) was a useful, scholarly book, especially about the literature of the Maritime provinces. But the aspersion cast on Ontario bothered me for many years and caused me to collect evidence to the contrary. In fact, it gave me a program: finding, sorting, and presenting the real bulk of the early literature, not only of Ontario, but of the English in Quebec.

Campbell was an early Canadian mythological poet who drew from the mythology of the Chippewa for his *Lake Lyrics and Other Poems* (1889), a fact that makes it a more important book than has been realized, because the lakes and waters are interpreted through Indian lore. His imagery is fresh, with overtones of Longfellow, but it is also post-Longfellow, in terms of Campbell's own inspiration and respect for the modern world's "lost youth." Evolutionary theory had not previously given the lakes an historical background. Campbell's early imagery seems to have been more completely inspired by the way of life of the Indians whom he knew and their natural environment. His descriptions defy substitution of other words or rhythms; they are the words and rhythms of his lakes and of his identification of himself with their moods.

Working on Campbell's biography caught me up in the excitement of genuine research. Once I had obtained access to Campbell's papers I was kept busy gathering papers, visiting the locales of the poems, and interviewing people Campbell had known. But I was already preparing my thesis when, according to Columbia's regulations, I should first have prepared for, and passed, my general orals. I had not received official approval of my thesis subject and little official supervision. Fortunately, my case was taken up by Emery Neff, not without a warning from him that my request to receive the Ph.D. was out of order, but he was willing to see what I could do in an examination.

Accordingly, I obtained leave from Waterloo College for a few months, paying a substitute, in order to prepare myself for the orals. Margaret and I lived happily in a sub-let room (and shared kitchen) overlooking Riverside Drive and the Hudson. Professor Neff was a specialist in Victorian literature; I listened to him and read his impressive *Carlyle and Mill: An Introduction to Victorian Thought* (1926). Oscar Campbell, who had recently come to Columbia, was to be on my examining committee.

When the time for my orals came, I was among friends. I think there was a general feeling that I needed to be treated well as a Canadian. The Americans were not in the war yet, but they knew the time was not far off, so probably there was also sympathy with someone from a British ally.

Professor Neff took me over the next hurdle. Being a specialist in comparative Victorian literature (in 1940 he published an excellent book on that subject, *A Revolution in European Poetry, 1660-1900*), he decided to take me under his wing. Henry Wells had evidently encouraged him to do so after examining my manuscript, and when I was back in Waterloo, he had sent me some good advice regarding final revision. I acknowledged this in letter of 5 April 1941: "I have built up both the European and American backgrounds—as you and Professor Neff advised—by writing the 'patriotic' chapter into a study of Toryism and by giving a more comprehensive setting for Campbell's ideas on Nature, Darwinism, and religion." At this time, Neff and Wells were reminding me that I could not expect to find many readers familiar with Canada generally, and Canadian literature particularly—especially since few among my Columbia professors would be final examiners of my dissertation.

I sent my completed manuscript to New York in April 1941, hoping to sit for the defence on 10 May. When the time came (about a year later), it was peculiar. It was held in a large room with a great round table surrounded by professors from various departments: English, comparative literature, Italian, French, and many others. I don't think they had read the thesis, but fortunately the defence was carried on by J.B. Brebner, a Canadian from Toronto, at that time professor of history at Columbia. Feeling, I suppose, that the others knew nothing about Canadian history or Canadian affairs, he spent perhaps half an hour explaining relevant matters, which certainly took me off the hook.

Columbia's Ph.D. requirements stipulated that seventy-five copies of the dissertation would have to be published and given to the Columbia University Library. Meanwhile, Lorne Pierce arranged to accept my Campbell manuscript for publication provided that I could produce $1,000 by way of a subvention. My father, who was always generous, gave me the required amount, and the book was published in 1943, also the year in which my Ph.D. was conferred. My first book! It looked good on my shelves, though I do not know how much it was read in Waterloo. However, the possession of a Ph.D. was soon to make me a dean.

When the book on Campbell was published I received a variety of responses. William Arthur Deacon, literary editor of *Saturday Night* confessed in a letter of 26 January 1943 that he was not sympathetic toward Canadian authors and warned me not "to fall into the isms": "Call a spade a spade—literature is neither a mystery nor a frill but a common and essential life expression, as necessary and utilitarian as potatoes growing out of the ground. It is communication or nothing.

Have no patience with the bogus; it is the universal bane of all art. Look through pretensions to plain worth." This period piece of Deacon's journalistic reviewing is a lamentable contrast to Henry Wells' critical remarks on Campbell in a letter of 9 September 1949:

> He began as a pure romantic, and ended to a considerable degree as a lesser Kipling (I am a great admirer of Barrack Room Ballads). But with advancing years it seems to me that he not only developed, as you say he did, from his beginnings, but gained a place among the poets at the turn of the century who were occasionally writing a powerful reflective and meditative poetry based on a disturbed consciousness of their times….There is substance, dignity and power in quite a little of this writing, as Campbell's poem on the comet shows. It is not the very finest verse, for it is quite didactic and lacking in taste and a firm grasp of language, but still it is sincere and represents a considerable advance on the tradition of Longfellow.

Looking back, I find little in the Campbell book that I would wish to erase or qualify—except the first four and a half foolish pages—for I thought I had made some observations of special and general value, and I tried to express them clearly. I found that Campbell had faced the great void of materialism and the implications of evolutionary theory more deeply and explicitly and had expressed them more vividly in *The Dread Voyage and Other Poems* (1889) than his contemporaries Roberts and Carman had done in their poems or Roberts even in his short stories.

Lorne Pierce figures largely in the story of my publication, as he does in my later correspondence and in Canadian literature. When I first met him he wasn't far from his own beginnings. He had become editor of Ryerson Press in 1920; thus, he had been there perhaps nine or ten years when I came along. He had accomplished much already, having been a patron to many Canadian writers, and by then he had published ten books of his own, notably *Marjorie Pickthall, A Book of Remembrance* (1925). He called it "a labour of love"—a biography of the woman who had been a librarian at Victoria College and who had died in 1922. I have often opened that book on Pickthall, a belated Victorian of the decorative poetry kind. Contemporary Irish poets, I am sure, had influenced her. No one has paid a greater tribute to her than did Pierce.

As an example of Pierce's prominence at this time, after Carman's death in 1929, Pierce had become Carman's literary executor and biographer. The bulk of the material, some of which is now listed in *A Catalogue of Canadian Manuscripts* (1946), Pierce collected and presented to Queen's University over several decades. Pierce told me that he was greatly worried about Carman's unconventional love letters, of which he had trunks full; Pierce was no prude, but he was a Methodist. He could be witty and spicy in his conversations, but he confessed to the results of an early commitment to conventional religion—in fact, ordination in the Methodist Church. Their ordination was never forgotten by men like Pierce, Campbell, Ned Pratt, and Northrop Frye, who all had strong theological backgrounds.

One of the best articles I have ever found concerning Lorne Pierce is called "Persona Grata—the Romantic Puritan." It appeared in *Saturday Night* on 26 November 1955. There is a typical picture of Pierce: "And notwithstanding the hushed devotion of his acolytes in the United Church Publishing House (on Toronto's Skid Row) [it was on Queen Street, near the Exhibition Grounds]," the writer said, "there is still something more of the imp and less of the saint than the picture indicates."

> He has no rivals. In a jealous world, people delight to do him honor. And though the delight may be mixed with a certain sense of remorse in those who have profited directly or indirectly from his faith in Canadian literature only to move on to fresh fields and new publishers, it is nevertheless a tribute to his influence that this consciousness of obligation exists so widely. Nor is it dependent on intimacy. "Lorne Pierce? No, I can't say I really know Dr. Pierce, but I have met him, of course, on different occasions...." The refrain is the penalty of his early rise. (He was just thirty when he became Editor of the Ryerson Press, so that most of his real contemporaries in achievement are now departed), and of his deafness.

In the early 1940s while I was negotiating with Lorne Pierce to print my manuscript the pace of my life quickened. A major event was the adoption of our son David, who was born on 6 December

1941. At Waterloo College, the autocratic reign of Willis Froats as dean had ended when the faculty men revolted against his arbitrary and peremptory demand that we should teach summer school without extra pay. When the war came, the Reverend Dr. Fred Clausen was president of the institution; he also served as dean. It was during this period that I was on leave during several autumn months to take my orals at Columbia.

Early in the spring of 1941, when the Campbell manuscript was nearly ready for Ryerson Press, I took stock of my position. For ten years I had been teaching at the College. Even when I got my doctorate, the years ahead appeared to hold no promise of a career elsewhere. I did not feel that spending years of my life there would be a vain enterprise, since I believed in the beneficent influence of literary study upon students' characters, and I recognized the high office of a teacher of the humanities. However, the special denominational nature of Waterloo College demanded in 1941-42 unusual service and leadership in Christian education. Feeling that I should prepare for a dual role, I enrolled in courses in the seminary, which was on the same campus as the College.

What I hoped to find was intellectual discussion of problems Campbell had raised for himself, some of which I shared. He was not a reliable guide: he agonized over doubts and then, quite properly perhaps, smothered them in poetry. On 27 February 1892, in *The Globe*, he had protested against "false religious prejudice" in Canada. While recommending John Fiske's writings on mythology, he also declared that stories "in much of the earlier part of the Old Testament" had "all been proved to belong to the class of literature called mythic." "The story of the Cross itself," he added, "is one of the most remarkable myths in the history of humanity; connected with the old phallic worship of some of our most remote ancestors." I had not been trained in evolutionary theory and had studied little of philosophy and biblical criticism. Indeed, I had succumbed to Emerson's idealism, but now I wanted to know where I should stand.

The United States was not yet actively in the war, and Nazi propagandists were actively advocating American neutrality. I remember one young German who called himself a Dane. He could see no iniquities in the Nazi position. He regarded Hitler's Germany as a model for North Americans. I was appalled when I found American opposition to President Roosevelt turned against sympathy for Britain even among Americans in our colleges and universities. I found, when I returned to teaching after my leave, that I had a new colleague, a replacement in economics, who left German propaganda lying around in the library. Another, supposedly a student but later unmasked as a spy, moved through our halls. My worries became acute after Dr. Clausen died in 1942 and I became acting dean, with no president yet appointed. I know that these infiltrators could not influence more than a few unthinking students. After taking steps to curtail un-Canadian activities, I spoke privately to the Mounted Police. I did not have the solid evidence to publicize a case, but the intruders moved elsewhere.

Under the influence of J.D. Jefferis, our classics professor, the College organized a unit of the University of Western Ontario's Canadian Officer Training Corps, whose graduates turned in the best performance in active service. Our enrolment increased; and the registration of women grew accordingly. As dean, I was both in the COTC and outside it. By the articles of affiliation I was the College liaison officer with UWO and an executive member of UWO's Senate. Fortunately I had a direct line to the University when the war and the draft of young men raised unusual problems. Like the dean of arts at Western, I had to certify the status of students as subject to military service or as temporarily exempt from such service while engaged in certain acceptable educational programs.

In order to avoid competition with members of my faculty who wanted instant commissions, I enrolled as a private in the COTC and never rose above the rank of sergeant. Consequently, I served under the officers of Western's COTC, but above them as an officer of civil law with regard to the rights of College personnel. When some of my decisions were challenged by the adjutant of the University's COTC, I went over his head to obtain confirmation of my civil rights stand from the dean in Western, and finally, from Area Military Headquarters at London. Such action did not improve my standing in the COTC.

Nevertheless, I enjoyed the winter routine of the unit and the summer camps in London. I taught military law and map reading and memorized the theory required for a commission. At camp I had a platoon of young men whose military acquirements included an amazing fund of indecent stories and songs. When I had passed the necessary examinations, I applied for a commission to serve abroad in the personnel or educational branch of the Army. I was interviewed but turned down because there were no vacancies.

College classes increased in size, and I was still a teacher in spite of new administrative responsibilities. R.J.E. Hirtle, the registrar, co-operated with me in stopping up loopholes in admission and examination practices, in improving conditions for the secretaries, and in sorting out timetables, which were a mess because of attempts to give each student exactly what he or she wanted. I suppose we were dealing with diseases common to small church-related colleges.

Also I had to perform some auxiliary services. One was visiting various parishes to drum up students. I was always well received in churches and local high schools, but results were not easily achieved. I also had to promote Christian education and report to the annual synodical meetings. The value of education in the humanities (humanism is a bad word among clergymen) had to be spelled out; it had a rather low rating when compared with theological concerns.

But there was also relief. I made my first recorded speech before a meeting of librarians in Guelph. It was entitled perhaps prophetically "Salvaging our Literary Past" and published in the *Ontario Library Review* in 1943. I also took on a series of studies of current books for a business and professional women's group.

Relations with the University of Western Ontario were cordial throughout my deanship. Sherwood Fox, the scholarly president, and Fred Landon, the historian and librarian, were friendly and interested in Waterloo. K.P.R. Neville, dean of arts, was always a last resort in problem-solving. Frank Stiling was a personal friend. But at Waterloo College itself I had been deeply dissatisfied with the influence of the secretaries of the United Lutheran Church, who repeatedly made great shows of their financial support to the College and seminary (chiefly the seminary, and meagre support at that), but treated us like colonials. Our professors were advised that their chief responsibility was to some American Lutheran standard of education. My last report to the Lutheran Synod of Canada regarding Waterloo College was given at a meeting in a rural parish. I spelled out the special contribution being made to the Church by our college of liberal education. The American representative confronted me and said, "That's not what the Synod wants to hear. Tell them how many of your faculty members are communing Lutherans."

I resigned at once, not because I despised Lutheranism, but because its entrenched defenders had little vision of Christian liberal education. This event happened in the spring of 1947. For three days after my resignation, I was without a job! Some kind friends threw a wild party to celebrate my unemployment. However, I had already been made aware that Professor James Spenceley had died and left a vacancy in the Department of English at Western. An invitation to join that department as an associate professor was soon made formally to me by Arthur Jewitt, who had succeeded W.F.Tamblyn, long-time head of English. Jewitt was a very able administrator. I believe that I was hired as a figure in his scheme to re-organize the department.

CHAPTER FIVE

Laying the Foundations

Margaret, David, Patsy (our Irish terrier) and I moved to London in the early autumn of 1947. Housing regulations were still in force, so we had to trade our good apartment in Waterloo for a poorly built house used by a London family moving to Waterloo. This house on Patricia Street was a burden for as long as we rented it. I never could persuade the coal-fired furnace to provide flame and heat in accordance with my schedule, and in the early spring flood, the water in the basement rose high enough to float boxes and other objects over the cellar steps and up to the level of the kitchen floor. Things were somewhat better in 1948 when we rented an upper flat on Wellington Street.

By this time, to my surprise, I was appointed head of the department. Frank Stiling, who deserved the position, was held over by the superior authorities to become Dean of arts.

In 1949, Margaret found a neglected lot on Grosvenor Street near old Huron College, where the park road inclined downhill toward the river. The lot was heavily wooded with at least a dozen great old white pines and maples, hemmed in by grapevines and shrubs. We decided to buy it and build our dream house. Don McGugan, an architect, corrected our rough drawings. We decided, for the sake of economy, to be our own contractors and to have the carpentry work done by the Suzuki family of Japanese boat-builders who had been forced out of British Columbia during the war. Our lack of knowledge about many aspects of building was an asset: experts enjoyed giving us advice. We did much of the work (such as hauling bricks, lathing, and painting) ourselves as the house at 8 Grosvenor was on its way to a measure of completion during the summer of 1950.

We moved in on 29 August, though a huge mound of soil outside the dining room window still showed where there was to be a lawn. The back yard gave no early promise of a garden, and much had still to be done in the interior. Our mortgage would seem small now, but it was all we could manage. My salary was satisfactory, but it was Margaret's thrift and household expertise and my supplementary teaching of summer school and extension classes that kept us financially afloat (funds from the University or from various granting bodies paid for my travel).

From 1947 until 1960, I did extracurricular teaching for the University in such centres as Listowel, Galt, St. Thomas, Sarnia, and Windsor. These courses helped introduce students to the humanities at Western, as did credit courses by correspondence. In 1951-52, for example, a group of such students in Sault Ste. Marie not only sent in answers to assignments, but also met locally as a group. At mid-term, I flew up to the Sault and delivered an intensive weekend lecture series on American and Canadian literature.

I gained additional information on secondary school education by serving as a marker for Grade XIII examinations for the Ontario Department of Education at various times between 1943 and 1954. It was not a position for someone like myself who hated routine, but living in Toronto was very pleasant. After everybody went home, I usually had hundreds of papers to read when I was chief examiner. I learned a good deal that way; for example, that composition was not well thought of and that there was no specific curriculum for it. Although it was required in the teaching program it was largely avoided, so I started applying Professor Baldwin's methods at Columbia more vigorously to the program at Western.

I didn't neglect teaching in the University. I did not always teach freshman English, but I did extend undergraduate American-Canadian and make Canadian literature a competitor with the Renaissance for postgraduate study. A.B. Conron, well-equipped in comparative literature, was a sturdy supporter in this respect.

I also enjoyed teaching criticism and benefited from attending the English Institute meetings at Columbia. I had joined the conference at its eighth annual meeting in 1949. The program could be described as "comparative criticism" of authors and works, both American and British. There I heard discussions by the best American critics, among them, Cleanth Brooks, Meyer Abrams, Hugh Kenner, Richard Altick, W.K. Wimsatt, and many others.

In New York we attended theatres as usual, but despite all these activities—including as many weeks of summer holidays as we could afford—my research did not suffer. In fact, it gained momentum as I prepared some speeches for local clubs and historical associations on such topics as Archibald MacMechan (a native of western Ontario) and "Early Theatres in Waterloo County."

My most enjoyable writing in the 1940s was a happy collaboration with Henry Wells, Ned Pratt, and Lorne Pierce, which resulted in the publication of *Edwin J. Pratt, The Man and His Poetry*. Pratt's reputation had grown steadily through the 1920s and the 1930s. I had had the privilege of being introduced to him by Pelham Edgar at Victoria College as early as 1929. And then I had heard his poem *The Roosevelt and the Antinoe* read before a large audience, with Pratt in attendance.

In the American and Canadian courses I had been teaching at Waterloo College since the early thirties, I had introduced selections from Pratt's work, using such anthologies as Garvin's *Canadian Poets* and Carman and Pierce's *Our Canadian Literature: Representative Verse English and French*. By 1940, too, Pratt had at least ten published volumes. He had begun with *Newfoundland Verse* in 1923; then *The Witches' Brew*, and so on to *Brébeuf and His Brethren* in 1940, *Dunkirk* in 1941, and *Still Life and Other Verse* in 1943. *Collected Poems* published in Toronto by Macmillan appeared in 1944, and another book, *They Are Returning*, in 1945. I have a copy of the Macmillan *Collected Poems* of Pratt, which I treasure because Henry Wells was consulted about it by the American critic, William Rose Benét, who thought there was a good American market for the book. The title page holds these words: "To my dear friend Carl Klinck, with much appreciation, Ned Pratt."

There were actually two *Collected Poems* of Pratt published at this time, the Toronto Macmillan one in 1944 and a somewhat briefer volume with the same title, *Collected Poems*, published the next year in New York by Knopf. The two volumes are not quite the same, and a comparison of them is very interesting. I believe that Henry Wells tried to persuade Alfred Knopf to keep *The Witches' Brew* in the New York book (evidently at the sacrifice of *The Great Feud* and the *The Fable of the Goats*). These two last poems had been dropped, but Henry had his way in keeping *The Witches' Brew*. The New York edition had an introduction, a friendly, enthusiastic account by Benét, which the Canadian edition had not.

In 1943 A.J.M. Smith's anthology, *The Book of Canadian Poetry*, devoting at least half its pages to contemporaries, was published in Chicago. Smith's anthology was a revelation of Canadian poetic achievement. He also made his readers aware of native traditions in a long historical introduction going back to the eighteenth century, and in biographical sketches he provided some information about the poets themselves. Not only did Smith thus gain a significant place in the history of Canadian studies, but also he provided in his acknowledgements a roll call of his contemporaries, who were attempting to crack the monopoly that the literature of England had held in the curricula of English departments in Canadian colleges and schools.

As I look back over it, I am inclined to name among the pioneers the editors of Canadian publishing houses such as Paul Corbett of W.J. Gage and Company, who published the Smith book in Canada, and Lorne Pierce of Ryerson Press, who held much of the copyright of the poems. Smith's bibliography left out little of importance, listing even my *Wilfred Campbell* and pointing out such significant earlier works as Baker's *A History of English-Canadian Literature to the Confederation*, W.E. Collin's *The White Savannahs* (1936), and E.K. Brown's essays, published in *On Canadian Poetry* (1943), which had an excellent chapter on Pratt.

Henry Wells was as impressed by Smith's anthology as was Benét. Wells was then publishing on a variety of subjects. *The American Way of Poetry* appeared in 1943, and he was preparing his *Introduction to Emily Dickinson* (1947). A specialist in comparative literature, he was now developing an interest in comparative North American literature. In an article in March 1945 in the *New England Quarterly* entitled "The Awakening in Canadian Poetry," he made many references to Smith's anthology and to major books of Canadian poets. In another article designed to acquaint American readers with Canadian poets, entitled "Canada's Best Known Poet, E.J. Pratt" and published in *College English* in May 1946, he wrote: "Clearly we need new voices, and various voices, serving the urgent aesthetic, spiritual and moral requirements of the times—one can hardly know from what quarter of the globe among English-speaking or non-English-speaking ones much of our new enlightenment will emanate...whatever Mencken wrote of the southern desert and Sinclair Lewis of the middle west has been commonly supposed to be in substance true ten-fold for Canada. Yet by one of the ironies of history, while we have slept, some unobserved northern lights have been streaming in the sky for at least a decade. We are even beginning to perceive them."

In a letter Wells wrote to me on 21 October 1945 he said he was planning to visit Ontario. It was his intention to visit me in Waterloo and, later, if possible, the "celebrated" art museum in Detroit. This was not his first visit to Canada, since he had gone to Newfoundland in 1923 with the painter Hugh Gray Lieber. In 1945 he was ready to write about Pratt.

This was only one of several visits across the border that brought Ned and Viola Pratt, and their daughter Claire, together with Henry and his wife Katharine. Margaret and I had our share in these meetings too, and I spent hours talking to Henry Wells and Ned. Wells and I agreed to do a book on Pratt jointly. I was to concentrate on the biographical chapters, while Henry would write the chapters of interpretive criticism. Ned was most gracious and generous. It is still a favourite book of mine.

One passage pleased me especially because I was able to write about Pelham Edgar and Pratt from my own experience. "Although registered as a philosophy student, Pratt had taken many optional English courses under Dr. Pelham Edgar, now to be his chief" (this was in the 1910s). "This noted professor and critic who had hailed the nature school of Canadian poets in their prime and who, living to this day, has directed his country's sanest criticism from ultra romantic to modern channels, opened the horizon of literature to E.J. Pratt" (and, if I may say so, also me). "I was thrilled," said Pratt, "by Edgar's lectures generally, especially on the Romantics, Shelley and Wordsworth." Pratt's *Rachel*, a volume privately printed in 1917, had been produced under this spell. Wordsworth and Tennyson account for most of the poems, as "Michael" and "Enoch Arden" resound to the seas of Newfoundland. Dr. Edgar had been heard to deplore the lack of a seaside odour in the laureate's tale about the fisher folk. *Rachel* should be credited with at least an advance toward realism. But Pratt was not yet ready to write "The Ice-Floes." Patiently he had yet to absorb the background of literature. Edgar knew better than to impose any opinions on Pratt. He strove for the poet's development by setting him to lecture, as E.K. Brown has recorded, "in the courses where he thought the material would be most valuable to Pratt's poetry." Nothing could be closer to my own experience of the way in which Dr. Edgar helped younger writers.

When our book was finished, the introduction was written by J.B. Brebner, who said: "Mr. Wells had used his own scholarship, wit and insight to set the principal poems against their archetypes in our literary tradition" and went on, "and in the process has arrived at a summation of the poet which is corroborated by Mr. Klinck's intimate, imaginative and affectionate inquiry into Pratt's life."

In his part of the book, Wells was not looking mainly for influences, but for parallels in the literary tradition. When the book came out, critics were difficult about this approach, claiming that Wells was trying to show that Pratt was the equal of Aristophanes, Shakespeare, the author of Reynard the Fox, Aesop, Melville, E.A. Robinson, or Hesiod. Yet the true nature of Wells' criticism was "to examine Pratt's work realistically against classical backgrounds," as Wells himself explains in his introduction. "Poem is matched with classical poem, each shedding light upon the other, to the writings of Pratt calling for entirely new elucidation." Finally, in his introduction to the succeeding series of essays, Wells says, "It may be well to note that not the slightest attempt is made to equate the merits of the masters of the past with the modern poet. Stature in art can best shift for itself. If he is not of their stature, he proves at least of their kind. The most which is claimed on Pratt's behalf is a family likeness to more illustrious predecessors."

With publication of *Edwin J. Pratt* I recognized that I was no longer an outsider in Toronto. In the world of Canadian literature of that day, I was to have a part; that part was to be the weaving of many threads into biographical and literary history. However, as my absorption in the systematic study of Canadian literature grew, especially in the writing of part of this book on Pratt, it became clear to me that in spite of two books bearing my name, I would never become an authoritative critic. I was evidently destined to follow my passion for discovery and to become a biographer and historian, serving the critics and philosophers. This was an office that I felt was near enough to creativity to satisfy my needs.

It may be that the wise and generous Henry Wells had eased me into recognizing that truth about myself. In 1945, when I had felt the urge to write an article on Pratt's lyrics, I had enough sense to send it to him before attempting publication. He replied on 26 November 1945, in a letter encouraging and frank: "Your letter on Ned's lyrics came this morning," he writes, "and has been read this evening. I am returning it at once. It seems to me that you have done a good job and given us something well worth printing. I add on the reverse side of the note a few random comments about a few passages. Generally I think you will agree that the essay lacks enthusiasm. The focus seems to me less sharp, the style less vivid [my focus, my style]—perhaps you wrote it when a bit weary on a hot summer day. I don't think it shows you at your best. But this is very frank, and not intended to give you any pause in pressing for publication. I should be mighty happy to see the essay in print." Chastened but undeterred, I sent him another article in summer of 1946, while we were both waiting for word about our Pratt book from the Ryerson Press.

The Pratt book was published by Lorne Pierce, with whom I had had little correspondence in this period. However, he had congratulated me on my appointment as dean of Waterloo College in May 1944. He had established a medal in his name, the Lorne Pierce Award, to be awarded by the Royal Society of Canada, of which he was a Fellow, for outstanding contributions to Canadian literature. He graciously predicted that I would in the future receive the award, though this prophecy was not to be fulfilled until 1978.

The educational opportunities that opened up for me after I became head at Western were renewed adventures in comparative literature. I do not know precisely how the idea of forming a committee on comparative Commonwealth literatures was initiated in Canada, but I do know that there were in our universities many scholars who were conscious of similarities and differences in English, American, and Canadian literatures because they had been educated or at least lived outside of English Canada. Although departments of English had programs almost exclusively devoted to British literature, many people who later became specialists in English-Canadian criticism and research had acquired a "comparative knowledge" of French-Canadian and American.

Some of those scholars were Ray Palmer Baker, with a doctorate from Harvard; Pelham Edgar, with a doctorate from Johns Hopkins and specializing in French; W.E. Collin, a professor at the University of Western Ontario and at Rennes and Toulouse in France, and known principally as a writer on French-Canadian literature; Lionel Stevenson, who did his undergraduate work at UBC and taught at Duke; A.J.M. Smith, educated at McGill and Edinburgh, who was for many years at Michigan State, where he wrote about Canadian literature; E.K. Brown, educated at the University of Toronto and the Sorbonne, later a professor at Toronto. I associate Brown with Cornell and Chicago and *On Canadian Poetry* (1943), not to mention other articles on Canadian literature; Desmond Pacey, who wrote *Creative Writing in Canada* (1952), took his D.Phil. at Cambridge, England; Northrop Frye studied at Toronto and Oxford and elsewhere; Reginald Watters, a graduate of Toronto, returned to Canada from the United States with a Ph.D. from Wisconsin as a specialist in American literature but who then contributed very largely to Canadian bibliography; Roy Daniells, who received his early education in England, came to Canada as a boy, was educated at the universities of British Columbia and Toronto, and contributed greatly to the study of Canadian literature; Alfred Bailey, born in Quebec, who studied at the London School of Economics and became a well-known Canadian historian and critic; Gordon Roper, who wrote a good deal on United States literature and was a professor of American literature, but who also wrote extensively on Canadian.

A Dominions Committee was appointed by the Humanities Research Council of Canada (John E. Robbins, secretary) in 1948. It had A.S.P. Woodhouse of Toronto as chairman and included in its membership Donald Creighton (History, Toronto), Alfred Bailey (Dean of arts at UNB), Claude Bissell (English, Toronto), and myself. Our task was to bring before Canadian humanities scholars knowledge of the other dominions in the Commonwealth.

Since I had demonstrated some interest in Australian material, I secured the committee's approval to work on a survey of Australian poetry. I had already discovered in our University of Western Ontario Library a recently published two-volume bibliography of Australian literature by E. Morris Miller, and I had begun corresponding with Australian authorities. We had had nothing in Canada like Miller's publication, which was in fact much more than a bibliography; it was a survey of the literature.

Woodhouse took the initiative to authorize work on a bibliography of Canadian literature. Watters, then at UBC, was appointed to start work in the summer of 1949 and to continue with the bibliography during 1949-50 and again in the summer of 1951 (when Robert McDougall of Carleton would assist him). As it happened, there was enough material to keep Reg busy in the east throughout the 1950s. This was fortunate for me because we met from time to time, corresponded a great deal, and produced our own *Canadian Anthology*, which I discuss in detail in a later chapter, in 1955.

My activities in the Dominions Committee did not end with Watters' appointment. During 1949, I put an enormous amount of time into the study of Australian literature, absorbing as many texts as I could lay my hands on and obtaining what I could from people in Australia. On 9 and 10 June, there was a humanities conference in the Maritimes. I was referred to as the Australian expert of the Committee, which was certainly an exaggeration, and in December 1949, was invited to give a research paper at the June 1950 Humanities Research Council regional conference at Royal Military College in Kingston.

Much of my material came from the Toronto Public Reference Library and the University of Toronto library. During meetings with the Dominions Committee and while I was preparing this paper, I lived at Hart House. I felt I was getting close to the University, only a few years after I had left a small college.

At the June meeting I met Roy Daniells, who asked me some difficult questions, and John Irving of the University of Toronto, who corrected some of my ideas and defined some terms for me. These men later became contributors to the *Literary History*, so I feel that this work for the Humanities Research Council was an excellent preparation for what would come later. In particular, through Reginald Watters, it became very practically an antecedent and a necessary foundation for the *Literary History*. Some of the difficulties I encountered resulted from my lack of experience of Australians and Australian literature. It was pretty obvious that I had never been to Australia, but my book information wasn't too bad.

Professors from Canada were soon to go abroad, Roy Daniells went to New Zealand; Claude Bissell and Reginald Watters went to Australia. From Australia came Brian Elliott of the University of Adelaide. He had been recommended by Norman (Derry) Jeffares of Leeds, a powerful figure in Commonwealth literature in Britain. Elliott wrote to me on 6 November 1958, when he was on his way home and had stopped off in Ottawa to see Rob McDougall:

> While in New York State I saw something of Henry Wells, to whom you introduced me, and we are now quite old friends. Rob showed me your letter this morning about the projected literary history of Canada, and I hope you won't mind my dropping you this line to say how interesting I find this proposition. It strikes me that I ought

to go home and advocate something along similar lines there.

Comparative literature was very definitely the theme of Henry Wells' letters to me in the late 1940s and the 1950s. In July and August 1948, he commented on my plans to publish an anthology. He gave advice regarding the usefulness of longer poems and some comments on suggested Canadian poets. He said that I should do the book alone: "But if, after some time and thought, you still wanted me to join you, I should love to do that, for scholarship tends to be lonely. I love collaboration—in that, and all other walks of life." I had told him about the "committee on the Dominions literature, with emphasis on the plural." He asked to be kept "posted."

Henry evidently went to work with his characteristic independence, brilliance, and speed to produce some relevant articles (unfortunately never published) that I have in manuscript under the title "British Poetry in the Dominions" or "New Poetry in the British Dominions." On 11 January 1951, I described the contents in a letter to A.S.P. Woodhouse: "I have now a portion of his manuscript...a study of new poets and movements in Canada, New Zealand and Australia...Wells' study is generally limited to criticism of books published in the last twenty years. I have parts one and two, on Canada and New Zealand. Production in the latter country is sketchy at present, but Wells gives a full treatment. The Canadian section, dealing with Pratt, Birney, Klein, Page, Livesay, Smith, Finch, Anderson, Hambleton and a few others, is brilliant." But Woodhouse said that he had had "no success" in trying to interest University of Toronto Press in Wells' anthology of New Zealand poetry, and he did "not think that the Rockefeller people [who gave grants to the Humanities Research Council] would allow us to spend money to subsidize work done in the United States."

At Western I had the influence to give a certain direction to our departmental program. It was no secret that I was trying to find a significant place (not merely as an option) for Canadian literature. But I never sponsored general or honours courses in Canadian alone: I held to a "comparative" system, which involved American in the first semester and Canadian in the second. And I defended this policy against the charge that it was neither American nor Canadian; I argued that there was an affinity between them as well as a common ancestry in the British literature that was more intensively studied. Also, by "comparison" the status of Canadian was better located and better appreciated.

Comparative literary history (British-Canadian-American) became more and more fascinating. I could not believe that Canada had no literary history paralleling the British and American at least as far back as 1800. Emigration had been an exercise in British or foreign literature finding a comparatively new environment. But the backgrounds of the many emigrants who became writers were only sketchily noted, and their Canadian works were neglected. My ambition to give English Canada a literary history going back through a hundred or more years impelled me to begin with study abroad into the English careers of Major John Richardson, William "Tiger" Dunlop, John Galt, and other writers of the early years about whom there were records in the British Museum Library. I also laid foundations at home, looking into the early creative literature of Western Ontario.

I was fortunately placed in my relationship with people in the Department of History and the Library, which contained some rare books of American and Canadian literature. Talman and others had responded to Western's proximity to the American border by engaging in cross-border history of the Quakers, slaves, emigrants, pioneers, and warring armies. As a practical result of my turning to Canadian literature, I raided findings, many of them local, from Canadian historical works in our library.

But the earliest documents for the British component in my research could only be found abroad. I applied for grants, describing what I intended to do; namely, to study "the British background of early Canadian literature." I felt that I needed many more documents: in fact, I knew what some of their titles were. I used what I had learned about William Dunlop as an example of what needed to be done. In my requests I pointed out that few writers had attempted to review even part of the early cultural history of Canada as revealed in the early literature or records of men like Dunlop.

John E. Robbins, with whom I had worked on the Dominions Committee supported my request, and the University offered me full salary (around $7,750) less the amount of the grant-in-aid from the Humanities Research Council of Canada. In addition, I received smaller grants from the Commonwealth University Interchange and the British Council, and so Margaret and I travelled abroad, from 6 April to 13 September 1955. In addition to the cultural and scenic glories, we enjoyed many experiences and privileges that only Britain could provide. Canada House was helpful. We had several talks with the distinguished Head of the House, Norman Robertson; attended the Queen's garden party, the 1 July party at Canada House, and a party for Beaverbrook scholars at the Senate House of the University of London, where we met Beaverbrook himself. There was little or no advertisement of Canadian books in London at this time, and there was no stock of them at all. In comparison, the Australians, especially the Angus and Robertson firm of Sydney, were getting a great deal of publicity and were easy to find.

The British Council was especially diligent in taking care of me. John Hampden, who had edited at least sixty books, took me under his wing and did many favours for me. His influence extended beyond London, to Cambridge, Edinburgh, and Glasgow. At Cambridge I was able to meet E.E. Rich, the authority on the Hudson's Bay Company. In Edinburgh I was greeted by Librarian William Beattie at the National Library of Scotland, and in Glasgow I talked with Peter Alexander, Regius Professor of English. He encouraged me to attend the summer school in modern English literature at Wadham College, Oxford. There were a number of French and German students, and we had provocative lectures by F.R. Leavis, W.W. Robson, a Fellow of Lincoln College, and F.W. Bateson.

Other lectures of great interest were by Father Vincent Turner on Graham Greene, whom he pictured as a writer of thrillers who chose to get extra effects from references to philosophy and the Church, and A. Alvarez who talked on William Empson, who was present. H.A. Mason discussed platitudes, and Elizabeth Sewell brought out all sorts of conflicts between fear and desire in W.H. Auden. Joyce Cary and Pamela Hansford lectured on fiction.

I came home full of all kinds of ideas and ambitions. In 1956, less than a year after my return, I resigned as head of the department, to become Senior Professor and Professor of Canadian literature. As if to justify this new, unique title, I used my new freedom from administration to provide evidence of the discoveries that my research abroad had yielded.

Before the end of the decade, I saw a *Literary History of Canada* project well on its way toward successful preparation. In addition, I had published a booklet on Major Richardson's *Kensington Gardens* (1957) and a book on the Scottish-English career of William "Tiger"

Dunlop (1958). Beginning a series of articles on early British-Canadian authors, I published "Some Anonymous Literature of the War of 1812" (1957); "John Galt's Canadian novels" (1957); "Adam Kidd" (1958); and "The Canadian Chiefs and 'Tiger' Dunlop" (1959). "The *Charivari* and Levi Adams" appeared in 1960.

Inevitably, I made speeches. In 1957, I gave a graduation address at Waterloo College, and I spoke about "The Literary Reputation of John Galt" at the Ontario Historical Society meeting in Galt's "home town" of Guelph (1957). The same year I addressed Section II of the Royal Society of Canada on "Some Anonymous Literature of the War of 1812."

In 1958, Margaret and I drove to Edmonton at the time of the Learned Societies meetings to publicize and explain the project for a literary history to members of the Humanities Association. We improved the occasion by going to Vancouver, and then down the Pacific coast to San Francisco, and across the United States to Denver, Chicago, and home. In the Christmas-New Year holiday I joined the Conference for British Commonwealth Literatures and gave a paper entitled "A Survey of Commonwealth Studies in Canadian Universities." My correspondence with Henry Wells from the beginning to the end of the 1950s was full of his suggestions for publications of books or articles on literature of the British Commonwealth, especially his desire to see his "New Poetry in the British Dominions" in print and an anthology of literature of the English-speaking world, which he hoped I would edit. We tried unsuccessfully to gain the interest of Canadian publishers, especially the University of Toronto Press, Oxford University Press, and Gage.

In 1958 also a new attempt to found a British Commonwealth Conference was made in the United States. It was sponsored by Joseph Jones of the University of Texas and Joan Corbett of the Department of English, Westhampton College, University of Richmond, Virginia. Jones was one of those genial, enterprising, and itinerant Texans who were cleaning out the used book stores of Britain and stocking the library of the University of Texas. He was also an adviser on authors to be assigned biographies to in the Twayne Publishers series. Miss Corbett was of Canadian origin, born in St. Catharines and a 1944 graduate of McMaster University.

The first meeting was to be held on 28 December in New York, since that date would be convenient for members of the Modern Language Association of America meeting, as they always did, in the

New Year holiday period. Munro Beattie of Carleton University, Ottawa, arranged the Canadian part of the program.

In preparation for the "Survey" I was to deliver, I sent out a questionnaire to universities and colleges across Canada regarding courses in the literature of Canada, English and French. Of the thirty-nine institutions involved, thirty-one offered courses in Canadian Literature. Fifteen of these offered French-Canadian only; eight offered neither.

Institutions offering English-Canadian literature in "combined" American-Canadian undergraduate courses were Acadia, Assumption, Bishop's, Carleton, Huron, McMaster, Mount St. Vincent, Ottawa, Royal Military College, St. Michael's, Trinity, United, Waterloo, and Western. Institutions offering English-Canadian literature in "separate" undergraduate courses were British Columbia, Carleton, Dalhousie, Laval, McGill, Mount Allison (with Commonwealth literature), Ontario Agricultural College, New Brunswick, Queen's, Saskatchewan, Sir George Williams, Toronto, and Victoria. Institutions offering postgraduate courses were Assumption, British Columbia, Carleton, New Brunswick, Toronto, Trinity, and Western. Institutions that had produced theses in Canadian literature were: M.A., Acadia, Alberta, Bishop's, British Columbia, Dalhousie, Laval, McGill, Montreal, Mount Allison, New Brunswick, Ottawa, Queen's, Saint Joseph, Saskatchewan, Toronto, and Western; Ph.D., Laval, McGill, Ottawa, Montreal, and Toronto. Institutions publishing specific postgraduate courses in Canadian literature in annual announcements were Assumption, British Columbia, Carleton, Laval, New Brunswick, Ottawa, Toronto, Western. Other universities that had official Faculties of Graduate Studies and therefore could "arrange" postgraduate study in Canadian literature were Alberta, Dalhousie, McGill, McMaster, Manitoba, Montreal, Queen's and Saskatchewan. Courses in Commonwealth studies were offered by Mount Allison (Literature of Canada and the Commonwealth) and Toronto (a proposed course involving the comparative study of Canadian and Australian letters and culture).

Conference members requested that a conference group on British Commonwealth literature be set up for the 1959 MLA meeting in Chicago. The CBCC became a recognized Group 12 of the MLA, but I do not know how long it continued. I do remember that for many years I subscribed to Joseph Jones' small periodical, *World Literature in English*. It was the Conference of Canadian Literature newsletter.

His advisory board included Northrop Frye, myself, and Lionel Stevenson. I continued in this honorary post until my retirement in 1973.

In 1959, I began compiling "Canadian Literature: Theses in Preparation," a project I conducted for the next thirteen years.

That same year I had the great good fortune to visit the Canadian North, in company with Air Commodore Fred Carpenter of the Canadian Air Force Transport Command. He picked up people from various universities and other "VIP's." Probably the most interesting of these was James N. Minifie, a remarkable journalist who also did radio broadcasts.

Our pilot, Bill Carr, was a very fine airman, who had been on the air geographical survey which had criss-crossed the whole North and mapped it out. He said, "they even named a lake after me." From Trenton we proceeded north over James Bay, to Churchill, where we saw the old Prince of Wales Fort and the rather rundown town. From there we flew north beyond the tree line. I kept looking out for notice of the magnetic pole. We passed it. It does strange things to compasses, and then we lost our radio connection with Resolute Bay.

We did get there in the late afternoon, before the residents knew that we were coming. But somewhere they had motorized snowmobiles that would hold a dozen people, and a number of these finally came out and took us in. We were made very comfortable. There were dormitory rooms for us, very private and very neat, and—their pride and joy—flush toilets, the farthest north in Canada; nowhere else could that be matched.

After we left Resolute we flew up to the tip of Ellesmere Island. We were only seven hundred miles from the Pole and somebody had the bright idea of serving orange juice, which was somehow symbolic, it seems to me, because every one of us felt that we were in a different world. It was vast—it was Canada, but it was like looking down a hole, looking at the far distance. It taught every one of us a lesson. From there we flew westward to Great Slave Lake and Yellowknife and then to Whitehorse.

I have never viewed a more magnificent scene than the Rocky Mountains at the point where the Mackenzie River meets them and proceeds down to the Arctic. It was fantastic and splendid. We went on to Edmonton, to Rivers, Manitoba, then back to Trenton and London. It was a profound experience, registering for me a wholly new concept of Canada's vastness. So much to see, so much to possess, so much to hold dear.

CHAPTER SIX

Research into the Literature of the Canadas

As is apparent, my subject of research was becoming the literary activities in the Canadas from 1820-80. This was a challenge because there was no reliable historical guide to the period. My own concentration during the 1950s on research into the literary backgrounds of such writers as Galt, Dunlop, and Richardson and into Scottish, English, and Canadian journalism enabled me to add depth and breadth to what had not been organized historically by my predecessors.

I had found it difficult to account for the remarkable burst of literary activity in Montreal in the 1820s and for the gap that ensued before the *Literary Garland* began in 1838. The 1820s had brought forth the *Scribbler*, the *Canadian Magazine*, and the *Canadian Review*, edited respectively by immigrants Samuel Hull Wilcocke, David Chisholme, and Dr. A.J. Christie, during a period notable also for books of verse by native-born Captain George Longmore and Levi Adams; and for the works of sojourners like Margaret Blennerhasset.

The *Literary Garland* of 1838 was different. It was developed on a genteel basis—a decided contrast with the *Scribbler*. It may have been largely for women, as the annuals and gift books were. The editor wished to publish what Canadians could and would write; he intended to encourage them. But he did not call necessarily for Canadian subjects. Susanna Moodie was an exception, although she mainly published novels about England.

The demise of the 1820s journals probably occurred because their editors had aims that could not be realized in the cultural conditions existing in Canada in their time. Wilcocke aimed both too low and too high—too low for common decency and too high for a literary response matching his own best, broad taste. Chisholme and Christie aimed too high at a Canadian parallel to the great contemporary British journals, the *Edinburgh Review*, the London *Quarterly Review*, and *Blackwood's*. Wilcocke's vogue declined with repetition; other journalists never really established a clientele for serious journalism.

I think part of the answer lies in successive waves of different kinds of immigration. In the 1820s Montreal's population was determined by its overwhelming fur trade and the belated results of the Napoleonic (and American) wars. But the second third of the century was characterized by immigrants of all sorts, who created a distinctive kind of Montreal "establishment" and, at the same time, made the city a gateway to Upper Canada for immigrants seeking land farther west. Montreal's prosperity brought immigrants, a goodly number of whom were educated and interested in social, as well as financial, progress.

Fresh and cheaper land sparked the movement westward. In the United States the same thing was happening. Many of the immigrants landing in Canada or crossing the border went through Upper Canada to Michigan. Many others stayed in what is now Ontario, having been sponsored by land companies such as the Canada Company. Many who came into that Company's lands were Scots, the kind of people John Galt and William "Tiger" Dunlop preferred. Dunlop had arrived in 1827. The Canada Company, formed at that time, operated in the townships north of Middlesex. The Bruce belonged to a later wave of immigrants.

People came in response to advertising by the land companies; but incentives were also provided by travel books. While there was a gap in the writing of creative literature, a hundred travel books describing parts of the Canadas were published in England. Very few were produced at home. It seems as if nearly every early traveller went back to England and wrote a book about his or her arrival at Quebec and the trip along the St. Lawrence, with some advice for immigrants and some mention of interesting facts.

The typical immigrant to Upper Canada differed from urban immigrants like Wilcocke, who had been professionally or technically trained before they had left the Old Country. Many of the potential farmers had been labourers or small tradesmen, and most had a limited amount of education. The Scots among them may have been exceptions, for they had a better level of popular education than the English had in those years. Some of these Scots had to start writing in

Canada at a quite low level. William Lyon Mackenzie and "Tiger" Dunlop were not typical: the former had read through a library of books, and the latter had practices writing with the Blackwoodians. So the gap between the agile "Regency" Wilcocke and early Victorians of *The Literary Garland* may be called a period largely of travel literature, Canadian of the Canadas only in content. Everyone came to Montreal, but for a time Adam Kidd and William Fitz Hawley, products of the 1820s, had few successors in a pragmatic society prospering on the people "passing through."

Rebellion came in 1837. And there was no notable inflow of Americans. By 1838, John Lovell set up a printing press and began publishing. He appears to have been involved with the directories of the population, but also with *The Literary Garland*. The editors of this Montreal publication wanted to present creative writing to match the English and New England writings. Canadians, it was supposed, could write in the high style. I have been criticized by some critics for saying that this was a bad thing, that the *Garland* didn't help the growth of Canadian literature at all. It still sounds foreign; it sounds like Godey's *Lady's Book*, and, in fact, it was Godey's *Lady's Book* that finally put the *Garland* out of commission in 1851.

Mary Markham Brown who was researching this area says that "80% of the material was written by Canadians in the *Garland*," but very little of it was "Canadian." In other words, the literary history of this period is colonial, showing a cultural lag. Many people suggest that marks the whole century, but really that isn't true. It's true of that period, and yet not wholly true even then; there was some writing of a Canadian kind. By the 1850s the railway came through. Canada became linked to the United States by trains; Canadians could then move rather freely between Montreal and Boston and New York— New York principally—and Buffalo. The railway made the connection with Britain more political than literary because of the competing American influences, the American magazines, and the American economic system which made books cheaper (for example, the dime novels). These books quickly penetrated Canada, and the result was a considerable North American tendency in the literature—except in the case of the recent immigrants.

In Montreal there were a number of Irish immigrants who had developed their literary know-how in the Old Country. Thomas D'Arcy McGee is the best example: he had to leave Ireland in 1848 because he had been a member of the Young Ireland movement, which was officially opposed. He went first to the United States and tried to be a spokesman for the Irish there. Then he moved up to Montreal, bringing with him Irish things that came into Canadian literature. His ballad about Jacques Cartier became a classic. In Ireland, he had been editor of *The Nation,* a newspaper politically aligned with Irish nationalism: all this he brought to the Montreal scene. He explored Canadian history and the political concerns which resulted in Confederation. There was a great deal of French-Canadian nationalism at that time. But there was some merging—Montreal is a city constantly affected by the nature of successive waves of immigration. Waves roll in like that, and in between the sand shows. I think *The Literary Garland* was the sand showing—the colonial attitude. But D'Arcy McGee had become a Canadian. Montreal had the lead in the 1820s; the gentility in the late 1830s and 1840s; and McGee and the Irish in the 1850s and 1860s.

He was not alone in creative writing. A Montreal Irish girl, Rosanna Eleanor Mullins, contributed fifteen poems, one sketch, and five serial novels to the *Garland* before she was twenty-three. After she married Dr. J.L. Leprohon, she wrote about both English and French society. Her poetry was published after her death, but her best books, *The Manor House of de Villerai* and *Antoinette de Mirecourt,* belong to 1859 and 1864. The subject matter was provincial, but not narrowly so, and the intention was evidently to bring together French and English upper class material in a way that was distinctly Canadian and not imitative of American works.

In Canada the journals were the outgrowth of newspapers. Politics and journalism were constants in the literary history of the nineteenth century in Canada. Various forms and traditions of contemporary Britain and Europe, brought in by one wave or another of immigration, helped neutralize the overshadowing influence of the United States. The result was a unique mixture, which, even in our later nineteenth-century life and literature, we can call "Canadian."

As a result of the intensive research for the *Canadian Anthology* (1955) which I was preparing with Reginald Watters, and for revisions of Lorne Pierce's *Outline* (1927), I wrote to the latter on 19 December 1953, about plans I had been shaping "in the hope of going to Britain to investigate British-Canadian literary relations."

> On the other hand, I have been going through a period of unsettling with regard to the traditional historical view of

Canadian literature. The categories for the colonial period do not seem right to me, and the bridge between the earlier and later periods in our literature has not been described in our books, not even by A.J.M. Smith. I have hesitated to voice possibly eccentric views in doing a standard work. But I hope to know where I am going by way of 1954 because Gregory Schultz (a graduate student) and I are battling it out on a broad front.

"Battling it out" meant attention to details that, together, would enlarge understanding. I had to know more about most of the early writers. The first public signal I gave of my intention to start what became a life-long crusade was at the Royal Society of Canada annual meeting at the University of Western Ontario in June 1953. Fred Landon had sponsored me to give a paper entitled "Early Creative Literature of Western Ontario." I went as far back as I could at that time, staying on my home ground and dealing with "some books of the first fifteen years, 1828-1843." I gave considerable space to Galt and Dunlop (along with Major John Richardson and A.S. Holmes' *Belinda*).

Galt's *Lawrie Todd* was slightly known, and slightly read, in Ontario. His fictional "Judiville" might have been derived from experiences either in Canada West or in New York State, but I was prepared to think of the novel as Canadian. Was not the river "Debit" actually the "Credit"? I then knew more about Canada and New York State than about Galt's Scottish classic, *Annals of the Parish* (1910). I still had to identify certain qualities of invention and characterization in *Lawrie Todd* in terms of Scott's Lowland fiction.

Galt's *Literary Life and Miscellanies* and his *Autobiography* (Edinburgh 1833) were of little help in understanding this many-sided Scottish novelist who had directed an emigration company. *Bogle Corbet* (1831), a compound of fiction and advice to emigrants, was, I thought, mostly dull. Much more entertaining and informing was a loving book of reminiscences—a kind of historical romance entitled *In the Days of the Canada Company, 1825-1850* (1896). This was the work of two sisters, Robina and Kathleen Lizars, both journalists, whose family's memories went back to the 1820s when Galt and Dunlop were in the Huron Tract at Goderich. Other gossipy on-the-spot reminiscences by settlers and travellers were also available, especially *Twenty-Seven Years in Canada West* (1853) by Samuel Strickland, brother of Catharine Parr Traill and Susanna Moodie.

I did not want to compete with these historical and legendary sources in Canada; I hoped to find and document many of the references loosely made in these books as experiences in Britain. I wanted to trace teasing quotations and anecdotes to their sources abroad and to find the historical Galt and "Tiger" Dunlop. On 18 March 1953, I had written to Lorne Pierce to ask, "Are you sure that you do not wish to publish a nicely edited abridged edition" of *In the Days of the Canada Company* (first published by William Briggs)? Pierce was unable to oblige.

When I went abroad in 1955, I found a new book, *Recollections of Literary Characters* (1854), by Katherine Thomson. She said that Galt had "the gift of narrative, so rare, so fine, so seemingly simple, but so inexplicably difficult; repartee is nothing to it; the power of relating a story, without affectation, or weariness to your listener, is one above all price." My efforts to apply this "rare," "fine" test to *Lawrie Todd* and *Bogle Corbet* provided, after my return, an article in *Ontario History* (Autumn 1957) entitled "John Galt's Canadian Novels." I valued his vivid characterization, exhibited, for example, in "Miss Beany Needles," who was "a tall atomy. Her acquaintance, on account of her meagre length, and for being still unmarried, called her the Spare-rib." My file of notes on Galt became heavy through the years, but I wrote little more about him.

On my first full day in London, I went to the British Museum Library to work on the ponderous central catalogue for references to William Dunlop, *Fraser's Magazine*, and *Blackwood's*. I also followed clues in the Lizars' *Canada Company* book, which hinted at Dunlop's early involvement in journalism. That day I bought a copy of F.D. Tredrey's *The House of Blackwood 1804-1954: The History of Publishing Firm* (1954). Dunlop was not mentioned, except on a page or two of speculation about the authorship of the "Canadian Boat-Song." This poem was quoted as it had appeared in the "Noctes" column of *Blackwood's* in September 1829. It ended with the words of James Hogg, "the Shepherd": "Well, Doctor, what say you? Another bowl." "Doctor" and "bowl" were terms suggestive of Dunlop who had trained as a medical doctor. My search was leading me into the fascinating world of Scottish journalism of the 1810s, 1820s, and 1830s.

That was the beginning. A few days later I was in Edinburgh, having conversation and morning coffee at the National Library of Scotland with William Beattie, the Librarian, and others. I soon had a great deal of information new to me, and, I am sure, to most Canadians: there was a set of three volumes on the Dunlop family, privately printed by J.G. Dunlop in Frome and London, and very rare. An interesting discovery also was George William Blackwood's *A Manuscript List of Early Contributors to Blackwood's Magazine 1826-1870*, which could be seen only at the National Library.

I eagerly paged through this manuscript, finding a few errors but also identifications of some of Dunlop's pseudonyms. Pseudonyms were so common in British journals of the day that identification of them was part of the scholars' game.

I was introduced to Alan Lang Strout from Texas, who was also playing this game. We compared notes and attempted to correct items showing in the Manuscript at the Library. It was possible to identify Dunlop as the author of four articles on India and other subjects that had appeared in *Blackwood's* in 1822 and 1823. Strout published his findings in *A Bibliography of Articles in Blackwoods Magazine, Volumes I through XVIII, 1817-1825* in 1959.

For my part, I was especially interested in the journalists who edited and wrote for *Blackwood's* from the time of the famous 1817 semi-biblical spoof called "Translation from an Ancient Chaldee Manuscript." When Dunlop moved to Edinburgh in 1823, he was welcomed into the circle of these lively editors, who rejoiced in fantasy as well as truth under such pseudonyms as "leopard" (John Wilson, also "Christopher North"), "scorpion" (John Gibson Lockhart, son-in-law of Walter Scott), "great wild boar" (James Hogg, also "the Etrick Shepherd"), and O'Doherty (William Maginn, who became editor of *Fraser's Magazine* in 1830). I was convinced that Dunlop was given his title "Tiger" by this group and not only because he had been in India.

I had to return to London to obtain accurate information about his career as a journalist in India and his wild scheme to rid the Island of Saugor of tigers. There were two sources: Calcutta newspapers, which took me into the Indian Library of the Foreign Office in Whitehall; and London newspapers, such as *The Telescope* and *The British Press*, which I could find and read only at the British Museum's Newspaper Library at Colindale.

I was astonished to learn from these sources about the low level of some newspaper journalism in London in 1825. *The Telescope*, which Dunlop edited, and to which Lockhart and Maginn may have contributed, went far beyond the spoofing of *Blackwood's* into vulgarity, gossip, and slander as a rival to *The Age*, edited by Charles Malloy Westmacott, also compiler of *The Spirit of the Public Journals for the Year MDCCCXXV*. I ploughed through a good deal of it with the feeling that I had learned more about the underside of London life than British fiction and history had revealed.

One of my most pleasant experiences concerned Dunlop's medical career, which he began at the University of Glasgow and practised as an assistant surgeon of the 89th Regiment of Foot (2nd Battalion) in Canada during the War of 1812. I also discovered that upon his return from India to Edinburgh, he had established a medical practice in that city and lectured on medical jurisprudence at the University.

I believe that readership and imitation of *Blackwood's* by Canadian provincial journalists was much greater than has been recognized. Adaptations of its easy-going style, use of pseudonyms, and fanciful dialogues resembling its famous feature, "Noctes Ambrosianae" (begun in March 1822), appeared in Canadian newspaper sketches and in inventions of local groups of convivial wits. A good example can be found in "The Editor's Shanty" in the *Streetsville Weekly Review*, edited by the Rev. Robert Jackson MacGeorge, known as the "Solomon of Streetsville," Upper Canada.

I also discovered pictures of Dunlop, especially in the black and white drawings in *Fraser's* magazine (that precursor of *Punch*) edited by "Tiger's" old friend William Maginn. One of the features of *Fraser's* was a series of drawings of celebrated characters made by Daniel Maclise ("Alfred Croquis"). Maginn wrote the accompanying sketches of their careers. Dunlop was celebrated in the thirty-fifth of the "Gallery Sketches" just before Benjamin Disraeli, Thomas Carlyle, and Samuel Taylor Coleridge. In Maclise's group of the "Fraserians" in a composite portrait, Dunlop is easy to recognize. Later I was allowed to use—through Lorne Pierce's influence—a frontispiece to my book about the "Blackwoodian Backwoodsman" derived from a portrait hanging in the Academy of Medicine of Toronto. My whole experience with Dunlop convinced me that his *Statistical Sketches of Upper Canada, For the Use of Emigrants* (1832) was an elaborate spoof of the current vogue in British emigrant and travel books in both title and details.

Finally, I was delighted to read in Volume 2 of *The Dunlop Papers* a note about William's "little cousin, Jeannie Walsh." When William visited her in 1833 she had become the wife of Thomas Carlyle, the famous writer, who described Dunlop as "one of the strangest men of his age, with an inexhaustible sense of fun." Dunlop described Carlyle, in a letter introducing Col. Fitzgibbon, with these words, "you are congenial spirits, both being crack-brain'd Enthusiasts." I cannot resist appending the account of William's visit in 1833; the Carlyles were staying with friends:

> The door opened, and there was ushered in an enormous giant of a man with long red hair: so strange and immense did he look at first sight, and like an Ogre, that Carlyle felt timorous, expecting he would proceed to devour some of the party: while his wife made one spring on this tremendous apparition and caught him round the neck and embraced him. For a few seconds Carlyle thought he had married a woman who was wrong in the head.

As I finished my research on Dunlop, I felt that I had stolen for Canada a writer worthy of a place in the annals of British literature.

On my return to Canada, I offered Pierce a book of extracts by and about Dunlop, in chronological or topical order, with brief bibliographical references by myself. I promised "valuable and wonderful additional material, especially from the pen of William Maginn"

> I have no end of new material, most of it still on microfilm," I added, "letters from Edinburgh; whimsical notes which Dunlop made for a standard medical textbook; records of literary friendships in Edinburgh and London; relations with Galt; most of the story of his [Dunlop's] career in India (including extracts from Calcutta newspapers); complete files of newspapers he edited in London, England. In all this, Dunlop the journalist and adventurer comes out strongly as he moves on intimate terms with the convivial geniuses who brought fame to Blackwood's and Fraser's. Aided and abetted by Maginn, Dunlop made his Telescope one of the notorious Sunday papers of the easy-going post-Napoleonic, pre-Victorian era. Into the story came vivid presentations of Blackwood, Galt, James Silk Buckingham (who started the Athenaeum), James Hogg, Lockhart, and even Carlyle.

Pierce wished to tone down my plan. "You have just about rounded out the canon," he said, but it seemed to him that "a brief, sound and exciting biography" would be the best plan. I countered by pointing out that a rival publishing house was being asked to publish a biography by a man who possessed very little of the information at my disposal. *William "Tiger" Dunlop: "Blackwoodian Backwoodsman"*, which contained extracts from and about Dunlop with my comments, was published late in 1958, much to my satisfaction. Nine years later, McClelland & Stewart published it in one paperback volume, with my introduction, "Recollections of the American War of 1812-1814" and "Statistical Sketches of Upper Canada for the Use of Emigrants," for which there had been no room in my *Blackwoodian Backwoodsman* volume.

In the 1950s when I began to go further back into Canada's literary history, I also devoted much research and writing to Indian themes. When I was a boy, Indians were creatures of fiction found only in books and represented in plays by bows and arrows. At school I was taught little about those who lived within reach of my home. Their historical geography remained vague although association of events with on-the-spot experience would have been my best way of learning. Not until my teens did I visit such places as the Mohawk Chapel at Brantford and, near Midland, the pile of stones that marked Ste. Marie among the Hurons.

In my early twenties I was introduced to general theories about Indians that had prevailed long before my time in England and the United States. At Columbia, Professor Fairchild lectured on "the noble savage," and Wright discussed "the meaning of Rousseau." I read such authors as Colden, Chinard, and Chateaubriand and followed the fascinating theme of "primitivism" to the Ossianic controversy and to commentators like Mrs. Anne Grant and William Richardson. Rusk's lectures on James Fenimore Cooper were vital for they led me to "good" Indians in books by John Heckewelder and other Moravians of Pennsylvania and southwestern Ontario.

I regarded Major John Richardson as a central figure because of his poem *Tecumseh* (1828), and his prose *Wacousta* (1832), as well as A.C. Casselman's *War of 1812 with Notes and a Life of the Author*, his 1902 edition of Richardson's experiences with the war of 1812. In my search in the British Museum, I came upon additional, anonymous poems on Tecumseh and a sketch on "Indian Warfare." Adam Kidd used a "Huron Chief" to satirize a bishop of Quebec. In

Frances Brooke's *The History of Emily Montague* (1769) were some comments on Rousseau and the Indians of Lorette. More subtle was the influence of Indians on Campbell's *Lake Lyrics and Other Poems* (1889), and more explicit Ned Pratt's use of *The Jesuit Relations* and the diggings at Ste. Marie. An article on William Richardson's "The Cacique of Ontario" in the *University of Toronto Quarterly* (1959) gave me my first opportunity to discuss philosophical and critical problems in Indian literature.

The story was ready-made for the "transatlantic" presentation I aspired to give it. From the beginning there was much to explain, for "cacique" did not seem to fit with "Ontario," or with the author, who had evidently no first-hand acquaintance with the Hurons. The subject appealed to me because the fortuitous circumstances of my training and my special interests enabled me to explain its diverse, yet unifying sources and features.

I had been prepared by my Columbia courses for the "noble" Indian characters in Richardson's tale. It was apparent to me that Richardson's setting, "an island in the Lake Ontario," was probably not Canadian but on the American side near Oswego or even farther west. In the story, Marano, a white girl, is rescued by the family of Ononthio (the cacique, or chief) when the Outagami "carried terror to the gates of Albany." When I discovered that Richardson knew Anne Grant of Laggan and had been named in one of her poems, much more fell into place, especially that the place or area was definintely northern New York state, more specifically the Indian lands between Albany and Oswego. Mrs. Grant's father had been in the garrison at Oswego, and she had been brought up by the Schuylers near Albany. Her early *Letters from the Mountains* told her story in the United States before she went to Scotland and married the Reverend Mr. Grant.

The plot was conventional. The language had the flavour of Ossian, perhaps as a result of Richardson's professed interest in Macpherson's *Fingal* and the controversies it aroused. I had long been interested in Cadwallader Colden's acknowledgment of Indian eloquence, which, I thought, suggested Ossianic rhythms or a common source for Macpherson and the translators of Indian speeches. There were several pirated editions of Richardson's "The Indians," a tale in prose published in *Poems Chiefly Rural* (1776) and later turned into a poetic play. For such details and textual differences I had to delve into the world—chiefly the London world—of journalism and such early journals as *The Monthly Review* which, indeed, reviewed Richardson in 1791.

Although the philosophical background of William Richardson's characterization required a review of the sentimental tradition behind the "noble savage" concept, I was pleased to find how it tied in with Shakespeare's principles of human conduct as Richardson presented them. I discovered to my satisfaction that the professor had achieved a comfortable reputation, still recognized, for his essays in Henry Mackenzie's *Mirror* (1779-80) and specially for his "Criticism on a Scene in Shakespeare's Richard III." Richardson wished to make both criticism and moral observation as scientific as possible.

I thought that I had found Richardson treating Indians (whom he knew chiefly by repute) by means of a deduction from his assessment of Shakespeare's characterization and dialogue—"a wishful application of principles concerning the passions of the inhabitants of a vaguely understood transatlantic community on the shores of Lake Ontario." "The tale," I added, "would thus owe more to Shakespeare studies than to a reading of the source books of Indian lore," although Richardson probably had not altogether neglected Hennepin, Lahontan, Lafitau, Charlevoix, or Colden. I would have been lost in understanding Richardson's and Shakespeare's imitation of the passions and affections of his characters—"human nature somewhat methodized," making poetry "subservient to philosophy" and employing it "in tracing the principles of human conduct" if it had not been part of my earlier studies.

I brought to this article all the resources of my professors' lectures about romantic criticism, my renewed reading of Coleridge, and what I had learned about Shakespeare from Hazelton Spencer's *The Art of William Shakespeare* (1940). This article marked the end of the 1950s, during which I had gained in confidence as a guide to the production of a literary history and seemed destined to become an unapologetic representative of literary Canada even in the British Museum Reading Room.

In 1959 I was commissioned by Prentice-Hall to compile a book of documents about Tecumseh. I knew that I must consider not only early American-British warfare but also contemporary American and Canadian nationalism. In the American tradition Tecumseh was a traitor and an enemy; in the Canadian tradition he was a patriot and hero.

I had to combat the received opinions of critics, and of school authorities. The book of "primary source materials" was to be provided for teaching composition and research to students in the upper high school grades and freshman English. It was called *A Guided Research Series*—there was one book on *Brook Farm*. I was very much taken up with *Brook Farm*, and it occurred to me that perhaps a Canadian subject would be possible, half historical and half literary, so I got in touch with Wallace Matheson in the Canadian office of Prentice-Hall. After some negotiation, I proposed to do a book to be called *Tecumseh: Fact and Fiction*, which would be interesting to those with little or no access to original books on the subject. As Tecumseh was more a "name" than a figure whom people could picture, there were a lot of questions to be raised. These questions could serve for classroom discussion and essay topics.

Tecumseh was later described as "the colorful story of the famous chief Tecumseh (1768-1813), presented through a generous selection of the earliest records. These letters, descriptions and narratives by men close to the Shawnee warrior and statesman must be the basis of any assessment of his role in the struggle of the Indian nation to maintain itself against the settlers. Since the Indians wrote nothing and the white men gave conflicting reports of Tecumseh's life and death, the legends and historical accounts leave much scope for fresh inquiry." This was the beauty of these "guided" books: the students could make an enquiry of their own and back up their opinions from actual documents.

This hero of the old northwest and Canadian border had not yet received the treatment he deserved. There were, of course, books on Tecumseh, but these were either superficial or American-oriented. Tecumseh was given biased treatment in American history. He had been killed by some of General Harrison's men in 1813 at Moraviantown, in what is now Ontario; and when Harrison ran for president of the United States in the 1840s, his reputation as the killer of Tecumseh and Tecumseh's brother, the Prophet, was made part of the campaign publicity.

I aimed my book at both American and Canadian readers, and although I became very much excited about the whole thing, I adopted a strictly objective approach. It could have been exploited—that is to say, the book could have had no circulation in the U.S. if I had presented only the Canadian position. Tecumseh had been the leader of an organized rebellion, you might say, of the Indians on this side of the Mississippi when the American settlers and America soldiers were driving them westward.

There was a very wide field to be covered—not only Upper Canada, which is now Ontario, but Indiana, Ohio, southern Michigan, and the old Northwest. Indian history is not something separate from early white man's history. I wanted to keep the discussion about Tecumseh open by providing a collection of documents chiefly written in, or not long after, Tecumseh's lifetime. I attempted to maintain a neutral position with regard to the local and dated issues which were so hotly contested about 150 years ago and to invite readers to approach the accounts of the past in an enlightened and objective spirit.

> The major issues will be recognizable because they are basically still with us today: the conflicts between coloured and white races; self-determination and colonialism; local leadership and centralized government; individual "natural" rights and general welfare; private contract and national policy; casual and efficient use of the land; the old order and the new; primitivism and progress; savagery and spirituality in our natures; cool discussion and open warfare; cruelty and humanity in the treatment of enemies; propaganda and respect for truth.

I could not help but feel that these problems were permanent in society of haves and have nots.

I was quite prepared by this time with regard to Canadian documents, but I had not read widely in American sources. Therefore, my main preparation lay finding out what the Americans had said. The books I found especially useful were, *The Life of Joseph Hunt* (1838), Moses Dawson's *A Historical Narrative of the Civil and Military Services of Major General William H. Harrison* (1824), Benjamin Drake's *Life of Tecumseh and His Brother the Prophet, with a historical sketch of the Shawanoe Indians* (1841), B.B. Thatcher's *Indian Biography; or, An historical account of those individuals who have been distinguished among North American natives as orators, warriors, statesmen, and other remarkable characters* (1832), Robert Breckenridge McAfee's *History of the Late War in the Western Country* (1816), and an amazing book, Benjamin J. Lossing's *The Pictorial Field-Book of the War of 1812* (1869). Lossing went from place to place where battles had been fought or where important events in the war of 1812 had occurred; he had both photographs and artifacts.

Also, I found material in the Public Archives of Canada [now National Archives], since Tecumseh in 1811 had tried to expand the influence of his confederacy all the way down into Georgia and Florida. The best book for this purpose I found was H.B. Cushman's *History of The Choctaw, Chicasaw and Natchez Indians* (1899). In it I found a record of Tecumseh's visit to the South. My discoveries delighted me.

There was one particularly valuable story about the trip of Tecumseh down to the South.

> On his return from Florida (he had been among the Florida Indians), he went among the Creeks in Alabama, urging them to unite with the Seminoles. Arriving in Tuckhabatchee, a Creek town on the Tallapoosa River, he made his way to the lodge of the chief called the "Big Warrior." He explained his object; delivered his war talk; presented a bundle of sticks; gave a piece of wampum and a war hatchet—all of which the Big Warrior took. When Tecumthe, reading the spirit and intentions of the Big Warrior, looked him in the eye, and pointing his finger towards his face, said 'Your blood is white. You have taken my talk, and the sticks, and the wampum and the hatchet, but you do not mean to fight. I know the reason. You do not believe the Great Spirit has sent me. You shall know. I leave Tuckhabatchee directly—and shall go straight to Detroit. When I arrive there, I will stamp on the ground with my foot, and shake down every house in Tuckhabatchee.'
>
> So saying, he turned and left the Big Warrior in utter amazement, at both his manner and his threat, and pursued his journey. The Indians were struck no less with his conduct than was the Big Warrior, and began to dread the arrival of the day when the threatened calamity would befall them. They met often, and talked over this matter—and counted the days carefully, to know the day when Tecumthe would reach Detroit. The morning they had fixed upon as the day of his arrival at last came. A mighty rumbling was heard—the Indians all ran out of their

houses—the earth began to shake; when at last, sure enough every house in Tuckhabatchee was shaken down! The exclamation was in every mouth: "Tecumthe has got to Detroit." The effect was electric. The message he had delivered to Big Warrior was believed, and many of the Indians took their rifles and prepared for war.

The reader will not be surprised to learn, that an earthquake had produced all this; but he will be doubtless surprised that it should happen on the very day on which Tecumthe arrived at Detroit in exact fulfillment of his threat. It was the famous earthquake of New Madrid on the Mississippi.

My book was published in 1961. I had a lot of satisfaction from this book, and I was to keep my interest in this Indian subject for a long time. I picked it up again in a different form when preparing the *Journal of Major John Norton* (1816). Perhaps I would not have found the manuscript of this *Journal* at all if I had not always been on the lookout for more interesting Indian material relative to early Ontario and Quebec.

When I got to Norton's manuscript, I realized that Norton had made his trip to the Cherokee and Creek country in 1809-10. Norton's intentions were much different, but he was also misunderstood sometimes because of the general movement among the Indians to prevent their being pushed across the Mississippi.

I had a greater supply of source material on Major John Richardson than on Dunlop or Galt or Holmes, author of *Belinda*. Our library had various editions of *Wacousta*, and they obtained for me microfilm or photographic copies of any books I needed, including Richardson's *Tecumseh* and *Ecarté*. His autobiographical *Eight Years in Canada* was also available. In addition, I had William Hamilton Merrit's copy of the elaborate edition of Richardson's *War of 1812 with Notes and a Life of the Author*, edited by Alexander Clark Casselman and published by the Historical Publishing Company of Toronto in 1902. This was an excellent scholarly work enriched by photographs, maps, and a good bibliographical section, listing some English publications Casselman had not seen and a number of others with American imprints. William Renwick Riddell's *John Richardson* in Pierce's series of *Makers of Canadian Literature* (1923) was useful, especially in the summaries of some unavailable books by Richardson with notes and bibliographical information.

Nevertheless there were more surprises ahead in 1955 when I went to England and again worked in the British Museum. I not only enlarged my knowledge of Richardson's life and filled in gaps regarding his career in Britain, but I also became a kind of Richardson authority by adding to the canon of his works. The first was *Kensington Gardens in 1830*, published in London in 1830, evidently a unique copy acquired by the British Museum in 1895 and bound with several other volumes, and therefore not easy to find. Later on, I came to the conclusion that there was no copy in North America. I was convinced that *Kensington Gardens in 1830*, although it was anonymous, was Richardson's, because the title-page announced that it was: "By the author of *Ecarté*." No reader of *Ecarté* would be surprised to find this Canadian officer having a fling at English-French social life.

I also discovered "A Canadian Campaign by a British Officer," an earlier form of Richardson's *War of 1812*, more or less casually in *The New Monthly Magazine and Literary Journal* published by Henry Colburn in London during the period 1826-27. There had been reference to the so-called "Canadian Campaign" before I found it in 1955, but its exact location had escaped other Richardson buffs. I was delighted to settle the question in 1966 before William F.E. Morley published his excellent *A Bibliographical Study of Major John Richardson* in 1973.

A third discovery was entitled *Jack Brag in Spain*. Part of this tale was published by Richardson in his own journal called *New Era* in Brockville in 1841-42. *Jack Brag* was his continuation of Theodore Edward Hook's 1837 *Jack Brag*. Indeed, Richardson's books have provided me with subjects for publication from 1953 to 1977.

During 1956-57, I published two papers I particularly enjoyed working on, but whose end results were disappointments. The first, entitled "Life in the Army 150 Years Ago," was published in the local newspaper, *The London Free Press*, on 29 September 1956. A callous editor chopped off the most intriguing portion of it before publication, and the book that formed its core has disappeared from the library. This book, called *Standing Orders of the 41st Regiment of Foot 1789*, owned by a Lieutenant John Hall, had been printed by A. Edwards in Cork, southern Ireland, in 1797. As handwritten notes showed, it had been carried from Ireland to Canada and through campaigns of the Forty-First Regiment on the Detroit border until the regiment was destroyed by Harrison's American army at Moraviantown (Richardson was one of the officers who was made a prisoner of war; he told his story in *War of 1812*, and there are oblique references to it in *Ecarté* and *The Canadian Brothers*). It is full of regulations for the good conduct of all ranks, especially of women who worked at the barracks, from details of dress to an injunction against throwing water or dirt of any kind out of the barrack doors or windows. It stressed sobriety and cleanliness and outlined the punishment for various offences. The following part of my article was removed by the editor, along with the most delightful of the book's quaint rules for conduct: "It would be illiberal to suppose that the surgeon and his mate could both be intoxicated at the same time— however joyous the occasion."

The second disappointment resulted from my efforts to pursue the subject of Tecumseh through the writings of contemporaries of Richardson who had made poetry or prose out of the life and death of the famous chief. In an article entitled "Some Anonymous Literature of the War of 1812," published by *Ontario History* in 1957, I was indeed in the mazes of anonymity, likely to make some good guesses and certainly some bad ones.

Three discoveries appeared to interlock. The first was *The Lucubrations of Humphrey Ravelin, Esq., Late Major in the... Regiment of Infantry*, containing a chapter on "Indian Warfare," published by G. and W.B. Whitaker of London, England, in 1823. Though the authorship should have been transparent, it had been successfully hidden. Neglect of the book is the more remarkable because it had enjoyed a considerable circulation in London in its time and was reviewed in the *Quarterly* (October 1822), *The Literary Gazette* (March 1823) and *The Monthly Review* (May 1823). Any Canadian who turned to the "Indian Warfare" chapter would notice the homage paid to Tecumseh (spelled Tecumthé), the naming of General Procter (Colonel of the 41st Regiment at Fort Malden), and the shrewd, perhaps eyewitness observations on military affairs. The British Museum identified the author as "G. Procter, Novelist." I spent a good deal of time speculating that G. Procter was Lieutenant George Procter, one-time Adjutant of the Royal Military College at Sandhurst, who had married General (earlier, Colonel) Henry Procter's daughter, Susannah Anne. This may have been a good guess, or a red herring, for no one has yet come up with an alternative.

Another discovery was truly exciting: I came upon a unique, anonymous book—*Tales of Chivalry and Romance*—306 pages of verse published in 1826 by James Robertson and Company in Edinburgh and Baldwin Craddock and Joy in London.

Had the much more recent findings of Mary Lu MacDonald, an independent researcher in Halifax, been available to me, I would have known that there was proof in the columns of the *Montreal Gazette* that the poems were by George Longmore, a Canadian by birth, a captain in the Royal Staff Corps in Montreal in the early 1820s, who had published poetry in Montreal journals. I thought in the 1950s that Levi Adams, a young Montreal lawyer, had written "The Charivari" and was therefore the poet of the other poems printed in the *Tales of Chivalry and Romance*.

Serious errors in matters like these show that the real joy is in digging out details. If they do not fit, one has still learned a great deal about the period, the setting, and the time.

Longmore, then, was the author of "Tecumthé," the other poems printed in *Tales of Chivalry and Romance*, and possibly of the prose chapter on "Indian Warfare" printed with "Tecumthé." The poet of "Tecumthé" acknowledged that the "Indian Warfare" chapter was an extract from a periodical journal, not identified, and it is not quite clear whether he is referring to an article he wrote by himself. If Longmore wrote that article on "Indian Warfare" from which he quotes, and in fact that article appeared also in full in *The Lucubrations of Humphrey Ravelin*, we have a very interesting circle of anonymity.

What the "Tecumthé" poet says is that he had taken the extract from a periodical journal "republished in *The Lucubrations of Humphrey Ravelin* under the head of 'Indian Warfare.' " Now, was the author of *The Lucubrations* Longmore? I don't know.

Meanwhile, I had good and bad results with an abbreviated edition of *Wacousta* published by McClelland and Stewart in its New Canadian Library Series in 1967. I protested from the beginning to the general editor of the series, Malcolm Ross, and to McClelland and Stewart about the decision to reduce the text to 300 pages. I could not, and did not, claim to offer a definitive text, only a popularized version. Only my introduction was scholarly. What I left, by cutting out chapters, was a fast-moving romance; in spite of everything, it gave many people pleasure, and *Wacousta* kept the name of Richardson before the public.

In my introduction I discussed Edward Young's *The Revenge* and Robert Rogers' *Ponteach* and the rhetoric and conventions of the sentimental romance, the succession of vivid narration of incidents followed shortly by chapters explaining feeling and action, the suddenness of happenings, the rhythm of intense situations—and I closed by saying that *Wacousta*, in spite of crudities, "may appeal to the poetically minded as a gigantic symbol for something in the frontier places of every mind."

In *Reviews and Criticisms* (1972), Carl Ballstadt says that I suggest that "*Wacousta* is psychological fiction." I do not believe that I use those technical terms, but I was impressed by the existence of "coverts" in *Wacousta* and in *The Canadian Brothers*, which I edited for Douglas Lochhead's Literature of Canada series (1976). In my introduction to that volume I found, once more, "sudden surprises, actions before explanations, mysterious happenings, terrors by night and day, deadly combats, pervading gloom, intriguing sexual encounters, haunted minds, and consuming passion."

In the midst of the violence, there was satisfaction in drawing up a genealogical table of the De Haldimar line based on Richardson's own belated clarity about the persons involved in his two novels, *The Prophecy* (that is, *Wacousta*) and *The Prophecy Fulfilled* (that is, *The Canadian Brothers*).

The Canadian Brothers was a project for which I was well prepared because I was entirely familiar with Richardson's *War of 1812*, which covered in biographical and historical form a good deal of the material he romanticized in *The Canadian Brothers*. I had, indeed, found the first publication of Richardson's "A Canadian Campaign," upon which the *War of 1812* was based. This article had been mentioned in Richardson's Preface to the London edition of *Tecumseh*, but it had not been found by other researchers. Paging through Henry Colburn's *The New Monthly Magazine and Literary Journal*, I suddenly found "a Canadian Campaign, by a British Officer" in the British Museum, in issues of December 1826 to June 1827. This was a real coup. I gave the information to William Morley for the *Bibliographical Society of Canada Papers* (Vol. 5, 1966).

The "Campaign" material, "a private memoir [rather] than a relation of the incidents of the war," and the enlarged version of *War of 1812* were exactly what I needed to comment on *The Canadian Brothers*. In addition, I read many American books regarding the "Beauchamp tragedy, which took place at or near Weiseger Hotel in

Frankfort, Kentucky," where, as Richardson recorded in his introduction to an 1851 edition of *Wacousta*, he "had been many years before confined as a prisoner of war."

My most useful contribution to Richardson studies, however, was a chart with details that identified the families who were the principal participants in the action of *Wacousta* and *The Canadian Brothers*. I do not know why Richardson did not clear up probable confusion about these characters in *Wacousta* but instead waited until the *Brothers* to give full genealogical information. I added this supplement to the more popular *Wacousta* published by McClelland and Stewart. In the year of my retirement, 1973, I welcomed two additions to the Richardson canon: *Frascati's; or, Scenes in Paris*, discovered through the Colburn papers by David Sinclair, and the full text of the long-awaited *Westbrook the Outlaw*, discovered by David R. Beasley, and edited by him for Grant Woolmer Books, Montreal. Will more be found?

I was always also interested in the writers of Canadian regions outside of Ontario, such as Adam Hood Burwell, a contemporary of the Maritime Oliver Goldsmith. And I had become acquainted with a valuable book about early Lower Canada, *The Life of the Right Reverend, the Honorable Charles James Stewart, D.D., Oxon., Second Lord Bishop of Quebec*, by Thomas R. Millman, who had been a professor of Church History at Huron College at Western. Its most valuable feature was the biographical sketches of missionaries and candidates for missionary work in the Canadas under the auspices of the Society for the Propagation of the Gospel. One was of Adam Hood Burwell (1790-1849); others were of Adam Kidd and Edward Lane.

The transatlantic nature of investigation was demonstrated when I visited the headquarters of the Society for the Propagation of the Gospel in the Dean's Yard at Westminster. In this Victorian setting I relived something of an earlier Canadian past. Here, Millman had gathered much of his information. Additional facts were derived from H.P. Hill's *History of Christ Cathedral (1832-1932)*.

In *Old Lamps Aglow* (1955), Montreal collector Lawrence Lande showed that he had consulted Millman and had found additional sources regarding Burwell, especially an article by Henry Scadding in the *Canadian Journal of Science, Literature and History* (1878) and a letter to Burwell in the John Macaulay Papers (Ontario Archives). Scadding had identified Burwell as "Erie-us," the author of poems in

The Canadian Review and Literary and Historical Journal (1825), but Lande understood that Scadding had confused *Adam* with *Mahlon* Burwell. It was Lande who fired my interest in "Talbot Road," one of the first of Burwell's poems. Lande's extracts from poems in the *Canadian Review* also sent me to that early journal and rival periodicals in Montreal.

W.S. Wallace's "The Literature Relating to the Selkirk Controversy" and his interest in Samuel Hull Wilcocke led me to Wilcocke's Montreal journal, *The Scribbler* (1821-27). When we finally succeeded, through W. Kaye Lamb, the first National Librarian, in obtaining a reasonably full set of the first six of ten volumes, it was possible to see how much "Erie-us" (Burwell) had contributed to Wilcocke's journal from Port Talbot, Ontario. I collected nineteen of Burwell's Port Talbot poems, and these, the poems Lande had found in *The Canadian Review*, and three poems from *The Literary Garland* (1849), were published with my introduction as a paperbound volume of 110 mimeographed pages in May 1963 by the Lawson Memorial Library of the University of Western Ontario.

Adam Burwell attracted me because his poetry was familiar and local, Adam Kidd because his book *The Huron Chief* (1830) had a title that would intrigue anyone interested in documentary or romantic literature. But when I approached Kidd's book, I also questioned his claim to have suffered "an accidental fall from the cloud-capped brows of a dangerous Mountain, over which [he] had heedlessly wandered, with all that open carelessness which is so peculiarly the characteristic of poetic feeling."

I noted that in *Old Lamps Aglow* Lande had expressed no doubts about this claim. He had made a strong point, however, about Kidd's championship of the Indian cause and quoted the poet's statement that he could "fairly and honestly plead for the correctness of [his] observations."

First, I studied maps for "Tullinagee, in the parish of Desertlyn, near Moneymore, in the southern part of the County of Derry"—his home before emigration to Quebec—and the neighboring mountain, Slievegallion (altitude 1735 feet!). Then I became sceptical, for the Slievegallion suggestion had been replaced by "a M...t...n" "that wears a gown." This sent me back to Quebec, Bishop Mountain, and that very different product of the Society for the Propagation of the Gospel, Adam Burwell.

I appealed to Professor Millman who replied:

> The only reference to Adam Kidd which I have been able to trace occurs in a document dated July 24, 1824, at Quebec, and sent by the writer, Archdeacon G.J. Mountain, to Archdeacon G.O. Stuart at Kingston. In this letter Mountain gives Stuart a list of divinity students which he divides into three classes: (a) Students actually enjoying scholarships; (b) Students not actually rejected, but proceeding at their own risk; (c) Possible candidates. Fourteenth in this last category is "Kidd, Adam, Quebec, Supporting himself."

In a copy of *The Huron Chief* in the Public Library in London that formerly belonged to the Reverend Job Deacon, someone known to Kidd has penciled a comment on page 64 opposite the lines:

> All looked so like the scenes and groves
> Through which the dreaming spirit roves,
> That my wrecked heart forgot the pain
> A <u>Mountain</u> demon flung before it—

The comment is:

> It was thine own foolish way and inclination and not "a mountain demon" that has blighted thy prospects. Justice to the <u>illustrious dead</u> whom thy heartless calumny cannot reach, requires this much to be said. The living is able, if inclined, to justify his own conduct; but I apprehend is too conscious of his integrity, and too exalted in mind, to condescend to notice your base scurrility contained in this inharmonious doggerel.

On pages 44 and 45 Kidd again writes:

> For me, I hate all whining cant,
> And, doubly so, the Churchman's rant,
> If even sent from sides of iron,

By hill, by dale, by grot, or fountain,
Against the great immortal Byron!

In all the poising of a M...t...n,
Who nothing loves, but what's his own,
Or some <u>thing</u> else that wears a gown.

However, the poet's discretion apparently overruled his lacerated feelings, and an address to the "Rev. Polyphemus" was replaced by a couple of innocuous rhymes. He refers to this omission in the preface.

Apparently Kidd contemplated studying for the ministry. For some reason he was rejected by Bishop Mountain and by Archdeacon Mountain, who tutored the theological students. He may have been refused because of carelessness. Because of his disappointment Kidd apparently conceived an intense dislike of the Mountains, father and son, whom Job Deacon defends.

In a poem in *The Huron Chief* addressed to Bishop Charles James Stewart, thanking him for "Gospel truths," "thy tender friendship oft on me bestowed / Throughout a sunny lapse of happier days / When this wrecked heart with pure devotion glowed," Kidd had evidently found a bishop whom he liked. In another poem there is a poetic confession that he loved an Indian girl "over well"—another version of a fall. Probably it was Job Deacon who wrote on p. 55 of his copy, "perverted taste, to be first attracted by a squaw!"

In terms of my studies in literature of the Indian, *The Huron Chief* presented "good Indians." Kidd's attitude was, no doubt, conditioned by the Indian girl, his acquaintance with the Huron people at nearby Lorette, and the dramatic requirement for a native chief to be idealized while the official chiefs of the Church were degraded.

I was pleased with Kidd's notes, for his reading in early literature of the Indian resembled my own; including the works of such authors as Cadwallader Colden, Loskiel, Heckewelder, Alexander MacKenzie, Alexander Henry, William Tudor, and William W. Campbell, and the later romancers, Moore and Cooper. I was also delighted by the echoes of Ossian.

In the early days when I tried to document the location of "Slievegallion," I had a delightful correspondence with the Rev. Ronald C.C. O'Connor, in Moneymore, Northern Ireland. I wrote to him about information concerning the Kidd family and the Workman family, who had come to Montreal and established a school and a newspaper. O'Connor had no record of an Adam Kidd, but he gave details about John and Anne Kidd and John and Sarah, their children. My wife and I later spent happy days visiting places associated with Kidd in Quebec and at Lorette, while we had a rented house on the Grande Allée in Quebec City, where the artist Krieghoff had lived. *Queen's Quarterly* published my article "Adam Kidd: An Early Canadian Poet" in 1958.

I did not get around to writing about Kidd's friend, William Fitz Hawley, author of *The Unknown or Lays of the Forest* (1831), until I was asked to do so for the *Dictionary of Canadian Biography* in 1978. The DCB editors also asked me to write on Edward Lane, author of *The Fugitives*.

Edward Lane, a minor novelist, figures in our literary history only as an historical figure. Perhaps this is the view he himself took in his sub-title, "or, A Trip to Canada," and in further detail "An interesting tale, chiefly founded on facts: interspersed with observations on the manners, customs, etc. of the colonists and Indians. By Edward Lane, formerly a resident in Lower Canada." He did not claim to be Canadian-born, and I could not identify him with any of the Lane families in Montreal, but his residence in Lower Canada was confirmed by Millman in his *The Life of The Right Reverend, The Honorable Charles James Stewart, Second Lord Bishop of Quebec*.

My first problem was geographical, for, when I began, I did not even know that Rivière du Loup-en-Haut, where Lane was appointed, was near Berthier and Trois-Rivières. Finding it in Joseph Bouchette's *A Topographical Dictionary of the Province of Lower Canada* (1832) also meant that I had pleasant reading in a great book, but that I was diverted from my main purpose. Lane's *The Fugitives* was manifestly also a geographical book, for the places visited by two characters in the story are described in detail. The parish of St. Antoine de Rivière du Loup, for example, is said to have had a population of about 2,000, "not above sixty of whom were Protestants" for "a small group met on the Sabbath in a private house."

The files of the Society for the Propagation of the Gospel were particularly useful. In the Quebec Museum there are archives of the Diocese of Quebec and in the National Archives of Canada an S.P.G. file on Lower Canada. A single sheet (1834) brings Lane the catechist into view. A "Report of Sunday Schools, in the District of Rivière du

Loup, County St. Maurice for the 6 months ending May 1, 1834" is signed by him. Further, there is information about "Sunday Stations for Reading, Parish Church of Rivière du Loup: School-house at Crit de Coq Parish of Maskinonge, dist. 8 miles." There another note indicates "Rotation of Reading": "At Rivière du Loup every Sunday morning at 10-; At Crit du Coq every Sunday afternoon at 1/2 past 3." The number attending at Rivière du Loup varied from 15 to 35 and at Crit du Coq from 12 to 36. The number of scholars attending Sunday School at 9 a.m. at Rivière du Loup was 12; and at 2:15 p.m. at Crit du Coq was 15 to 25. "The Catechist," he reported, "has been detained from Church one Sunday through illness & from Crit du Coq twice from bad roads."

The information from Bouchette, the S.P.G. files at Ottawa, and the S.P.G. archives in London confirms details in *The Fugitives*. Mr. White, who speaks to the travellers at some length, had a farm southwest of great Rivière du Loup (parish of St. Antoine de Rivière du Loup). His conversation shows Lane's own views about English and French residents of Quebec. Mr. White says:

> Yes, gentlemen, if England wishes to preserve the sovereignty of these provinces, let her be careful to provide the Canadians with just and merciful magistrates—let her still allow them to enjoy their ancient forms and language...and, indeed [let] every thing be, as heretofore, transacted in <u>French</u>, and bear as great a resemblance as possible to the former state of things:...It is therefore the interest of England to keep the Canadians, a <u>distinct</u> people, as different in language, as in manners, from the Americans. (pp. 169-70)

The wife of *The Fugitives'* Strickland, a captain in the Navy, has eloped with a seducer. She thought her husband was unfaithful. Strickland comes to Canada to find her and their son, who had been left with a foster-mother. They are re-united in Montreal. My principal discovery was a review of *The Fugitives* in *The Gentleman's Magazine*. "The plot of this tale," said the reviewer, "is taken from Kotzebue's celebrated drama, the Stranger." At the time I was totally ignorant of a play that had been popular in England and the United States since 1798. It was an English version of August von

Kotzebue's romantic German drama, *Menschenhaus und Reue* (Misanthropy and Repentance).

The Fugitives, therefore, made me learn a great many things about the geography and English emigrants of Lower Canada and compelled me to acquaint myself with Church and theatrical affairs. I was tempted to study Lane's use of language, especially in conversations: I suspected that some North Americanisms had been described.

To the able young researchers now sleuthing in Canada and Britain, I leave Edward Lane's promise to publish another novel which he said, "shortly will be ready for the Press." Who will find this book (if it was ever published)? *The Cabin Boy; or Life in a French Prison*, "An authentic account of Five Years' Captivity in Cumbray, and other parts of the Continent, from 1809-1814." Lane claimed that he had included in *The Fugitives* a few chapters "from the pen of the 'Cabin Boy,' " which he declared, "contain real facts, and are correctly copied from his own manuscript, now in my possession."

CHAPTER SEVEN

Canadian Anthology

While I was pursuing my interests in early Canadian writing I was also involved in preparing *Canadian Anthology* with Reginald E. Watters, whom I first met in 1949 when he came to Toronto to work on his checklist of Canadian literature. At this time Clara Thomas was preparing to collaborate with me on a book we intended to call "Writers of the Colonial Period in Canada: Extracts of the Prose Works of Authors Writing in English before Confederation." The authors we favoured were Hakluyt, Brooke, Bailey, Galt, Richardson, Howe, Haliburton, Jameson, Dunlop, Moodie, and McGee. We wrote a foreword, claiming that ours was to be "the first anthology devoted to English prose in the pre-Confederation period in Canada, and restricted to authors who attempted creative writing. Their literary activities were centered in this country. The material chosen was that of active human interest," and we also said that "so far as these sketches afford human experiences and…the flavor of the land, they give depth to our vital knowledge of Canada." Clara then carried our proposal to various Toronto publishers, but she had no success.

Watters' suggestion for an anthology of a different kind came toward the end of that year. I had consulted him about classifications and subclassifications that he was using for the "bibliography," as it was then called. He wrote me a lengthy reply on 23 November 1949 that began: "I am taking the liberty of inviting your opinion upon the possible publication of an inexpensive anthology of Canadian writing which might be of general value in university courses." He had experience with anthologies, having collaborated on an anthology, *The Creative Reader*, with Robert W. Stallman of Wisconsin. He was involved with Rinehart Publishers, but he was thinking of switching to Gage, which was very active across Canada. Reg had met their representative at the University of British Columbia, and I had met Robert Verner at Western. In April 1951 Verner wrote to me and said, "When I talked with him [Reg] in March he seemed to be interested in collaborating with you."

There were many reasons why Reg Watters and I undertook a *Canadian Anthology* in the 1950s. One reason for our friendship was devotion to the cause of Canadian literary scholarship. We were keenly aware of what needed to be done, and we were both dedicated to digging up facts. We aimed to present the most reliable information. Our biographical sketches of the authors we included were based on records made for us by the authors themselves. Using questionnaires, we made a fresh survey, asking for proper dates, places, and events. We did not ask for opinions. As we composed our biographical sketches, we expressed the facts without interpretation or judgment. The whole principle of selection was to give people facts and let them form their own judgments and opinions. We included a few earlier writers of special interest to suggest the historical context of writing in Canada, but we did not impose fixed classifications of periods or genres. Authors appeared in chronological order based on birth dates.

In a preface to a later edition of the *Anthology*, Reg and I referred to the original publication in 1955 as a time "when courses in our national literature were few and far between." The two of us, however, were teaching university courses, for which a volume of readings in prose and verse was urgently needed. Our book was well received by general readers as well as by teachers and students. I still believe that the amazing success of the *Anthology* was a result in large part of the excellent bibliography that remained a feature of the book and that only Reg, slaving over the *Check List*, could have produced. We helped establish a canon.

When Reg first contacted me he wanted to have my advice on whether an anthology of poetry and prose or of poetry alone would be the more desirable and whether such an anthology would fill a real need for university students and even possibly for the general reader. I told him: "Very frankly, what I should like to have is a really good selection from six or seven representative poets without any prose. Such a book would leave us, where we are now, without any satisfactory prose anthology. I am not at all convinced that one can make an anthology for general use and also for closer study in university courses. I am convinced that anything which will bring Canadian literature before any sort of public is a useful effort."

When I told Reg that Gage's editor, Robert Verner, had become interested, he replied that he had talked about "a Canadian anthology to every Canadian publisher or his representative that I've encountered—and this is the first and only nibble....If the book actually comes to publication, the one thing I know is that it will not make our fortunes—but it will provide us with a useful textbook for our courses." We then set out to define the parameters of the book. In a letter to Gage on 4 May Reg explained:

> The kind of book Klinck and I would plan would obviously be affected by the approximate size and number of pages—which would determine the number of authors represented and the amount of their material included. What about a book about the size of A.J.M. Smith's BOOK OF CANADIAN POETRY? I think a very good anthology could be put together, of both prose and poetry, within such limits—not only a reasonably wide selection of authors but reasonably comprehensive representation of each author. A smaller book would mean reducing the number of authors, since both Klinck and I are of the opinion that Canadian anthologies tend to offer snippets from a great many authors rather than usable and adequate blocks of material.

Because we had other commitments, we did want to provide a detailed outline without a contract, but we were under way. However, we began to discuss authors to be included. Reg wrote:

> What do you think of a 15-20 page section headed "Pre-Confederation Poetry," in which we could show samples from Goldsmith, Howe, Heavysege, Crawford and Cameron. It should be our only departure from the idea of a large block representation, but I myself would find such a section useful in my course. How fond are you of Carman and Roberts, the latter as poet I mean? Both leave me pretty unmoved. In fact when I was reading for the Rinehart book I found it difficult to discover more than 400 lines by each

that I would want, and 400 lines is only ten pages. I imagine there would be a howl if we omitted them entirely, though my heart wouldn't break.

Early on, we decided what we wanted to do, in the light of our experience as teachers of courses in Canadian literature:

1. Not less than three-quarters of the book will be devoted to <u>Major</u> Canadian poets and prose writers, texts of their works and editorial comment. There are for this purpose approximately fifteen "major" authors.
2. One-quarter of the book, or less than one-quarter, will be given to early and later "minor" writers.
3. Significant writers of earlier periods will be included. Appeal to our generation will not be the chief criterion.
4. Care will be taken to prevent duplication with the contents of A.J.M. Smith's Anthology.
5. A special effort will be made to print important literary works not readily available to the student or general reader.
6. It will be planned for use as the standard textbook for college courses in Canadian Literature.
7. The editorial comment will be brief but, we hope, scholarly, revealing the personality, thought, critical theory, and technique belonging to the work at its inception, and offering guidance to an understanding at the present time. A review of Canadian critical opinion concerning the work will be included.
8. Dates of publication and, wherever possible, dates of composition will be indicated.
9. The book will illustrate the history of Canadian Literature but will not represent an attempt to write a systematic history.
10. The bibliographies will be better than any now provided for the study of Canadian writers.

On 26 May 1951, Reg wrote to Verner stressing the importance of a bibliography and adequate scope.

> If Klinck and I have 400 to 500 pages to work with, we can produce a very readable as well as significant volume. If

we confine ourselves to somewhere between 15 and 30 authors we will also be able to represent each with a sufficiently large block of material to enable a reader to get the "flavour" of the writer and to enable a student to form a sound judgement of the range and ability of the author. The great fault of all other anthologies of Canadian literature—even including Smith's—is, in my opinion, that they offer too little from too many.

On 5 June I wrote to Reg a letter on editorial policy:

i. The number of authors was to be severely limited.
ii. An author who survived the critical sifting was to be given the full treatment as an interesting individual, with a fair, varied and "genetic" (the phrase is [Harry Hayden] Clark's) representation.
iii. If possible, no snippets.
iv. If a distinction had to be made at any time, choice of teachable, rather than esoteric, selections.
v. Some regard for selections which show interesting relations with American or British literature, history and philosophy.
vi. Inclusion of any writings which reveal the author's literary theories.
vii. Recognition in the notes of weaknesses in otherwise valuable selections.
viii. In the notes, swift introductions to the point of view of the author and his times.

Gage's Verner suggested that we not aim the book at high school students. "Experience has taught us that when attempting to place a book on two markets you invariably lose both. Pending further discussion then, we [that is, Gage] are chiefly interested in the college text." And about point five, he said: "I think we should publish in Canada only those materials which otherwise would not be published. This would be a labour of love, both for ourselves and the authors. The aim being to contribute a really needed book. We are perfectly willing to go ahead on this basis and should dramatic sales possibilities materialize, exploit them." He agreed that the book should be about 500 pages and have the major writers' approach. All the way along we found Gage's editors to be generous, thoughtful, and willing to share their publication know-how.

While the contract was still being actively discussed, I was worried about the cost of reprint rights. When I talked with Lorne Pierce I gathered, perhaps wrongly, that Ryerson would not drive too hard a bargain. I decided, therefore, to unfold certain details of our plan to Pierce. Ryerson held, or controlled, the royalties for most of our poets—even Lampman, who was apparently still on the active list. Republishing rights for men like Birney might run as high as $25 a poem. Months of discouraging and protracted exchanges of letters then ensued on how to estimate the copyright fees without preparing a complete table of contents. Gage became more insistent that it be done, and Reg was equally adamant we should not do so without a contract.

Along the way Reg made some very useful comments about pioneering in our selection. Perhaps we could revive William Dunlop or James DeMille or Sara Jeannette Duncan or others. "But," he says:

> I don't really see how we can do so in this particular book. We could, of course, have a bibliographical "List of Selections Unfortunately Squeezed Out" or something of the sort (and I'm more than half serious about such a List), but I don't see how we can do what needs to be done. Actually, of course, the whole of Canadian writing needs to be re-assessed and a decent History of the subject written. But that's a vast job, and one that must wait at least until the Can. Bibliog. is completed; then we ought to have a co-operative project such as the Spiller-Thorp-et-al. Literary History of the U. S. But until that is done I'm afraid we can allow ourselves little of the luxury of "discovery," or "rediscovery."

This, of course, was also brewing in my mind, but it was 1957 before our *Literary History* got under way and I could ask Reg to take part in it.

Though the contract was not signed until December, a compromise was worked out in the late spring. Gage would pay us each $250 in advance. If the book was completed, this advance would be deducted from royalties. But if the book was dropped, Gage would lose $500. As Reg put it, "We risk time, energy and knowledge. Gage risks money." Gage now began to plan the marketing strategy for the book. By June I was sending Reg "trial flights." He, however, was much occupied with *The Creative Reader* he was co-editing for the Ronald Press, and we did not really expect to be able to provide the final table of contents before the spring of 1953.

Then on 9 February 1953, Gage president, Wilfred Wees, wrote to Reg: "Do you suppose we could have your manuscript by mid-July 1953?" On 12 February Reg replied to me indignantly:

> I don't know whether or not Wees sent you a copy of his letter of Feb. 9—making the incredible inquiry about whether we could have THE MANUSCRIPT by mid-July! And he's the guy I had to persuade, almost, to set a deadline of late spring for the table of contents! I haven't answered his letter yet—but when I do I shall say we can't possibly do it. Apparently his desire is to start promoting the book "for use in schools in 1954"! But he can "promote" with the table of contents. He doesn't seem to realize how much work is involved after we finalize the table of contents. Locating, cutting or copying the text, writing introductory material, compiling bibliographical lists, etc., just cannot be done in a week or two—unless the Gage office undertakes to do some of it—and quite a bit of it, too. If the Gage office would undertake to compile the copy, and leave us free to do the biographical and bibliographical stuff, we'd still be rushed to meet a deadline of mid-July. Maybe end of August might be barely possible, though how I'll find time to do my share while working on the Canadian Bibliography for the Humanities Research Council I can't readily foresee....I should get Gage to write to UBC saying that I must be excused from the chore of earning a living by teaching!

In his letter to Wees on the same day Reg was no less blunt. He wondered: "What weasel has got into the Gage dovecote to stir up such haste about the Canadian anthology?"

> Let's look at a time schedule. After we submit for your approval a final table of contents (by the end of April, let's say—being optimistic types), there's the business of

getting permissions. Unless Gage is willing to pay whatever is insisted upon, changes in selections may have to be made to drop pieces that are either refused or that cost too much. My experience with other publishers Permissions' departments suggests that at least a month will elapse after the permissions letters go out before we know exactly what we will have in the book.

Meanwhile, Klinck and I can be doing some work on the biographical and bibliographical material that will accompany each author's work. After we know what selections are really going in, the job of locating copy commences. As you know, many of the books we draw upon are out of print (thanks to Canadian publishers!). Finding copies we can cut up takes time. Getting typists to transcribe from library copies takes a hellish amount of money—enough to eat up royalties at a feverish rate, if Klinck and I pay for it—and also needs careful checking to ensure accuracy. Even the pasting-up job easily consumes a week—if you want neat copy.

At this time, the project suffered a serious blow when Bob Verner was killed at the end of April in a highway accident.

By the next spring I was also worried about arrangement of selections.

If we arrange our authors, major and minor, merely in order of birth-dates, how can we defend ourselves against charges of excluding people who did not fall within our original terms of reference? Will we not appear to be promising a completeness in coverage of Canadian writers which we never did pretend to aim at? If we have no plan to present major authors with some completeness and to skip most of the others—or at least disregard their claims—why are we doing the book at all? Unless you can suggest some clear line of reasoning—something clear-cut for our statement of policy in the Foreword—we shall not only lose some friends, but also run the risk of being called muddle-headed. I have not aimed at completeness; I have been trying to provide more than we can use (to assist in the elimination process), but I have aimed at including good chunks of the best authors' works, and providing enough before and after for cross-reference and "depth" as we teach the best teachable things.

On 16 February Reg wrote: "The shape our book has taken has impressed me about the fact that we face a surplus of good stuff, not a dearth; and we're providing, in effect, a whole library of Can. lit. There isn't now, and never has been, anything comparable." "The shape our book has taken" is a phrase I wish was my own because it expresses my own theory—superimposed categories go wrong or don't tell the truth. A book takes its own shape.

By 22 February we had almost completed gathering copy for *Canadian Anthology*. I told Wees that we would "promise that the copy could be in your hands by mid March, complete with biographical and bibliographical notes on the authors. But if you wish your production editor to start work on the format earlier than that, we could send in a week or so, the copy of the selections, with copy of biographical and bibliographical notes to come as soon as possible thereafter." That Don Ritchie would edit the book is confirmed in a letter from Wees on 24 February 1954.

Now Gage was eager to press on with the job and Reg worked hard at the editing while I agreed to take on the permissions. Concerns about format were raised as I wrote to Reg on 5 May 1954. "Another thing, Our policy of dating selections, especially poems—and possibly prescribing a hard-and-fast order for, say, short poems—will cause a hardship for the editor who will try to set such things in the most economical positions on the page. That is to say, the breaks between poems as we set them up may come at most uneconomical places. Perhaps we should indicate, wherever possible, permission for the publisher to arrange poems <u>with the same dates</u> in whatever order he wishes."

On 8 May in a letter to Wees, Reg protests "I hate," he says, "double-column prose!" and has two underlinings of it, and that is meant to be emphatic. And on 27 May he commented on the biographical sketches which I had sent:

> The chief difference between yours and mine is that you include critical or evaluative comments, whereas I try to confine myself to what might be called the purely factual. I thought we had agreed several months ago to avoid

> comment? Art Smith uses a lot of critical comment, but I'm not in favour of our doing so, simply because for such comments to be worthwhile, a lot more thought should go into them than we have time for. Moreover, in a joint production, such as ours is, we'd have to send sketches back and forth several times, because naturally you and I don't always see eye to eye on every author. Some of your comments, for instance, I'd have to rephrase in order to agree exactly with them; and the same would be true of mine for you. That's why I was very happy when (as I thought) we agreed to be strictly factual in our biogs. I know that, occasionally, a descriptive statement verges closely on an interpretive one, but if we tried hard to avoid interpretive or critical comments, we'd be as safe and sound as human beings can be.

I think he was quite right about that, and in theory at least I was completely with him from the start.

On 4 June Reg had seen sample pages, which he thoroughly disliked because they seemed to belong to "primer-type" books: "It's as bad as I feared it might be, I'm afraid....Canadian literature deserves better than the format of a juvenile's book, and I intend to squawk! I want richness and lavishness in the selections, not in wide-open waste spaces or other things designed to coax non-readers to read. Non-readers won't buy or use our book. Those who do, want lots of matter in a dignified and decent format. More later." Royalties to the Clarke Irwin authors continued to cause problems for months. But by 22 October Katherine McCool was sending to me the first batch of proofs of the *Anthology*, and on 28 October Reg sent me the bibliographies with the request that I go over them and send them on to Gage. He says: "I don't know how Gage will react at the length of the bibliography. I myself think this feature very important indeed and would, if necessary, drop some selections to make room. (I cringe to think of all my work on these lists going unused!) But I believe the bibliogs. will make it almost imperative that libraries in the U.S., for instance, which might not buy 'just another anthology' will buy this one."

A letter of 14 November provides an example of the way in which we handled almost everything: "Here at last is the draft of the preface—which I'm calling 'Foreword' because of its somewhat greater length than usual. You can tear it apart and assemble it differently, if you wish. I found it a difficult thing to write—as usual." On 28 December, Reg wrote: "We could probably go on for ever revising the damned Foreword, but what I'm enclosing is a slight reworking of your version. I'm sending it direct to Ritchie....If you have objections, a word to him will stop it. Word-substitutions can, of course, be handled in proof stage, unless the length of the line is much affected." On another matter he wrote: "Since proof-reading the bibliography will be a foul job—which I'll have to do—will you take on two equivalent chores: proof-reading the acknowledgements, and preparing the index?" I became more grateful every day for Reg's careful editing on our part of the manuscript to be sent to Gage. He not only helped to select but he edited, because I had done the work on permissions.

We spent the early weeks of January 1955 making deletions, in response to Gage's request. On 4 March I told Don Ritchie that on 6 April I would be sailing from New York for five months in Britain. Upon my return on 19 September, Ritchie wrote to say that copies of the book were soon due: "I think you will agree that we have a fine book. I will now be working [on] adoptions right across the country, and I think it will do fairly well even this year." Our genuine satisfaction with our collaboration on this book was voiced by Reg in a letter of 8 October 1955: "We can surely be proud of our work. I for one even swing towards smugness, only slightly qualified by the realization that there may still be room for improvement in subsequent revised editions."

Later on 22 January 1956, he speculated about some of these possibilities when reporting another project:

> I've been having a fine old time reading for the project, in between other duties. Strange holes in Canadian writing turn up, too. For instance, there seems to be almost nothing in prose or verse that gives the texture of life in big cities—stuff about skyscrapers, night clubs, department stores, thick traffic, etc. etc. Do you know of anything? Or about air transport—bush pilots, etc. And surprisingly little fiction or poetry about sports, hockey, curling, football, and the like. Or about orthodox religion and the spiritual experiences of Christian belief. The religious emotions which Canadians have are attached to aspects of our

geography, rather than traditional doctrines, to judge by our writers. There are heaps of things about our northland, our bush, our prairies, our waterways and oceans—but where there are dozens of things about fishermen, there are none about hard-rock miners, construction-workers, electrical workers, pipeline-layers, etc. I haven't found anything good about teachers or professors, for that matter. Or railway workers, or truck drivers, or Great Lakes shipping.

Canadian writers haven't scratched the surface of Canada, as yet! Poetry that fits is easier to find than prose. All 20th century, since it's to be a portrait of Canada today.

I was now beginning to develop what was to become our most important enterprise, the *Literary History of Canada*, but, unfortunately, Reg could not join us. About this time, he took a year off. In a letter of 13 March 1958, he wrote, saying: "First I want to say that I received the Senior Fellowship I asked for from the Canada Council, and I plan to leave with my family for Australia next June [1958]. I think I said in my last letter something about my project—which is to study Australian literature, both for itself and for the light its developments and achievement may reflect upon the Canadian equivalents."

A year later, on 30 March 1959, he sent a long letter from Australia:

My reading in Australian literature has convinced me that the lit. of the Commonwealth is very well worth serious study—and very enjoyable study, too. I'm having a splendid time both with Aussie books and Aussie people. I'd need pages to tell you the whole of it. My first impressions are that in several ways the Australians are ahead of us. Not always is it because of anything other than sheer necessity. They have no neighbor to provide the "near enough" or the overwhelming example, for one thing. I wish I could get to New Zealand to discover whether or not the N.Z.'ers versus Australians are like Canadians-versus the Americans. I feel this year has been illuminating to me, not only for what I'm beginning to know about Aust. lit., but—more important—what I'm beginning to think about Can. lit. We're a lot more complicated a people than the Australians, but they seem to have accomplished a more successful <u>national</u> lit. than we have—because they're less complicated.

My impression is that Australians know (and care) even less about Can. lit. than we do about Australian. But I suppose interest always must begin at near zero. Generally speaking, Aust. universities are less interested, also, in courses in Aust. lit. than ours are in Canadian. Part of the reason is the more rigid course-structure here. The elective system does make the introduction of new subjects much easier. Another reason is that too many of the heads of English depts. here are Englishmen, than whom few are more provincial for dear old England. In this respect, Aust. universities are one or two generations behind Canadian. Aust. authors seem far more anti-academic than Canadian, as a result; they have reason. At the same time, the average Aust. reader seems more pro-Australian than the average Canadian seems pro-Canadian.

Soon after the Watters were back in Kingston the need for a third printing of the *Anthology* had become apparent. Don Ritchie sent me a list of the universities that had used *Canadian Anthology* as a required text for one or more years from 1955 to 1960. Reg agreed and my ongoing work on *The Literary History* showed me that significant revision was required. On 23 September 1962, I wrote to Reg:

With regard to the <u>Anthology</u>, which will be used in our part of the country by at least 500 students this year, I feel pressure for revision. The articles which are coming in for the <u>Literary History</u> are giving me a very good picture of other scholars' selections of the best in our literature. We might be enabled to serve our public better if we were at least aware of these opinions. I am planning to spend a week or ten days at Toronto (probably at Hart House) during the middle of October for the purpose of polishing off my own article for the <u>LHC</u>. I shall give you more accurate information about the dates. Do you think that you could meet me there at that time for a full session on revision?

In a letter I wrote to him on 27 October 1964, I mention that there was a new editor at Gage for *Canadian Anthology*, Irmgard Weiller. This was the beginning of a very long story of difficulties. Something of our problems with the new editor emerged from this part of a letter Reg wrote her on 19 September 1965:

> Like Carl, I have my moments of unease and unhappiness about editorial changes in punctuation, spelling, etc. As he says, blame (if any) will fall on him and me, not upon Gage Ltd., regardless of the paragraph in our Preface. When I agreed to Gage house-style standardization, I was thinking mainly of prose, rather than poetry, and of early 19th century stuff rather than modern—apart, of course, from the "our"—"or" in "honour" etc., or the "ize" for "ise," etc. Something very different in spirit is involved when we undertake the "correction" of the punctuation practices of Pratt or Frye or Birney—professors of English all, as well as men whose lives have been devoted to good prose or verse writing. Any changes in such work should be absolutely minimal, since it can be assumed that their practice is conscious practice, not slapdash.
>
> For myself, I don't believe punctuation is a science, or that it can in all uses be reduced to hard-and-fast rules. It is mostly an art, and is related to the rhythms of a writer's style, and "style is the man", I believe. Some things about punctuation are unimportant—for example, whether that last comma of mine should be put inside the quot. marks or outside. That kind of thing should be consistent within a book, and the publisher's house-style can determine that.
>
> Personally, I can detect a difference between "a tall, red house" and "a tall red house"—the latter suggesting to me a class of "red houses" of which the one specified is a "tall"example, whereas "tall, red" denotes a "house" which happens to be both "tall" <u>and</u> "red."

I have tried to show through his letters and actions how generous and co-operative Reg was. Of course we disagreed; he was aggressive and strong-minded in argument, but we always co-operated happily. He was also an interesting, compelling talker, who had a peculiar kind of chuckle. It was his smile and the tone in which he talked which compelled: his smile was broad as a picture and his voice a bit loud. He was always very convincing. Personally he was a very good friend, and so was his wife Beth. Both were generous, hospitable, eager to have us come to visit, and I deeply lament his early death.

On 15 July 1979, a letter from Beth says:

> This is Beth, writing at Reg's dictation, while I am visiting him in hospital....
>
> Thank you very much for your very warm congratulations on my receiving the Tremaine Medal [this was a medal of the Bibliographical Society of Canada]. Your citing of my "many achievements" was indeed generous and I very much appreciate what you said.
>
> Beth was with me in Ottawa and we expected to see you there, only to be disappointed that you were not present in person to receive your honorable membership. We could have had a long chat together. I have been in hospital since shortly after the Society meeting for tests and surgery, to be followed by radiation treatment for cancer of the bowel—a very unpleasant business, and, of course, totally undeserved!
>
> We are on the verge of selling our farm and moving back into Kingston where we hope to be installed by August 31st. Perhaps you could visit us on your way to Spain for next winter?

Reg was always a hard worker, though perhaps too meticulous. I was pleased that the nomination that first proposed him for election as a Fellow of the Royal Society of Canada was signed by Roy Daniells and Northrop Frye. We were unsuccessful, and I have always been most unhappy that he did not receive the honours he deserved such as election to the Royal Society and appointment to the Order of Canada. He "ranks securely as one of the inspirers of the current upsurge of interest and scholarship in Canadian literature." As the citation for his nomination pointed out: "his *Check List* was a basic survey which enabled research specialists to proceed with the *Literary History of Canada* and critics to build on a comprehensive view of their materials." It is perhaps little known that he also gave a talk called "A Quest for National Identity, Canadian Literature vis-à-vis the Literatures of Great Britain and the United States" at the International

Comparative Literature Association's third congress, held in The Hague in 1962. But for an accident of timing—he was invited to Australia at the time an editor was required—he would have been the first editor of *Canadian Literature*.

Reg died on 19 December 1979, not long after the second edition of the *Check List* was published. Much of his other work is contained in a booklet published at the Royal Military College in Kingston by the Department of English and Philosophy, to which he had contributed so much. This booklet has a preface by Gordon Elliott, then an English professor at Simon Fraser University. It includes the text of articles Reg published that demonstrate his expertise really lay in North American literature generally, as well as Australian and other Commonwealth literatures. Elliot's preface is a fine description of Reg's capacity for work and friendship:

> He was foremost a scholar furthering scholarship....As a boss he was a driver, but with his Puritan attitudes, he was also a worker himself. He looked on work as fun, as satisfaction, as contribution. He never seemed to tire and while working along with him one often cursed him for his ability to talk all night and work all day. At the end of the day, though, when the two of you were all in, dog tired, half blind from reading microfilm, you often seemed to achieve some kind of nirvana, with the work itself as a sort of universal spirit absorbing you. And then again, just as often you did not.
>
> His writing techniques, too, were infuriating, and he could not understand those poor people like me, and many others, who write draft after draft after draft, correcting, chipping, changing. He would stay up all night talking, drinking, arguing, his voice and his laughter becoming louder and louder and louder, his wits sharper and sharper as he became involved in the subject, as he analysed it, debated it, shredded it, and put it back together. When he came to write he would by then know what he wanted and exactly how he wanted it, and he would have shaped it in his logical mind, every comma, every word, every sentence, every paragraph. He would then write a draft which would require hardly any correction.

CHAPTER EIGHT

Literary History of Canada

In September 1956, at the English Institute meetings at Columbia University, Northrop Frye delivered a brilliant paper entitled "Lexis and Melos," which later became the introductory paper in the Institute's 1956 collection called *Sound and Poetry*. That day after lunch I met him as we entered the building for the afternoon session. We had a brief, but for me a very significant, conversation. Full of my own subject, I asked him whether Canadian literature could be tested against international standards. Norrie replied, in effect, "Of course, why not?" He added, "First of all there must be a great deal of research in basic facts." That was precisely what I wanted to hear.

Early in October I crossed the University of Toronto campus to the office of Marsh Jeanneret, director of the University of Toronto Press. Here at a conference with Jeanneret, George Brown, Eleanor Harmon, and Francess Halpenny, I suggested publication of a *Literary History of Canada*. I was received cordially and a bit incredulously with generosity by George Brown, who favoured a joint venture with French-Canadian scholars (always a dream of mine, too); with administrative caution by Marsh Jeanneret and Eleanor Harmon; and with editorial imagination by Francess Halpenny.

A few weeks later, on 17 October 1956, I wrote a detailed follow-up letter to Jeanneret. This letter contained a proposal regarding procedures, authorities in the field, a comparison to *Literary History of the United States*, an advisory committee, financing of meetings and editorial expenses, together with an invitation to the University of Toronto Press to consider publication. That was a rather bold invitation. A few days later, Jeanneret replied and invited me to another chat, to be followed by some further observations "just as soon as is practicable." "Professor George Brown, for one," he said, "I know, would be glad of an opportunity to discuss the subject further with me."

George Brown had stated the importance of producing a unified, stylistically smooth book. "The editor," he had advised, "must have a firm hand, even to rewrite if necessary—and this must be understood from the first." Much as I was delighted by Brown's enthusiasm and help, these were two things I *wasn't* going to do. I wasn't going to "rewrite if necessary" nor was I going to carry things on with "a firm hand." That opinion was not only Brown's; it filtered into the Humanities Research Council (which was to become a major supporter) where, I think, the point was debated. It was not the last time I heard this piece of advice. Donald Creighton asserted the same opinion, less generously, to the Humanities Research Council and to me.

I was disturbed, but not unsettled, for I believed that the discovery of a sufficient basis of research was far too much for any one man, that several dozen researchers would have to be enlisted as diggers and recognized, therefore, as authorities entitled to write chapters. For one thing, I had seen what an enormous task Reg Watters had undertaken in his *Check List of Canadian Literature and Background Materials* (1959), sections of which were incorporated into the bibliography of *Canadian Anthology*. I knew that any book by one man would have to be, because of time and energy, a skimming off the top instead of a digging to the bottom. I was determined not to have a mere skimming off from the obviously inadequate stock of what passed for our knowledge of Canadian literature at that time.

There had been some signs of improvement in conditions for teaching and scholarship in Canadian literature in the late 1950s when we started our project. At this time we were all using A.J.M. Smith's *The Book of Canadian Poetry* (1943) in our classrooms. A companion book on prose was promised by Smith, but in fact it was delayed for many years, not being published until 1965. His anthology of poetry contained a great deal of fresh information. The selected poems were critically chosen, and the book was neatly arranged, with a useful bibliography and an introduction that extended our knowledge of early and modern poetry. Some of Smith's views on the course of that history were controversial; his hopes of finding a *cosmopolitan* tradition in Canadian poetry were demonstrated in a division of the book with that title. He was only partly successful in making this point, which, I think, was vital to his own creative policy and practice. Yet we were very happy to have the book in our classrooms and on our desks in the 1940s and 1950s. It caused a ripple in American criticism through Henry Wells and William Rose Benét, both of whom felt that Ned Pratt shone brightest in the Canadian skies.

By 1952 we had *Creative Writing in Canada* by Desmond Pacey of the University of New Brunswick. Subtitled *A Short History of English-Canadian Literature*, this valuable book covered modern poetry as well as prose; it had a good bibliography and was definitely an improvement over earlier books of this kind, such as Logan and French's *Highways of Canadian Literature*. There was also great improvement in the criticism of Canadian literature through the *University of Toronto Quarterly*, which from 1936 on included an annual section entitled "Letters in Canada." Although it was not comprehensive, it had a definite critical basis and was written by A.S.P. Woodhouse, chairman of the Department of English at Toronto, and others. Moreover, the success of E.J. Pratt's poems during the 1930s, 40s, and 50s also helped to create interest in Canadian poetry among academics.

Of equal importance to all these literary efforts was the establishment in 1944 of the Humanities Research Council. This organization, which continued until 1978, was advisory, and gave some financial aid to scholarship in the humanities. It received some of its money from American sources, such as the Ford, Rockefeller, and Carnegie foundations. Its primary purpose was to encourage scholarship in Canadian literature. In addition, there was also the Dominions Committee of the Humanities Research Council. The committee operated from 1947 to 1953 under Woodhouse and John E. Robbins, secretary-treasurer of the HRC. At that time I was very excited by a book of criticism, *Australian Literature: A Bibliography* (1956), edited by E. Morris Miller. This was much more than a bibliography because it included a great deal of biographical and historical material. I brought my excitement about the bibliography to the Dominions Committee, where I was supported by Roy Daniells of UBC. As I mentioned earlier, the members of the committee were so impressed by what the Australians had done in their *Bibliography* that Reg Watters, then at UBC, was invited to do a thorough bibliographical study of Canadian literature.

In 1948, Robert E. Spiller, Willard Thorp, Thomas Johnson, and Henry Seidel Canby had produced *Literary History of the United*

States, designed so that "we may now understand better the recorders of the American experiences." This literary history had as an adjunct a whole volume of bibliography—a very useful thing. The analogy with Canada struck me forcibly. Here was Reg Watters working on a bibliography. Why not a companion volume, a *Literary History of Canada*?

One thing that was involved in Reg Watters' work was the establishment of a canon of major works. Spiller, Thorp, and Johnson could write the *Literary History of the United States* with a reasonable understanding of who the major American writers were. But Reg, by the very terms under which he was working, was going to list every remotely literary publication he could find that had been published in Canada. His title, therefore, became *A Check List of Canadian Literature and Background Materials 1628-1960*, including history books and other volumes in economics and social science. So this work, while it was a fairly complete list of what had been published, made no critical distinction between books listed. Reg did not necessarily even read the books; he merely recorded their existence. Although it was a very useful and important book, it needed a literary history supplement. In 1958 Woodhouse wrote a foreword to the *Check List* while we were organizing the *Literary History*. He described the *Check List* as an "indispensable instrument for further exploration in the Canadian field, and for the writing of the Literary History of Canada now being planned." So, when I speculated about a literary history of Canada, I had a kind of blessing from the University of Toronto and the Humanities Research Council because both were involved in a Canadian project related to what *I* wanted to do.

When I first proposed the *Literary History of Canada*, there was no Canada Council to provide funding. The Massey *Report*, which recommended its establishment, was issued in 1951, but the Council did not exist until 1957. When we began to organize the *Literary History*, nobody knew how the Canada Council would operate. Would they give grants in block amounts to universities? As it turned out, what they wanted to do in 1957 was to give money to individual applicants—a policy that, as it turned out, was exactly what we needed.

For people wanting to go abroad, as I did in 1955, to research early Canadian literature there were the Nuffield Foundation and the British Council in England, which distributed travelling fellowships. So it wasn't an entirely hopeless affair to get some money for travel, chiefly for research. The Nuffield Foundation, for example, had a Canadian liaison committee, and when I applied to go to England, I was offered a Nuffield Fellowship. As it turned out, there were other sources, too, and I received a travel grant from the British Council under the Commonwealth Universities Exchange scheme. The Royal Society also had some fellowships available. Most importantly, I was encouraged to begin on this project because I had been working in the field for three decades.

As I mentioned earlier, my first discussion about the new book had been with Reg Watters. On 14 October 1956, he wrote me a letter I treasure:

> Is your magnificent plan of a *LITERARY HISTORY OF CANADA* the kind of thing heads of departments who escape from routine dream up in their new uncharted freedom? If so, we non-heads may owe routine a debt for our more or less untroubled sleeps of the past!
>
> Seriously, I think your scheme <u>is</u> splendid—but, oh, brother, it's ambitious! Unquestionably it's what we all need—but it's a vast undertaking, as witness the Lit. Hist. of the U.S. I'd like a part in it, to be sure—but I'm over my ears in a number of projects now, and I simply couldn't add to them by plunging into the organizational features of LHC almost immediately. Having just about finished the seven-year check list of Can. Lit., the thought of another protracted sentence of five or more years appalls me.
>
> Like you, I'm troubled by the fear that Jeanneret and Brown might rush at the production of a less than satisfactory kind of book. We don't need another general one-man or two-man survey type of history—like Pacey's, for instance. Pacey's book is useful and the best of its kind—but a thoroughly sound book of the survey kind is really <u>impossible</u> for any one or two or three persons to produce at this stage of Canadian studies. It's impossible because the basic investigation of our writers upon which the <u>surveyers</u> must depend has simply not been made. You could give illustrations yourself, by the dozen, of this sort: consider the actual knowledge we have of Frances Brooke's Canadian residence and experience. Who has read everything she wrote? Or take Richardson—Pacey is

doing the first full study of his life and works—but he hadn't adequate knowledge when he produced *CREATIVE WRITING IN CANADA*. Think of the gaps in our knowledge even of Susanna Moodie—and who has read all her novels, poems, and magazine articles? Look at the holes in Baker's account of Frances Brooke, of John Richardson, of Rosanna Leprohon—worse than Pacey's because in the intervening years a little additional investigation had been done that Pacey could profit by.

The tremendous advantage of a joint project such as yours is that with well-planned division of labour some of this primary digging can be demanded and carried out. The person writing on the Loyalist poets, for instance, could be expected to dig out the periodicals in which their stuff still lies buried and <u>read in full</u> what they wrote; to dig out the manuscripts of unpublished stuff—e.g., Jacob Bailey—and really do a job on him. To try to track down the manuscripts of George Frederick Cameron and, if they were found, to correct or supplement what is shown by his published work. To read the novels of Isabella V. Crawford and relate them to her life and poetry. And so on, and on.

This, as I see it, is the kind of thing that would have to be done—if we are to avoid going on indefinitely with slightly-better-but-still-quite-inadequate surveys or histories of our literature. It was to help make this <u>thoroughness</u> possible that I undertook the check list of Can. lit., the manuscript of which is now ready with the exception of an index of the titles published anonymously. I can't see this check list getting into print in less than two years at best, printers and publishers being what they are. And until it is printed, I doubt any history could be either written or fully planned.

Your emphasis on a literary history of Canada rather than a history of Canadian literature is in my view the exactly right one. Our available histories of Canadian literature show clearly that when the scholarly foundations are still weak or even wholly lacking the only kind of literary judgements possible are impressionistic "appreciations" or superficial "evaluative criticism." How can we see a writer in the current of his times when so little investigation of intellectual and social climate has been done? How much effect did the Darwinian and Bishop Colenso controversies have upon such writers as Lampman and Roberts—both sons of clergymen—for instance? From my work on the check list I happen to know that quite a number of publications were concerned with the Colenso affair, but I fail to recall any treatment of it in our literary histories or articles. Pacey's index lists neither Darwin nor Colenso. Now imagine if you can a history of English literature in the 19th century with the same omissions!...

The "five year" span you envisage would be a minimum if the history should seek to supply the kind of knowledge I'm thinking of. Like you, I would oppose any hasty job, despite the impatience of entrepreneurs and publishers, who tend to think that good work can be rushed into existence. It can't—and the swift shoddy invariably postpones or destroys the chances of the properly-matured good.

I was disappointed that Reg could not join us in the enterprise. On 10 December 1956, I wrote to him: "First of all thank you very much for your letter concerning my project for a <u>Literary History of Canada</u>. I shall explain developments, but I wish to say at once that I should like to keep you on my 'special list.' Don't say 'no,' please say 'maybe.' " At the end of the letter I said:

> Getting back to my project for the <u>Literary History</u>, I might say that I had a long talk with Norrie Frye about it. He would consent to act in an advisory capacity. I think the title-page could be arranged to give recognition to several advisers, as well as to the active editors, and then also the contributors. I shall send you a prospectus in some detail during the next few weeks. I am now trying to find out how the Canada Council and the various foundations propose to divide the work of sponsorship for such tasks of national significance.

Apart from wanting to provide a resource for teachers, especially university teachers, in Canadian literature courses in universities, we needed authentic background information for teaching and study at various levels in general arts, honours in literature, and especially postgraduate work in literature. I did not wish to *teach* literary history, but rather to have comprehensive information about the personal and cultural conditions in which individual works had been produced. My purpose was to know what the history was so that we could discuss the classroom materials in their proper setting. This was clearly stated, for example, in the introduction Reg and I wrote for *Canadian Anthology*.

Another incentive was that I was beginning to have very good relations with publishers, such as Lorne Pierce at Ryerson Press, who had published my *Wilfred Campbell* and also Henry Wells' and my *E.J. Pratt*. I felt rather cocky about my association with Ryerson; also we had very amicable relations with Gage, who published *Canadian Anthology*. I had not yet, of course, invaded the University of Toronto Press, but that was in the offing. Also I had a little experience in publishing in journals by this time. All in all I was making good connections in the publishing field.

My visit to England and Scotland in 1955 had also given me an immense amount of material, the first part of which I published in *William "Tiger" Dunlop* in 1958. Another factor was relief from my duties as head of the Department of English at Western in the spring of 1956. This gave me more opportunity to work, especially in my own field, and I was appointed professor of Canadian literature, which indicated that I had a certain independence, not only to work, but also to lead Canadian literature studies at the University. More and more students in the honours and graduate fields were interested in Canadian literature, but we simply didn't have enough original material. The Western library was surprisingly good, but much of what we needed was catalogued as social history and had never been identified as literature.

Another personal incentive to undertake the *Literary History* was my friendship with Reg Watters and our work on *Canadian Anthology*. Both grew in part with our hunger for information. If I felt myself qualified to do a *Literary History*, I owed a great deal to the strenuous efforts Reg and I had made in the preparation of *Canadian Anthology*. It required a moderately tight selection based on testing in classrooms. The *Check List*, on the other hand, was designed to be comprehensive and more than merely *belles lettres*. Reg Watters and, fortunately, Northrop Frye, supported the idea of providing a good grounding in basic facts before eventual achievement of critical definition of a Canadian canon of poetry and prose. It was apparent to me that before you could establish such a canon, it was necessary to have the information. You might say, "Well, isn't that what everybody would believe?" but that was not the case.

Some of the battles I had to fight while planning the *Literary History* were against well-informed, learned, experienced people such as George Brown, Donald Creighton, and others who contended that such a book ought to be written by one person. I thought unity would come out of the materials, out of Canada, so to speak, not necessarily from one author. Fortunately Reg agreed and so did Norrie, who was able to persuade almost everyone—certainly before we were finished we had persuaded everybody—that if the *Literary History* was not all one piece, it would be full of very interesting variety and still be a unit. I insisted that "if we do not launch out from a studied knowledge of ourselves and our own ways, no one else will."

Among the personal influences on me was Francess Halpenny, then humanities editor for the University of Toronto Press, who edited both Reg's *Check List* and the *Literary History of Canada*. Among many other aids, she provided proofs of the *Check List* to the *Literary History* editors and contributors. She saw, as we did, that the bibliography and the literary history were indispensable companion volumes. We wanted to produce what *Australian Literature: A Bibliography* and the *Literary History of the United States* twenty years earlier had achieved: a literary history with a companion bibliography. And that's how our books appeared, although in different formats.

To prepare the *Literary History*, I needed people who could write well—Northrop Frye, Roy Daniells, Desmond Pacey, Robert McDougall, Reg Watters, Claude Bissell, and others—and I hoped to enlist them in a crusade against "old wives' tales." That was the only way to get fresh material. I wanted what we eventually got in most chapters of the *Literary History*: such original studies as Frank Watt's "Literature of Protest" or John Irving and Al Johnson's "Philosophical Writings (1910-64)." My own chapters, too, were fresh. I had to convince Brown and others that the various topics would stimulate researchers' own essential treatments. We didn't want to impose a pattern, because people would write to it, that is, write up an old concept, instead of letting the concept issue from the facts.

As General Editor, I wanted to promote depth and imaginative revelation and not limit the materials themselves. What sometimes happened was that, in circulating the manuscripts, I stimulated somebody else, which of course is not imposing a pattern at all, but just giving an incentive.

Fortunately, Norrie Frye was not inclined to tighten the reins. Early on in preparations, I sent him a letter and a copy of the project that I had outlined for Jeanneret. Norrie's reply three days later was most encouraging. A meeting with him, arranged for 30 November 1956 at Victoria College, put the project into motion. At this point we had no contract with the University of Toronto Press or any other publisher, but we began to organize an Advisory Committee. On 18 December 1956, I wrote to Roy Daniells of the University of British Columbia and Alfred Bailey of the University of New Brunswick, who both promptly accepted roles as advisers.

On 28 January 1957, I reported to Jeanneret that we had an advisory committee of Frye, Daniells, and Bailey, that I was to be on a four-man editorial board, and that we would restrict our project to English-Canadian literature. In a long letter of 22 January 1957, Bailey warned against "territorial fallacy," and said he would be happy to ask Desmond Pacey of the University of New Brunswick to be one of the editors. Daniells wrote on 15 February that he saw "no point in selecting editors on a geographical basis." "The literary history of the country," he said, "is so concentrated into a few small regions and the writers of this century move so far and so often that I myself would favour selecting the best editors you can find, regardless of geography." He suggested George Woodcock as a possible contributor. A distinction between "adviser," "editor," and "contributor" was maintained for some time, but it was later obscured.

Norrie reported that McDougall was probably too busy to take part, and it was obvious that Reg Watters was fully occupied with the *Check List*. In a constructive letter written on 2 March 1957, Norrie said, "I agree with Daniells that geography isn't so important for editors, but I agree with you that it ought to have some weight in the choice of advisers."

In his letter Frye presented thoughts about organization, proposing as editors Pacey, McDougall, and Watters. If Watters was too busy, perhaps Munro Beattie would serve. More suitable for advisory capacities would be Earle Birney, Malcolm Ross, Roy Daniells, and perhaps A.J.M. Smith, Gordon Roper, George Whalley, and Millar MacLure. In March, Pacey became one of the editors, and I was described as co-ordinator. McDougall was not available. Frye also proposed Claude Bissell and Alf Bailey for the Advisory Board. Smith showed some interest, and it was probable that fourth and fifth editors should be named.

The prospectus was being generally accepted. While the slate of advisers was merging into a single editorial board, the most urgent matter was to obtain financial assistance through the Humanities Research Council. I proposed to go to Ottawa after the HRC's annual meeting in June to put our case before John Robbins.

Robbins was interested in the project and suggested we submit our plans to the HRC, with a request for support, not only for the initial year but also for future financial requirements. This Council was the obvious one to approach at that time. It had encouraged scholars since its foundation in 1944. Its members included such people as Alfred Bailey and Roy Daniells, W.L. Morton, D.G. Creighton, Maurice Lebel of Laval, J.D. Ralph of the University of Western Ontario, W.S. Rogers of Trinity College, George Whalley of Queen's, and A.S.P. Woodhouse.

I sent each member a copy of our proposal and made a special appeal to Woodhouse to sponsor a companion volume to Watters' *Check List*, which, of course, Woodhouse had initiated and sponsored. His reply was full of good advice on ways and means, his principal point being that the general rule in such scholarly ventures was to obtain grants in aid of expenses, but not to pay contributors. He cited as examples of projects similarly treated: the Columbia centenary edition of Milton's poems and the Yale edition of Milton's prose and declared that "the proper course would be to write into the contract with the publishers a provision that when royalties commence, they should be divided on some fixed scale among the contributors."

I certainly was hopeful of having some powerful friends at the meeting of the Humanities Research Council—among them, of course, Roy Daniells. Roy allowed himself to be drafted to serve as trustee and financial expert for our project. He proposed asking for a series of grants over a period of years (as Reg did for his *Check List*) and seeking advice from Woodhouse. Woodhouse in turn wrote to Robbins "that any expenses in connection with the <u>Literary History of</u>

Canada up to the $500.00 granted by the HRC would be legitimate." "As to ensuring a grant for next year," he wrote, "I have asked Dr. Robbins to put it on the agenda for the meeting of the HRC itself." Roy's reply to me was, "To some degree I must do what other people ask when I am in Ottawa, but so far as I can see at the moment, the 10th and the 15th are clear and the 14th if necessary." In the end we did attend the HRC meeting.

Robbins, of course, was invariably good to us; the HRC, he reported, would be glad to meet our expenses, up to $500, for a meeting in August of the editors and advisers on the *Literary History* project. Always thoughtful, he sent expense account forms and said that he would be pleased to send a travel advance if he was notified.

We still had no contract. However, I scrupulously kept in touch with Jeanneret at UTP by mail; his replies were cautious. On 1 April 1956 he had said, "If there are any details you require regarding the operation of our Publications Fund (which I often say is at once generous and not generous enough), I shall be glad to answer your questions. I think we discussed this matter in a general way, however, during your last visit here." Understandably, he had to withhold a final commitment to publish our proposed work. A week or two later, on 16 April, he informed me that the Press had, at least conditionally, undertaken to publish the Watters' *Check List*, and he explained what he meant by "conditionally": "I imply only that there are editorial and production aspects to be worked out. We are hopeful that we can vote the necessary additional and sizable subsidies necessary to solve the financial problems."

Probably there was some discussion in the HRC about our policies, and Marsh Jeanneret's interest and support, however cautious, must have played an important part in securing its favour. It became my policy to keep Jeanneret informed of our progress, which he called "as much crystallizing of the editorial thinking as possible." I also kept Robbins and Woodhouse informed. As well, my own position in the project was becoming clearer. My colleagues entrusted to me the writing of the chapters for which I was best fitted, namely "The Canadas before 1880." Norrie's influence was as strong in balancing the various topics and emphases in content as Roy's continued to be as our trustee for financial matters. I temporarily remained "Co-ordinator" for the Board of Editors.

One regret was that Reg Watters could not join us. On 6 November 1957, I wrote him a last letter inviting him to join the group of contributors and said, "We know that you cannot us give much of your time during the next two years, when most of the writing will have to be done. We hope, therefore, that you can help us at a more advanced stage, say in 1959, by preparing a bibliographical essay. We have in mind a discussion of books rather than any sort of list competing with the *Bibliography of Canadian Literature* [as the *Check List* was then called]." The members of the committee are unanimous in hoping that you will join us." His reply came on 12 November 1957, and he said he was hastening to answer it, to give at least some first impressions. He was not then, he said, so overwhelmed with the *Check List* and the book he was editing called *British Columbia: A Centennial Anthology*—both of these were at the printers—as he had been when my first letter about the *Literary History* arrived, and it pleased him that a great deal of the work on the history would not be done until 1959 or 1960.

Regarding the bibliographical essay, he was not quite sure what we wanted. He thought that in order to handle it properly he would have to read everything all the other contributors had read—an impossible task. "I am not," he said, "I'm afraid, entirely enthusiastic about the division of responsibilities listed for the breakdown of the book. In the first place, I think Pacey is taking on, or has been assigned, too much. He contributed a good deal to the study of Canadian literature in his *CREATIVE WRITING*. Is it likely that he has anything very different to say in this new book? Would it not be better to have a fresh appraisal on the material which he covered in his *CREATIVE WRITING?*"and so on. "At the root of these comments or questions," he said, "is the concern I originally voiced—that a great deal of primary slogging through completely untouched wilderness is required for a first-rate job."

> Otherwise, the *LITERARY HISTORY* should be preceded in time by a great many highly specialized investigations published as articles. For instance, in fiction, in the period 1880-1920, somebody should read all of the titles written by DeMille and all the titles written by Sara Jeannette Duncan, and so on. Pacey did not do this for his *CREATIVE WRITING*—and no one blames him for not doing so, since his book was not the scholarly work that the *LITERARY HISTORY* aims to be. But can Bissell and Roper alone do all of this basic investigation themselves? I

assume we do not want another book generalizing on only partial acquaintance with authors. Similarly with the poetry of the period 1880-1920. Will either Daniells or Pacey have time to look at the manuscripts of I. V. Crawford at Queens? And what about the fiction she wrote which appeared only in newspapers, and some of it remains only in manuscript. I repeat, this kind of fundamental research should, I think, be incorporated in this *HISTORY*. Perhaps the only way to do it is to greatly increase the number of persons involved in each of the categories and require whoever writes about Crawford to have read everything, and whoever writes about Sara Jeannette Duncan to have read everything.

"I must stop this," he said, "but may write again, and would be glad indeed to hear from you further." I don't know what I should have said because he was articulating very clearly one of my own nightmares—nevertheless I could only say, or think, or dream that, if we couldn't go the whole way that he had in mind, it would be something to go part way, and indeed many of our writers might go much further than he had expected. He noted in a postscript that in the *Literary History of the United States* "there were four editors, three associate editors, and about 55 'contributors.' And American literature is well supplied with all sorts of basic studies in books and articles which we lack for Can. Lit. Perhaps we don't need as many as 60 participants (for one thing, too, where would we find them?), but I'm certainly unhappy that the literary core (fiction, poetry, and drama since 1880) seems to have been allotted to so few—when there's so much digging to do."

While I lamented the loss of Reg from our project, I nevertheless persevered, and so did the rest of us. However, I wrote him a long letter on 21 November 1957 responding to the problems he had raised. My own worries were expressed in this letter too. I said, "I almost dropped the project when I was unable to count on you for work on the committee." I explained that

> Our schedule of contributors probably wants explanation. I have been won to the conviction that our publishers and our public will want a book written and edited with a high degree of unity. The members of the committee are

committed to that end. They, and a limited number of others named on the schedule of contributors, "in the first instance," will do the writing. Still others, named but not in a primary position, will do much of the digging. Finally, others not yet named, will put in their share. All will be cited for work done, and not in small print, I might add. We hope in the spring to be able to offer these people reasonable financial protection against loss of time and expense money. We shall not, therefore, abandon the policy of doing "ground" work—basic research—for the book. Here again the members of the Committee are in agreement and will present a solid front.

I have no time for specific detail, but I might mention Pacey's assignment to a large section of recent literature. In the first place, he might have held out for the position of editor-in-chief, and I would have yielded in the interests of the enterprise. But he made no personal suggestion of any kind, and he has indeed taken the general view of the necessity for grass-roots research. His new book will show that he has dug out what one needs for, say, Sangster and Richardson.

When all contributors have been won to the kind of solidarity which exists in the committee we shall be in a position to make demands for more and detailed research—in short, for reading everything....

This does not answer all your questions, nor all of mine....

It is very late to-night. and I cannot think my way through all the important matter of the Bibliographical essay. I shall write again about that. I know that the Committee had in mind an essay which would say the last word on the bibliography of Canadian Literature, by way of informed, mature and helpful comments, rather than by way of repeating your major <u>Bibliography</u>, to which we are merely supplying a supplement.

A word about procedure may help. You will observe that the Introductions to the three <u>Parts</u> have not been assigned to anyone. They will be written by the most suitable person after the various sub-sections have been completed and all the various results of digging have been shared. We expect to exchange a good deal of information; for example, my finding regarding Settlers for Bailey's sub-section. I feel that, for the present, I have a big enough part in digging up the information on the most obscure, but the really "generative", period of literature in the Canadas. I hope to make revelations qualitatively, and I believe that is what will count most heavily when the book goes before the public.

Despite these continuing concerns, by 5 September 1957, I could report unanimous approval by the editorial and advisory committee of the *Literary History* for a book of about "600 pages divided into 50,000 words from the Beginnings to 1880." Contributors were to be Galloway, Hopwood, Bailey, Cogswell, Chittick, and myself. There were 80,000 words allotted for 1880-1920—covered by Bissell, Roper, Daniells, Pacey, Watt, Ross, McDougall, and Lucas—and 100,000 words for "1920 to the Present"—Pacey, McPherson, Frye, Beattie, Jay Macpherson, Irving, and MacLure. Mention of John Irving indicates that there was a growing inclination to include not only poetry, fiction and drama, but also literature of other disciplines. Frye was to write a conclusion and Watters a bibliographical essay. I was named editor-in-chief at the August meeting. The other editors were Bissell and Pacey.

It would have been easier, but not better, to have had an advisory and/or editorial committee made up of people living only a few hours apart. But various factors were in our favour. The meetings of the Learned Societies provided opportunities and usually funds from university or society sources for most committee members to come together. Daniells was in the far West and Bailey in the far East, but they both served on national organizations, which usually met in what Bailey called "the centre"—Toronto, Ottawa, or Montreal—places Frye, Bissell, and I could reach easily. If no other source of money for expenses was available, the HRC could be called upon. On the other hand, attendance at our meetings was frequently reduced by the requirements of each member's full-time job. For example, Alfred Bailey was dean of arts at the University of New Brunswick; Norrie Frye was on leave from Victoria College at the University of Toronto to lecture at Harvard; Roy Daniells, head of the Department of English at UBC, was in England; and Claude Bissell was president of Carleton

University until January 1958, when he was appointed president of the University of Toronto!

If Bissell does not appear often in my story, one may rightly assume that he was deeply involved in the affairs of a great university. But he consistently did all he could for us. He had joined our project as an adviser in June 1957. On being appointed at Toronto, he nominated Gordon Roper to serve in his place and, with his help, to write on "Fiction, 1880-1920." He remained as editor and all bulletins were sent to him, but he was spared the minutiae. He had expressed his "fervent desire" not to cut himself off from scholarly interests. On 13 December 1958, he said that he simply could not write a chapter for the *Literary History*; the demands of his office were too great, but he offered to continue as an editor and to comment on various contributions.

Without extensive correspondence, we could scarcely have carried on. I owed my own university and its English Department a great deal for office supplies and secretarial aid. Personal attention to the needs of contributors was given by every member of the committee, often by letter, and often in person. Exceptional duties were also performed by each adviser. Alfred Bailey, for example, was our most meticulous copy-reader. He also manned the eastern frontiers by enlisting such expert contributors as Desmond Pacey, David Galloway, and Fred Cogswell. Norrie Frye, with an amazing grasp of the entire field of operations, provided wisdom and know-how in every aspect of policy and financial support. The payment of expenses incurred by contributors and editors, that is, editors who were writing as contributors, now became an issue. The Ford Foundation was mentioned. Everyone wondered about the policies which would be put into practice by the Canada Council, which had just been created. In a memorandum I sent to contributors on 31 October, I suggested that individual contributors requiring grants for out-of-pocket expenses should apply directly to the Canada Council, to the HRC, and to other bodies. Members of the *Literary History* committee would be pleased to support such applications by writing recommendations. Our tentative deadline for submission of chapters was then 1959.

In November 1957, enlistment of contributors went on, Norrie approached John Irving, Millar MacLure, Munro Beattie, and Jay Macpherson. I wrote long letters to Reg Watters, Hugo McPherson, Alec Lucas, Frank Watt, Malcolm Ross, and others. We talked personally to most of them. At this time we were assured of grants for organizational expenses in 1958 by the HRC. This was about the time when the Council appointed F.E.L. Priestley to survey the plans and requirements for aid (particularly by younger scholars). In 1958 I took advantage of the opportunity to advance the claims of junior assistants to contributors to the *Literary History* for grants. These research assistants might later be acknowledged in the book, though the principal contributor was the named author.

On 28 January 1958, I sent to the secretary of the Canada Council a statement about *Literary History* contributors and assistants desiring short-term grants to work on chapters. There were seven of these in 1958. By then we had a full slate of writers. Bissell's appointment as president of the University of Toronto gave a great deal of prestige to our project, and his advice was always very useful. It was the inevitable limitations upon his participation in our discussions, together with our knowledge that advisers and editors would also be contributing chapters to the *LHC*, that led to the merging of the advisory board with the editors in a common "Editorial Board."

On 3 February 1958, a different question arose. I wrote to Robert E. Spiller, an editor of the *Literary History of the United States*, to ask about his experience with publication rights. Publication by UTP had not yet been assured, but it was almost certain. In whom should ownership of the manuscript be vested? "In the University Press?" I asked. "In the Committee members?" "In a Board of Trustees?" "In the Humanities Research Council?" Spiller's reply was very helpful, although he had been confronted by quite different circumstances and problems.

About February 1958, John Robbins offered to receive our list of applications for grants from the Canada Council. I was grateful, though I had written several weeks earlier directly to the Canada Council about this matter, as Priestley had suggested. We were the first to ask the Canada Council for support for such a project and thus set a precedent for how such things could be handled—our way being through expenses for organization from the HRC and grants to individual writers and/or their assistants from the Canada Council. In April I thanked A.W. Trueman, director of the Canada Council, for grants made to us, and also thanked Woodhouse and Robbins for their support.

As the Learned Societies meetings in Edmonton approached, I had to find a way to deal with the apparent overlap between areas. In addition, unfortunately, both Malcolm Ross and Rob McDougall had both withdrawn from the project. Late in May 1958, Marsh Jeanneret announced that the Press had sent proofs of approximately half of Reg Watters' *Check List* to us. Additional pages were sent by Francess Halpenny on 15 October 1958.

On 19 February 1959, Frank Watt was invited to write about "Literature of Protest." This was a new start, not only in our plans, but in Canada. About this time Watters' *Check List of Canadian Literature* was published, and in March five contributors applied to the Canada Council for summer grants. Since we were allowing the divisions of the book to develop according to emerging needs, we had some growing pains regarding what we were calling "prose of thought and learning," as distinguished from fiction or drama. The Right Reverend James Thomson agreed to write about theology, and Peter Mitchum about travel and description. I negotiated a solution for handling historiography.

Francess Halpenny replied on 13 March that our procedures and schedules were working well. By 25 May 1959, William Kilbourn had agreed to write "Historiography" in place of Mitchum, who had withdrawn, A. Vibert Douglas was to do "Scientific Writings," and M.H. Scargill "The Growth of Canadian English." The tentative list of divisions, compiled in June 1960, is very like what finally emerged. Ultimately, neither Lorne Pierce, who was ill, nor John Robbins did "Publishing and Book Selling," and Frank Stiling could not write on "Essays." Meanwhile a chapter on "Folk Tales" was planned as well as one on "Autobiography." Marsh Jeanneret was pleased with our report and passed it along to Francess Halpenny, who met with us at RMC in Kingston in June 1960. By now bulletins were beginning to frighten some contributors, who were worrying about not completing their work before the autumn 1961 deadline.

Roy Wiles was chairman of the HRCC in 1961, to which we applied for an increase for expenses in that year. Roy proposed that we ask for $3,000. About $1,500 was proposed to be allotted to a translation of the *Literary History* into French by Maurice LeBel, professor of classics at Laval University.

Inevitably the question of compiling an index arose. Francess Halpenny's letter of 30 September 1960 was full of anxiety and warning. "Who is going to compile the Index?" she asked. I could have joined her in tears. "No doubt," she suggested happily, hopefully, "you are thinking of a person or persons, not the authors of sections, in order to get proper uniformity. Would it be possible for this person or persons to set to work making out cards as soon as the first manuscript arrives?" Francess was unfailingly helpful, but I fear that I was guilty of putting this matter on the back burner. Getting the first manuscript in was still absorbing my time and energy. I promised, nevertheless, in a letter of 4 November, that we would follow her advice, and I wish now that we had done so. At the time it seemed impossible for us to do the final editorial work which we had in mind for the autumn and winter of 1961. I did not even know whether we would have everything in hand before February 1962. I did, however, hope that I could let Francess have a fair sample of the material by the end of January 1961. "We are getting quality," I wrote. "We are stirring up Canadian literary research....Just think of the mountain of note-cards in various desks across Canada!"

It was unthinkable that we should cut ourselves off from UTP, but I had to repel the unprovoked challenge to it made in several letters by a rival Toronto publisher. "I can see many reasons," I wrote, "for considering the University of Toronto Press strictly on its own merits." Meanwhile, we were still struggling with allocating unassigned or new chapters on such topics as "Bibliography," "Autobiography," "Travel and Description," "Political Journalism," and "The Canadian Theatre." By 3 February 1961, however, we had enlisted Michael Tait for "Drama and Theatre," Edith Fowke for "Folktales and Folk Songs," Kenneth Windsor for some of the "Historical Writing in Canada (to 1920)," and Elizabeth Waterston for "Travel and Description." Editorial conferences had much business to consider, but there were asides of critical and even philosophical insight arising out of our discoveries and future needs.

I was unable to attend the meeting in Montreal in June 1961. Francess wrote to inform me that Norrie Frye had suggested that "Canada should be considered as an environment, a place where something happened." This seemed to settle the relevance of authors, birthplaces, places of death, and so on. How much of the special genius of Northrop Frye and of Francess Halpenny is revealed by this event?

Alfred Bailey, whom distance sometimes kept from the conferences, remained a conscientious, indefatigable, and useful critic of stylistic and factual problems in the draft copies of chapters, which were always circulated to all the editors. I do not remember precisely when the distinction between advisers and editors merged into a single board, but Alfred Bailey was both a contributor and adviser and Des Pacey was both a contributor and editor.

Roy Daniells was an independent spirit. Writing on "Confederation to the First World War" and helping us maintain critical standards, he was as frank as the others and always gave his opinions a humorous twist. Indeed, I should mention Bailey and Daniells in the same breath, although their contributions were extraordinarily different. Bailey was meticulous in copy editing. He took his job very seriously—so much so that Roy complained about the flood of editorial comments on the chapters passed on to him. I had to tell him that many of them proceeded not from me, but from Bailey. "He is working at the articles in detail."

I received from Daniells on 16 November 1962 a letter in which he said he was sorry that I was having troubles and offered me his sympathy. I replied, "I am not unhappy, only exhausted, hanging on the ropes. We are happy to know that we may still look forward to seeing you in London. It will be something for the New Year….My own chapter, greatly revised, is being typed this week-end. When a copy reaches you, please be so good as to send me the earlier draft copy (which was incomplete and now useful only to remind me of my shortcomings)." The letter contained a reminder that I was still performing my duties as a professor at Western. I said, "Perhaps you will like London well enough to join us here. That would be wonderful. We put up one building per week!" An example of Roy's humour occurred in a letter of 18 October 1961 concerning his "wrestling" with Charles G.D. Roberts. "I find both Roberts and Carman distressing people to deal with," he said, "they evoke either pity or anger and not much else. I should add that they are now my relatives; a wedding last month forged the vital link."

Although he had to cross the continent to attend *Literary History* meetings, Roy was usually present. And he kept in close touch with me through correspondence. Sometimes he confided his worries about the lack of a critical stance in individual chapters. He insisted upon high standards and, in practical terms, upon locating "the boundary between Canadian literature and Canadian writing."

He knew exactly what he would do with his own chapters for the *Literary History*, no matter what anyone else would choose to do: he would assemble enough basic facts to deal with major authors and works and disregard the minor ones. With sly humour he asked for my advice about various difficulties arising out of the general policy of the editors, and then he would write in accordance with his own principles! Through a curious kind of harmless sparring, Roy and I became good friends, and I began to appreciate the complexity of this "high-spirited and sensitive man"—as Earle Birney described him on the jacket of Roy's *Deeper into the Forest* (1948). He was also the "puckish, serious, essentially human man" described on the jacket of *The Chequered Shade* (1963).

Correspondence with the other editors contained little personal matter. Anecdotes, academic gossip, and good-natured cynicism punctured serious business during meetings, but the letters I received were devoted largely to assessing and correcting style in chapters submitted.

Letters from Claude Bissell and Norrie Frye were always brief, to the point, and very helpful. There is one letter of Norrie's (8 June 1964) that exhibits an interlude of wit, a spoof on the zealous copy-editing of his associates on our board. The composition in question is not named: "I dislike very much the style of the mass obituary, the use of the smarmy adverb. I dislike having a man four feet ten inches in height described as a 'towering figure' (page nine) and I dislike the use of such unreconstructed clichés as 'rendered yeoman service' and 'the dawn of what promises to be a great new era.' "

Des Pacey's letters were the most lively of all in their co-operative spirit and their candid response to what he considered nonsense. In contrast, Alfred Bailey, who also held his own among the conversationalists at our meetings, rarely broke away from businesslike correspondence. An exception to his restrained style occurred on 28 February 1964, however, when he was aroused by a challenge to his knowledge of Huronia, a subject on which he considered himself an expert. I was delighted to read his defence: "A niece of one of my ancestors married a Huron chief of Lorette in the eighteenth century and I know some of their descendants....The story of my ancestor's niece's marriage with the Huron is a romantic tale!" It was a great privilege to have such friends. If anyone should ask how we managed the creation of a literary history, the answer would be, "There was a meeting of minds."

Before Christmas 1961 I had told Marsh Jeanneret that we planned to submit the complete manuscript to the Press for publication in 1963. Early in 1962, I informed Roy that I had some well-written articles on "Canadian English," "Drama," "Folk Songs," "Radical Literature," and the like, but only the promise of early delivery of some more, including two-thirds of my own. I believed that I could have a large portion of the book in a semi-final state by mid-May 1962. Good will prevailed. Roy wrote to say that he had seen Norrie and Alf in Ottawa "two days ago, looking calm, benevolent, almost majestic." He doubted that the efforts of the advisers who were also writing introductions to the four parts of the *Literary History* could successfully "address the various excesses and defects of the contributors to some degree." He asked, "Does the Editor rewrite, or does he ask the contributor to do his own revision? He should," he thought, "at the very least reserve the right to recast or re-emphasize." My own policy was to use every ounce of tact to suggest to contributors to do their own revision. In this policy I was resolutely supported by my colleagues, who often carried the burden.

Roy's own example was very important: sensitivity, judgment, insight and grace of style were demonstrated. His work as an adviser was generous, comprehensive, and vital. In the inspired manner of distinguished scholar, he shed the light of universal traditions of excellence and acted as a counter to my sense of the possible. Graciously, he tried to give the grass roots approach all that it deserved. This was in March 1963, when the book was moving toward publication. He agreed that it could produce "whole meadows of fresh pasture unknown to himself" and unknown, he was sure, to virtually all readers of the *Literary History*. He liked writing in "close texture," "constant contact with fresh research," and "continuous marshalling of evidence and the modification of European sensibility by colonialism or its very persistence."

In her 1965 address to the Bibliographical Society of Canada, Francess described the general policy of the *Literary History*, or at least that of a few of the editors (including myself): "The editors were reluctant to set a formula and anxious that each contributor should be able to give his best effort in the manner dictated to him by his materials. They refrained from setting up anything as uniform as a sample article. Thus contributors were encouraged to make their presentation in their own individual style of writing, and it was thought undesirable to try in the final editing to smooth out the presentation into one anonymous style. Individuality of response was to express itself in individuality of treatment and word. There was an evident risk here of which the editors were conscious: would the result be wildly uneven?" It was a pleasure, I might interject here, to have someone like Francess working with us, someone who not only understood the Canadian field but who also understood what we were trying to do. Many people earlier on had not done so. In her address, Francess went on to quote from my Introduction as follows: "The first and overall plan of the Contents of the book was allowed to develop slowly and as it would, and how gradually a shape emerged in four main parts."

She had been doubtful, as I think even I was, that it would all come out, into a recognizable shape and more or less with unity and style. In rereading the history for her talk in 1965, she said, "After a lapse of time, so that the book [was] now much more at a distance," her conclusion remained "that in a great many of the essays, the gamble of freedom was successful. The analysis had been presented with vigour and aptness, often with wit; these essays were general and specific, philosophical and exact, scholarly and human, 'Canadian' in the best sense." This was the finest tribute, I think, the book ever received. When I thought that the end of preparation was in sight, I wrote to Munro Beattie, whose chapter was to be last in the book, that the copy-editing of the *Literary History* had been completed and that the typesetters were at work.

The index problem, which I had neglected, became urgent in April 1964; our typist, Pauline Campbell, could cope with only a few chapters, having no experience in indexing a work of this magnitude—867 pages of text. I started out one evening at home with a devoted group of Canadian literature enthusiasts, including Mary Markham Brown, Elizabeth Waterston, and my wife. Before midnight, we had accomplished little and we knew that we were beaten. I had to confess to Francess, already overburdened by proofs, that we would have to leave the task to UTP. She then came to London to help for a day or two. Characteristically, she found a way to success. She turned her editorial department upside-down, stopping other work there for a day or two, and making indexers of all members of her staff. The result was excellent. The same could be said of the whole book. We were all deeply indebted to Francess and her associates. I spoke for all of us when I wrote in the Introduction that Francess's "editorial competence, dedication, and firmness had made this almost her own book."

The *Literary History* was published in February 1965. Preparing it had been a colossal task. I recall what Claude Bissell once said to me as we walked across the University of Toronto campus, watching construction on a vast new building. He said, "Sometimes I feel as if I were producing Ben Hur." I had mixed feelings. In spite of my objections, the Press had put my name as General Editor in large letters on a line by itself, while the names of Bailey, Bissell, Daniells, Frye, and Pacey were below in smaller letters. Without them there would have been no book. Each had made a unique contribution, either by securing financial support, or by advice, persuasion, enlistment of writers, copy-editing, criticism, submission of chapters, or in all of these.

I suppose that the rewards for them were like those which I experienced: the excitement of discovery, of sharing information with one another, of passing on fresh insights to our students, and of revealing something of our nation's soul, what Norrie called in the last sentence of the *Literary History* "an imaginative legacy of dignity and high courage."

Between 1957 and 1965, there were days of frustration because facts were often hard to find and time for assessment even harder to find. But there was also the satisfaction of belonging to a national movement working toward recognition of a Canadian literature, and the joy of associating with old and new friends. One learned that generosity was a strong ingredient in scholarship and that there were so many more devotees of Canadian literature than one had supposed.

There were happy reunions every year, and a victory celebration at Charlottetown in June 1964. William Kilbourn, who had so little time to write, informed me that his paper was completed while we were in a line-up for the ferry to Prince Edward Island. Upon our return, he delivered his paper to me in the parking lot of Eaton's College Street store in Toronto.

The official celebration by the Press for those who had helped create the book took place in Toronto on 5 January 1965, in the form of "a reception and dinner in honor of Professor and Mrs. Carl Klinck." Of course, I was embarrassed, but delighted with this opportunity to bring Margaret to meet my colleagues and members of UTP.

The most amusing review of the book was published in *Saturday Night* in May 1965 and was written by Philip Stratford, formerly my colleague at the University of Western Ontario. Under *Presentation*, he said,

> "Monumental. Tall, clean, solid, 2 3/4 pounds." Under Price: "Moderate. Less than 1.9¢ per page or about the

same as the average novel. Bargain number of words per page (468 on the average)." Under <u>Range</u>: "Encyclopaedic. Over 3,500 authors cited 3,000 titles. Covers 450 years from the first literary hint at Newfoundland (1510) to the present. No trespassing in French-Canadian Literature as a twin volume, in French, is forecast." <u>Contents</u>: "Eclectic. Only a little over half the book deals with strictly literary matters." Under <u>Organization</u>: "Orderly and optimistic— 22 percent to Exploration and Settlement (to 1880), 33 percent to Emergence of a Tradition (1880-1920), 44 percent to Realization of a Tradition (1920-1960), one percent to Blank Pages." Under <u>Emphasis</u>: "Archaeological. Despite the foregoing, more frequent attention to roots than branches. 'Fiction 1880-1920' merits 79 pages. 'Fiction 1920-1940' gets 35 pages, 'Fiction 1940-1960' only 28 pages." Under Limitations: "Conservative and Isolationist. Though over half the book deals with the twentieth century, there are more references to Wordsworth, Dickens and Arnold than to Freud, Jung, Marx, Einstein, Churchill, Chaplin, Kafka, Sartre, Dostoyevsky, Gide, Proust, Eliot, Pound and Joyce combined. The same inward and backward look restricts any comparison with contemporary U.S.A. Henry James is the most mentioned foreign author (out-topping Shakespeare), but there are more references to him than to all major modern American novelists together, from Dreiser to Steinbeck. Moreover, there is almost no reference to modern British novelists." Under <u>Treatment</u>: "Exhaustive. The record for Exhaustion goes to Chapter 16 in which 477 novels are named in 28 pages." Under <u>Quality</u>: "Variable. Though there is a bawdy joke on the first page, the rest of the work does not live up to this Elizabethan promise. But then the matter rarely lends itself to sprightly treatment. On the one hand it tends, perforce, to be as full of titles and dates as a herring is of bones, and it is difficult to cut a clean filet. On the other, the raw literary is often watery and bland and it is hard to get enthusiastic about custard. Most critics, however, do a good job despite these handicaps. Some outstanding work is done on the least tractable subjects; Elizabeth Waterston is very bright on travel literature; William Kilbourn makes contemporary historical writing seem compelling; Carl Klinck treats early Canadiana with dry humour, and Millar MacLure gives a crisp account of literary scholarship. Other contributors, too numerous to single out, are authoritative, informative, generally interesting, and careful, in picking over the attic, not to stir up too much dust." Under <u>Conclusion</u>: "Brilliant. The book contains its own best review in the closing essay in which Northrop Frye brings this vast project into the focus of his sympathetic and assimilating eye. He answers many of the Computer's objections and presents the work in its best light as a profound study by a real community of scholars. His conclusion makes an excellent introduction to the book. It is a fine example of the enlightened use of this valuable reference work." And under the final category labelled <u>A Find</u>: "Canadiana We Would Most Like to See Reissued—Twok: A Novel (1887), and Tisab-Tsing; or The Electric Kiss (1896)."

It would be a betrayal of excellence and gratitude to pass casually over this slight reference to Norrie Frye's "Conclusion" to the *Literary History*. It was exactly what was needed to capture the spirit of the book; and it was written in Norrie's inimitable style. No one else could have said this as well; it was quoted often in the future:

> For present and future writers in Canada and their readers, what is important in Canadian literature, beyond the merits of the individual works in it, is the inheritance of the entire enterprise. The writers featured in this book have identified the habits and attitudes of the country, as Fraser and Mackenzie have identified its rivers. They have also left an imaginative legacy of dignity and of high courage.

The reviews were nearly all favourable, although they were frequently written without understanding of what we had hoped to accomplish. The popular need for criticism was demonstrated in some reviews by a neglect of historical material and by attention focused on chapters more critical than factual. Roy Daniells, Alfred Bailey, and Northrop Frye were recognized for their distinguished contributions. Dissatisfaction, if any, was expressed concerning efforts to catalogue creative works or to regard related prose of philosophy, history, and the like as unworthy of the name "literature." I especially regretted that the major contribution made by Desmond Pacey was not always appreciated.

Roy Daniells wrote to me from Rome in November 1965, after reading a review by Douglas Grant in the *Journal of Commonwealth Literature*; he was disturbed by the implied neglect of Pacey. "To see Frye and the two of us so warmly praised and his own part left unmentioned, indeed by inference condemned," was "indeed," as Daniells said, "going to upset him very badly." I also was disturbed. I now think that Grant, a scholar trained in the literary traditions of the United Kingdom, did not, at the time of this review, understand the conditions under which we were working to bring our basic scholarship up to par, something to which Desmond Pacey gave his talents and his life.

I felt that the *Literary History* raised questions as well as some answers—indeed, enough questions to keep many future generations of Canadian scholars digging and assessing. Next to acquiring many more facts was the question of critical judgments upon major Canadian writers, as distinguished from the minor ones crowding the pages of our book. My Introduction to the *Literary History* was only the first round of my skirmish between the primary needs of discovery and the sophisticated task of sorting out excellence from writings that would receive their "first and last" mention in this book. I know that my associates had similar worries and that Roy rarely failed to point out the defaults resulting from our pragmatic intentions.

The book went into a second printing in the spring of 1965. Initial sale had exceeded all expectations. But unhappy despite the success, Roy wrote to me on 25 October 1971, mentioning a book about which I had never heard—not a Canadian one. He had been told that it was important, but, on reading it, he found it to be only "an interesting sociological document in crudely fictionalized form." "I mention this," he said, "not with any thought of diverting the main-stream of opinion in the committee and without disrespect to those, like my dear friend Desmond, who hold to the historico-informative concept." He spared me in this context, although he knew my views. He continued, "But I do think that problems remain and that some effort should be made to spotlight the best we can offer the world, perhaps in a penultimate brief summing-up of a character and intent different from

Norrie's. Or, more likely, it is simply not feasible to graft praise-and-blame on the main trunk of historical record."

"In the fullness of time," he added, "I shall be immensely interested to learn of the shape of things to come in respect of CHC." The reference here was to a proposed "History of Canadian Culture," dreamed up by Desmond and myself over luncheon one day. We may never get credit for this idea because our proposal of it to the Royal Society of Canada was immediately swept into the area presided over by the Honorary Editor, Sandy MacKay. Desmond may never get credit for his support of the idea, and my still being alive may not qualify me for credit in initiating speculation such a monumental project. An entry of Roy's of 16 October 1970 notes that "you and Desmond had, at lunch that day, agreed that a cultural history of Canada, to be undertaken by the humanities side of the Royal Society, would be a GOOD THING. An historic moment of combined ingestion and inspiration!!"

The *Literary History* was widely distributed nationally by UTP and abroad either by the Canada Council or the Department of External Affairs. Roy Wiles of McMaster told me that there were only two Canadian literature books on the open shelves of the British Museum. One was his on Canadian folklore and the other was the *Literary History*. The latter was reprinted with corrections in 1966, 1967, 1970, and 1973. General editorship and the board of editors remained the same throughout these years, and for the second edition in 1976, which made two volumes of our original book and added a third volume concerned with the years 1960-73.

I have frequently mentioned the support the project received from the HRC, the Canada Council, and the UTP. I should also mention the Royal Society of Canada and the prestige that fellowship in the Society lent to our endeavours. Roy Daniells had been made a Fellow in 1950, Northrop Frye in 1957, and myself in 1961. Roy Daniells was president of Section II in 1962-63, and of the whole Society in 1970-71. Roy also received the Lorne Pierce Medal in 1970, as Northrop Frye had, earlier, in 1957, Desmond Pacey, later, in 1972, and myself in 1978.

It would be unforgivable if I did not mention in more detail a prominent French-Canadian of Section II of the Royal Society, Maurice Lebel, who became a Fellow in 1947, president of the whole Society in 1963-64, and winner of the Chauveau Medal in 1962. Lebel was a member of the HRCC in 1957-58, when it made its first grant to us, and he remained a supporter throughout the years. He was appropriately described as "perfectly bilingual," although he was born "French" in Quebec and had received a typical classical education at Laval and the University of Paris. His specialization was ancient and modern Greek. In order to master English he enrolled at King's College, London, where he earned an honours degree. He "never ceased to promote the cause of the humanities in Canada as a whole."

His influence was strong among his colleagues, not only as a professor of classics and the author of many learned publications, but also as an advocate of French-English cultural relationships. The hope expressed in the introduction to the *Literary History* that "Canadian literature in French" would receive treatment parallel to "Canadian literature in English" was, unfortunately, not realized, but a proposal for a "Histoire de la littérature canadienne-française," directed by Léopold Lamontagne of Laval, assisted by Paul Wyczynski of Ottawa and Albert LeGrand of Montreal, went forward.

Lebel attributed to George Brown the first suggestion that the *Literary History* ought to be translated into French. Lebel accepted this challenge in 1963 and in 1964 began his translation with the hope of completing it by Christmas that year. The task was enormous, complicated by the irregularity and complexity of decisions and revisions of chapters currently being made by *Literary History* editors and contributors and communicated to him at what were probably inconvenient intervals. The book was published by Les Presses de l'Université Laval in 1967 with financial support from the Canada Council and the Minister of Cultural Affairs of Quebec—truly hands across the border!

In anticipation of publication, Lebel told the story of the *Literary History* and the projected French translation in a paper delivered at the Charlottetown meeting of the Royal Society of Canada (13 July 1964). He told me, "For half an hour, I had to reply to their questions, so much interested were they in your Literary History." In concluding, he had advocated comparative study of literature "canadienne-anglaise et canadienne-française." "Professors of Canadian literature," he said, "are more and more aware of our traditions and of our literary patrimony. Without being chauvinistic, we have begun to appreciate and to study our literary works. It is a happy sign of the times."

Through all the vicissitudes of making a translation with uncertain deliveries of relevant manuscript, this admirable, learned gentleman and scholar maintained his devotion to the cause of French-English understanding and his friendly acceptance of us as colleagues. I was honoured by his friendship. He had put aside his own scholarly work to help us. On 26 August 1975, he asked for galley proofs of Volume III for translation. We hesitated; it added too much to his load.

Publication of the *Literary History* in 1965 gave us a certain reputation in Canada and in the United Kingdom. By virtue of A. Norman Jeffares' interest in Commonwealth literature—and the program for such studies centred at the University of Leeds—I was appointed Commonwealth Visiting Lecturer in the School of English there from 15 January to the end of March 1965. I was very generously treated: my lecturing schedule on Canadian literature was light, consisting of only one seminar. A very satisfactory house at Scholes had been rented for Margaret and me, and the Yorkshire moors and York were nearby. I visited Alnwick Castle and had my first view of the original manuscript of John Norton's *Journal*.

The relevance of all this to the *Literary History* story lies in the speech that I was invited to give to the English graduate students (especially the Commonwealth students) at Leeds on 3 March 1965. It turned out to be a great success, partly, I think, because I told them how we had compiled the *Literary History of Canada*. Of course, I had to explain Canada to them. "Canada," I said, "is that country which receives occasional mention in the *Times Literary Supplement* and the *New Statesman* when African and Australian articles are scarce"; and "Canada is a country classified in the Leeds University Library under the sub-heading of 'colonial.'" At least half the paper reflected Northrop Frye's opinions or were quoted from Frye's "Preface to an Uncollected Anthology." I left them with the key words: "this is the environment that Canadian poets have to grapple with, and many of the imaginative problems it presents have no counterpart in the United States, or anywhere else."

This was only a brief respite for we were soon revising the text. The publishers of the *Literary History of Canada* knew, and the editors realized, that we had an ongoing project. In the reviews of the 1965 edition there were suggestions for improvement of the book, and some correspondents had no hesitation in objecting to alleged omissions. These suggestions were filed in the editorial Department of the University of Toronto Press, where Jean Jamieson had succeeded Francess Halpenny as humanities editor. Plans for a second edition, designed to bring the *Literary History* up to date, took shape as a result of successful sales and the many reprints, in 1966, 1967, 1970, and 1973. After a conversation with Norrie Frye in April 1971, I sent out a bulletin to the editors of the 1965 edition, giving notice of a luncheon to be held during the Royal Society meetings in Ottawa in June. Jean Jamieson was invited to attend and some provocative suggestions for revision were made.

The editorial routine began again. By common consent, or probably by habit, I was still co-ordinator. I had once more the skilful, thoughtful, and salutary secretarial assistance of Pauline Campbell, graduate secretary of the Philosophy Department at Western, and an excellent response from the editors to my letters and bulletins. My colleagues also had excellent secretaries. Claude and Norrie, each being a "University Professor" at the University of Toronto, corresponded on the letterhead of Massey College. Their positions required attendance at national committee meetings, writing books, and lecturing to the most learned audiences in Canada, the United States, and abroad. Their programs, which generally included some teaching, were often complicated by the necessity to accept appointments elsewhere for various lengths of time. Alfred Bailey continued to be part of the Department of History while he was also vice-president (Academic) at the University of New Brunswick; so did Desmond Pacey in the Department of English when, in October 1971, he succeeded Alfred as vice-president. Roy Daniells was still head of the large Department of English at the University of British Columbia.

When a contributor had problems there was thus always an editor nearby to give personal assistance and advice. Alfred was particularly zealous and prompt in scanning submissions and suggesting corrections. On several occasions, when I was ill or not in London, Desmond took over with great success as co-ordinator. Norrie was our Solomon, our last court of appeal.

There was always a centre of operations at the University of Toronto Press, where the genial, shrewd, kindly, invaluable Jean Jamieson, a friend to each of us, kept us on schedule with the help of her alert and agreeable assistant, Jean Wilson, who was the copy-editor of the second, enlarged edition. Jamie's letters, like those of Roy Daniells, always conveyed wisdom with a touch (or thrust) of amusement. In our company, where good will prevailed and progress was friendly, it was a great pleasure to find infectious humour also at the centre of a Press with such an illustrious reputation.

Yet there was also sadness because of the fatal cancer threatening Desmond. We had scarcely started our planning when, in July 1972, Des was in hospital for an abdominal operation. Loyal as always, he came to London for the "Canadian Conference" in October 1972. On 2 June 1975, he wrote to say that his health was "not terribly good." At that time he hoped to get a six-month leave from his office as vice-president. Alas, on 4 July 1975, he died at the age of fifty-eight. We dedicated Volume III of the 1976 edition of the *Literary History* to him, but nothing we wrote could fully convey our deep personal sense of loss and our admiration of all he had done for us and for his country.

I shall now record briefly the principal topics and events of the years 1971-75 leading to the publication of the revised edition of the *Literary History*. At the first meeting, in a discussion regarding funds, Jean Jamieson insisted that there should be "an accurate and useful index" and money to pay an expert to do the job. In March 1972, therefore, we met with Harald Bohne, associate director of the Press. We had the Press's support and speculated about publication by 1975! On 3 August 1972, we were awarded a Canada Council research grant of $4,812 for the first year of revision, subject to a later application for further grants. One of our first bulletins asked for co-operation and suggestions from the contributors to the 1965 edition. At this time we proposed 30 November 1973 as the first deadline. In September 1972, Jean Jamieson informed us that the Press needed "to reprint the *LHC* in order to tide us over until the revised edition is ready. Success!"

In November 1972 Claude Bissell left for Leeds, but he continued his correspondence regarding our activities. There were administrative problems to be solved during 1972-73. We offered each contributor to the 1965 volume an opportunity to make corrections and minor revisions or, if he or she wished, to do no more writing for the *Literary History*. A. Vibert Douglas was one who had no desire to update her review of "Scientific Writings," but Henry B. Mayo was prepared to write an extension of his "Writing in the Social Sciences" into the 1960s and 1970s. Several others were unable to respond: we lamented the deaths of John Irving and James S. Thomson.

Since A.H. Johnson did not wish to adapt the "Philosophical Literature" chapter, we called upon Thomas Goudge to write a new chapter for 1960-73. A new chapter on "Religious and Theological Writings" was written by John Webster Grant. Kenneth N. Windsor and William Kilbourn being unable to serve again, Michael S. Cross took over "Canadian History," and Sheila A. Egoff wrote on her specialty, "Children's Literature."

There were thus twelve new contributors. Assignment of scholars to write for the 1960-73 edition was a pleasant task because of a new wealth of experts. A glance at the table of contents of Volume III will show that we put pressure on three of our editors—Bissell, Pacey, and Frye—to provide key chapters. The enlistment of other Canadian literature specialists such as Malcolm Ross, Clara Thomas, John Ripley, William New, and George Woodcock had long been anticipated. A chapter on "Literary Criticism and Scholarship" by Lauriat Lane, Jr., was also an appropriate addition. In spite of limitations in the editors' knowledge of writings on the sciences, we found authoritative and co-operative writers in John E. Chapman, assistant deputy minister, Research, Department of Communications, Ottawa, and William M. Swinton of Massey College.

In July 1973, a deadline of 31 October for completion of new chapters was considered unrealistic. In November 1973 Jean Jamieson noted that "we are still at the assigning and judging stage." She did not attend the Ottawa meeting, but "saved [her] steam for later."

Most of the chapters were submitted in 1974, and the correspondence of that year was full of co-operative editorial comment. On 11 March 1974 I wrote: "I have such a fat volume of Part V material (1960-1973) that I think it could become volume two of the <u>LHC</u>." Speculation about having two volumes and how to divide the material continued in spite of a warning that "the Press cannot see its way clear to making it in two volumes." On 17 February 1975 I reported to Norrie Frye that "the University of Toronto Press cannot see its way clear to putting all of our <u>LHC</u> material (beginning to 1973) in one volume or even into two volumes." However, the Press did not ask us to cut down our submissions; instead, they suggested doing three volumes. Volume III would be the first one published. Volume I would be a reprint of Parts I-III of the 1965 issue (with required revisions). Volume II would be a reprint of Part V of the 1965 issue (with some replacements around chapters 28-33). This was startling—but pleasing—news for our editors, who felt that our 1960-73 material had yielded something different from the existing *Literary History*: it was "a unique revelation of the last decade and a half." Norrie reluctantly agreed to write a new concluding chapter for the third volume.

Thanks to the memory of the hectic, some say hilarious, spree of indexing conducted at the editorial offices of the Press in 1965 and to Jamie's foresight in asking in advance for part of our grant, the Press was able to appoint a professional indexer. A supplementary grant of $1,000 was allowed for this purpose in April 1976 by the Canada Council. Sally Wismer, a former editor at the Press, did a smooth and accurate job of overhauling and updating indexes for Volumes I and II and of making a new one for Volume III. It was not an easy task because of the irregularity with which chapters came to her. Meanwhile, Jean Wilson was busy to the very end, pulling everything together. Norrie was writing his Conclusion. Alfred was still a valuable critic and meticulous copy-reader. Claude Bissell was taking part in questions concerning the order of chapters: "literature" first and "related" writing next? or the other way around? There was never any disagreement about putting his "Politics and Literature in the 1960's" in first place and Des Pacey's "The Course of Canadian Criticism" at the head of the "literature" chapters.

For myself, I feel most satisfied when I see our books on the shelves of historians, philosophers, and other academics. I hope that the *Literary History* will inspire others with fulfilment of Desmond's dream and mine, of having a "Cultural History of Canada."

The Press sent complimentary copies to all contributors. Roy accepted his set with a note of apology to me for what he thought was his insufficient participation in the work of the second edition. I could not accept his apology, for he had indeed, although ill, contributed a great deal of what he called "the arduous task of revision, expansion and reconsolidation." Evidence of his participation lies in my files of correspondence for 1974-76. "After a couple of hours of intense inspection of the elements making for a new whole," he had sardonically concluded "that we could now abolish all courses in Canadian Literature and turn the professors loose for tasks of research and the like; simply to hand prospective students the three volumes and to provide them with an easy chair and a good light would be enough."

In the year of publication of the second edition, Claude, Norrie, and I held an editors' luncheon at the York Club in Toronto. Roy was unavoidably absent. It was 10 November 1976. It was agreed that a fourth edition of the *Literary History* should be published about 1987;

that the other editors and I should retire from active service; that each of us should become members of an advisory board for the next volume, that Malcolm Ross should be added to this board; and that William H. New should be invited to accept the position of general editor. On 17 November I received Bill New's acceptance by telephone and on 1 December by letter. By 31 January 1978, the new general editor had assembled a new board, consisting of Carl Berger, Francess Halpenny, Henry Kreisel, Douglas Lochhead, Philip Stratford, and Clara Thomas. "About 1987" had been changed to "about 1985." The *Literary History of Canada* was becoming an institution! And in good hands!

When Jean Jamieson, soon to retire from the Press, was given the news about what had been decided, she wrote as follows:

> For all its seeming reasonableness, the action which you and your board of editors have taken has left me feeling deserted. Silently and in good order you have withdrawn from the floor and climbed to the mezzanine gallery, where you can arrange yourselves in comfort on chaises-longues (or whatever the plural is), commenting with infinite sophistication on the plays that are made, cheering genteelly at clever footwork, deploring the occasional outbreaks of violence, and altogether looking calm, respectable, and at leisure. What about me, left to deal with this new person whose name is so appropriate for the occasion? I have lost my good companions, as I now think of you and your board despite your eminence as scholars. We will certainly be in touch now and then about the present volumes, and I will welcome warmly and co-operate fully with Professor New and his associates, but there is no good pretending that the work will be anything like as enterprising and joyful without the pioneers.
>
> Not that I claim membership for myself in that company. I have been looking at our first file (there are now three or four) and taking pride in the fact that the Press did not back down from what was a very large and complicated project in proportion to the strength and experience of this institution at the time. Enthusiasm for the history overcame the very real worry of how it was to be financed and coped with. All hands fell to with a will (as

the best books of my childhood used to say), and I remember well the keenness of the men at the Plant which they were careful to disguise as nonchalance. The major responsibility was carried by Francess Halpenny, who must sometimes, I feel sure, be revisited by the nightmares that plagued her then, but that is a small price to pay for the great satisfaction she must take in the history. In your prefaces you have paid tribute to her and to Jean Wilson, who did the work of putting through the revised versions of I and II, and the new III. The nice things you have said about me are quite out of proportion; I only minded the shop in between.

This is a historic moment in the culture of Canada, and it feels odd, and undeniably sad, to be marking it. This Press is deeply grateful on its own behalf and on behalf of this country for a splendid idea splendidly carried out. And for all the fun. There will be more to be done every now and then on the present volumes, but we need not wait for that to write or talk, especially whenever you're in Toronto and can spare a bit of time.

In celebration of the second edition of the *Literary History of Canada*, Roy wrote some of his affectionate "unpublished doggerel verses," a long poem marked "Park Plaza, Plaza Room, 12:30." It was "a song of praise" for Margaret and myself at a dinner of celebration attended, as he said, by "ladies fair of high degree (like M.A. or like Ph.D.)" and "learned gents, with wisdom crested." Since I heard myself and my program for the *Literary History* irreverently treated in every stanza, I offer these to posterity as an ironic commentary upon my "introduction" to the first volume:

> Cheer for our Carl! for he's a hoarder
> of Can. Lit. in its fine disorder:
> From vivid tales that shock the censors
> To gentle hymns, like Edmund Spenser's;
>
> Tales that Sir Walter Scott's may rival
> Of hero's triumph all unaided,
> Or tales on Atwood's theme, Survival,

> With heroines who've barely made it.
> ....

The temptation to go on is too strong:

> Even such a gulf our Carl can span
> Encompass in one reasoned plan
> What Fate so far asunder hurled.
> He stands, still centre of the turning world,
> Reads offerings cheerfully or sadly
> And suffers fools—well, not <u>quite</u> gladly.

That was the gentle, fun-loving Roy whom we knew, to the very end, which unhappily was not far off. To our great sorrow he died on Good Friday in 1979.

CHAPTER NINE

Canadian Writers and the New Canadian Library

In the 1960s my principal books, *Canadian Writers / Ecrivains Canadiens* (1964), the *Literary History of Canada* (1965), and the revised *Canadian Anthology* (1966), were all results of co-operative editing begun in the 1950s. And two others for which I was sole author, *Tecumseh: Fact and Fiction in Early Records* (1961) and *The Poems of Adam Hood Burwell* (1963), came out of my early work on the Canadas. In addition, I did several introductions for early sketches and novels published in McClelland and Stewart's New Canadian Library reprint series.

I have described the foundations and development of the *Literary History* and the *Canadian Anthology* at length because they were integral to the work that so many of us were doing in establishing Canadian literature as a formal discipline. But *Canadian Writers* was important to me because it at last saw the completion of the revision of his *Outline of Canadian Literature* that Lorne Pierce had wanted to see in print for so many years, and the NCL helped fulfil my longtime program to bring together out of print books and our students.

Canadian Writers was a complicated project. In June 1948 Lorne Pierce had written to me: "I think we shall drop the Outline of Canadian Literature business and later I shall take up the matter again and commence from the beginning. I am hoping I can dig myself out of my present morass and be able to think consecutively about such things for an undisturbed hour." Evidently he was a bit impatient about delays that first winter of our discussions; I don't blame him. It was his book and he was eager to revise it. I had, I believe, mentioned to him the possibility of an anthology of major authors. He thought it was a good idea, but expensive. Six months passed, and then on 23

December 1948, I told him that I would be delighted to collaborate with him, but I reported that I had another project that must run concurrently, namely, the Australian project for the Humanities Research Council Dominions Committee. Characteristically, Pierce replied on 4 January 1949 that he wanted to have a long talk with me, though he sent me a copy of *Creative Writing in Australia.* The next month he reminded me that he had "not forgotten that we are pledged to complete the revision of the Outline."

On 5 May 1949, Pierce told me about a series of selected poems of major Canadian poets he was doing that had begun with Roberts and Lampman. He wanted me to edit the *Selected Poems of Wilfred Campbell* and provide a memoir. On 10 May I agreed to do it, and Pierce found me a copy of Sykes' *Poetical Works of Wilfred Campbell*, which had many of the poems. In November 1949, he had that manuscript, but even by January 1951 the problem of having an expert in French-Canadian literature do the French-Canadian writers for the "Outline" was still with us. Thomas Greenwood of the University of Montreal had proposed that he take some part in the revision, but he wanted to use Pierce's notes, which shook the latter somewhat.

In October 1951, Pierce wrote enclosing a contract, so that I could proceed with his book. He had seen the earlier unsuccessful proposal Clara Thomas and I had drawn up for a prose anthology of Canadian literature, but now he had learned of the anthology on which I was by then engaged with Reg Watters, so he raised a question—always the businessman as well as the enthusiast for Canadian literature—would Ryerson be a suitable publisher for *Canadian Anthology*? However, while our negotiations with Gage were far from complete, we were to stay with them.

Pierce cast about for ways and means and suggested that the "Outline" could be a companion volume to Reg's bibliography (I had sent him a typed prospectus). I was preparing a list for the "Outline," that is, I was still writing up sketches on authors. On 26 January 1952, Pierce submitted a list of Canadian writers and suggested more detailed plans for what was beginning to have the title "Encyclopedia of Canadian Writers." About this time I informed Pierce that I wanted to edit an anthology of standard Canadian poets. He was interested: "It will not be possible for me to edit it," he said, "that would be your job of course" (29 January). He was going to become a collaborator. "How many copies a year would your classes be likely to use? And what would be maximum price students would pay? This sounds threatening, but in these days of high costs of manufacture and high cost of copyright, that will be far from a mythical problem."

At that time, and for some time after, W.E. Collin was a possible collaborator on the "Outline." Then another candidate turned up, V.B. Rhodenizer. At Acadia University he was revising a previously published history of Canadian literature. I didn't want that arrangement, but Pierce, almost desperate, thought that it might be a kind of bibliography and encyclopedia, without the French for the time being, though that would have hurt him very much. He said in a letter of 13 February 1952, "I am keeping faith with you," and he was. On 22 April I expressed many doubts. Meanwhile, I was still sending bio-bibliographical studies, which convinced Pierce that we had better let Rhodenizer proceed on his own.

We continued to hunt for a collaborator while Pierce pursued his work on Ryerson's *Makers of Canadian Literature* series. I suppose the intermittent flow of sketches I sent to him kept up his faith in me; and he still hoped to collaborate as editor. "First there ought to be worked out a tentative introduction," he said on 12 May, "which would state for all of us the core of the scheme, our objectives and methods. This is the concept," he said. "Then we should divide the royalties. There will be 10% on the list price of, say, $4. Your share 6%, Greenwood 4%, Lorne Pierce nothing. I am interested in having the book revised and eager to help, but will forego all royalties. How's that?" he said. "Write to me and let us get going."

From 1953 to 1957 the Greenwood proposal was still alive. In December 1953, Greenwood phoned Pierce and said he could complete his work by December 1954. Pierce rejoiced: "This sounds as if we are indeed at last on our way." A few days later, I had some proposals of my own. I had a graduate student, Gregory Schultz, who was working on the poets Smith, Scott, Klein, and others; he also could work on the "Outline" for me. As well, Jacques Metford had expressed interest. Soon *Canadian Anthology* would be ready, so I would be released from that burden. Moreover, I would have to work with greater speed, because I was planning to go to Britain. One paragraph in this letter of 19 December to Pierce is interesting:

> There is no more valuable book on recent Canadian poetry than the section on Smith, Klein and the others in Henry Wells' unpublished work on the poets of the British

Dominions. The manuscript has been a very great assistance to me. I wish that Henry would revise it slightly and publish it. Please do not think that I am asking for a long reply. But the question whether Greenwood will do the job, or Metford is to be approached again is vital to my answer.

I was feeling rushed. Among other things, I was trying to complete the *Dunlop* and also to prepare my paper on the "Early Literature of Western Ontario." I must have been a thorn in Lorne Pierce's side by the great number of projects I had in mind. But I hadn't forgotten him. He kept up the letters, and I kept up the replies and kept sending him sketches.

In January 1957, a letter from Pierce informed me that he had been ill, and a new period in our negotiations began. He had a brilliant new idea, namely to talk to Father Morisset and "ask his opinion about a collaborator." Father Morisset was librarian of the University of Ottawa; as it turned out, he had "approached the Assistant Librarian of Parliament, Mr. Sylvestre, who is an outstanding writer in French and one of our leading critics in French Canada and an admirable man." Pierce went on, quoting Father Morisset, that "Mr. Sylvestre would be happy and honored to be one of the collaborators." And Pierce was "dropping a line today" to tell him how pleased we are, and "very shortly we shall be writing him." He said "I think this completes the team, you and Sylvestre will be excellent."

By 28 March we had an excellent, efficient collaborator. I called on Sylvestre on 30 April, and we agreed on "some broad principles," as he said in a letter to Pierce on 2 May 1957. But he added, significantly: "I cannot actually start writing anything before I know whether my text should be in one language or the other." On 22 May 1957, Pierce wrote a long reply to Sylvestre, saying that he was not in favour of a bilingual book. "There are not enough with a working knowledge of both languages to warrant our making the book bi-lingual." And then Pierce wanted to have a talk at the Royal Society meetings in Ottawa with Sylvestre and myself, but he thought he had settled the language question: "In a sense this will climax my long years of work in trying to build a covered bridge between our two principal cultures."

We met at the Chateau in early June, and Pierce wrote afterwards to say that he thought we had had a good meeting. He mentioned knowing that I was involved in a *Literary History of Canada* project, which he called interesting, and he must have realized that some of my time would be taken away from revision of the "Outline."

On 16 December 1957 he went over some of the problems, asking me for suggestions and a schedule. On 6 January 1958, I sent him a list of writers to be included in the new "Outline." Sylvestre had evidently not yet done so. Pierce had said that he would like to retire before the end of 1958. I had no doubt that he was worrying about getting the "Outline" finished by then. On 29 November 1957, I had given him some of my own views, which may or may not have pleased him. He would like to have paid me, I think, to ensure completion of his book. And he did think of it as *his* book. I remarked in my letter:

> I have never taken seriously the question of any profit accruing to me financially for being editor of the Outline, and I have never thought that I needed a contract to ensure good-will in such an enterprise. The book ought to be called Pierce's Outline of Canadian Literature English and French—if the French language can be made to say that same thing....Second, I cannot make a contract with an exact dead-line, and I can do better without it. If I did set a date, I would knock myself out to meet it, unnecessarily perhaps because I might get ahead of any French collaborator.

And I go on: "I have actually accomplished a great deal toward the end we have in view. Students have checked and rechecked data for articles on well over a hundred authors. My files are bulging all over the place. An increasing number of graduate students, as I had planned, have helped me by discussion to achieve critical convictions about the standard authors."

On 24 September 1959, I wrote again to Pierce: "I think that the Outline is well worth revising, or altering in a Dictionary type of publication, principally because it will carry on the excellent work done by your Outline through the years. I could not see myself participating in something quite different, something unrelated to you, even if it were to become all my own. You will recognize this idea as one that has run through all my letters on the subject. Secondly, therefore, I have always regarded myself as an assistant to you, rather than as an editor supervising the work of a French-Canadian helper."

He was eager, and I was eager, to have some difficulties settled before his retirement. However, on 12 December 1958, he had insisted on a contract, and publication in the fall of 1960. This would have coincided, I guess, with the new date set for his retirement. On 13 February 1959 I wrote to Sylvestre and said: "I have consistently sought to avoid taking the principal responsibility with regard to editorship of the <u>Outline</u> or <u>Dictionary</u>." And on 18 February to Pierce, "We have a letter from Sylvestre, a defence of his busy life as an author, as a reason for not much communication."

On 20 February 1959 I wrote to Pierce: "My main incentive can be only to have the material actually in print....Do you think that the Ryerson Press would pay out $600.00 ($200.00 per month) to a student who would work from my notes and under my supervision....I am actually suggesting that the money be paid to the student and deducted from future royalties accruing to me." The next day Pierce wrote saying he would be going to Jamaica for a month, as he was ill. "My successor will arrive in July," he observed, and he [Pierce] would be leaving at the end of the year.

He thought so highly of the necessity for a revision of the "Outline" that he was almost desperate in 1959 and throughout 1960. On 19 December 1959, he wrote saying: "My reason for haste is that I am near the exit. I must take it much easier, for my angina at times cripples body and will." On 14 March 1961, he wrote, "I had a coronary, and was sent to the hospital for six weeks. Then more weeks at home with a nurse. Saturday will be three and a half months of incarceration." I had mentioned to Pierce that to get the job done I thought I could persuade one of my colleagues, Brandon Conron, to join me on the English part of the work. Moreover, Conron was quite capable of working in French.

On 20 June 1961, Ryerson Press's Grant reported that he had a very pleasant talk with Sylvestre regarding the *Dictionary*. What was more important to me at this point was that evidently he and Pierce had agreed with me that I should turn over much of my work to an assistant, to do what was necessary to ensure a sound product. A co-worker "would supply the drive and steady production. To be fair then, both names," I said, should go in the title: "I have full confidence in this man [Conron] although his research and writing has not yet been done in the Canadian field." I was delighted to welcome Brandy Conron to take over largely from me, with any assistance I could give him.

147—The New Canadian Library

On 27 June, Grant had asked for the name of the man and said that Pierce was likely to agree, although he had "offered to continue to cooperate in the project." I suppose the team had grown a bit large for Dr. Pierce. I described Dr. Conron and then his role:

> Dr. Conron would make himself responsible for the writing of the articles on English-Canadian authors. My part would consist in supplying notes and files, which have been collected, in helping to establish the canon of authors to be covered, in advising concerning extent and emphasis in coverage of authors, in checking when asked to do so and in supporting whatever will make the project a sound and authoritative one. I believe that certain authors should be re-considered with a view to ensuring substantial royalties for an unusual number of editors. I include Dr. Pierce in this statement because he did the basic book of which the Dictionary is a kind of revision. In short, I think that the budget for the book should include an exceptional item, or an author's (editor's) expense payment, or an honorarium upon signing plus royalties. Mr. Sylvestre and Dr. Conron will be of course the major participants. Dr. Conron and I would hope to work closely with Mr. Sylvestre, and have the benefit of frequent exchange of views. Additional details, I feel sure, can be brought into line with the intention to get the job done which this letter signifies.

On August 10th, 1961, I learned that Pierce had made a generous offer from his Pierce Fund for Canadiana, that is, the offer of an honorarium.

On 19 September 1961, Grant was still sending us information about Pierce's views. "What would you do with a book called a Dictionary?" "He," Grant said, "favours the appendix." On 21 September Pierce sent his last letter to me:

> I am phoning Frank [Flemington, his assistant] that I have the selected list of authors here, and to come over and see it. I have insisted that this book is what we call it—a Dictionary. I have also said that the arrangement big, medium & small fish in alphabetical order is sound, and a

supplemental list of mere minnows is also sound. I will see him and try to iron out the thing. Of course it conflicts with <u>nothing</u>, and Ryerson can go it alone without any Council aid. The letter is a thesis! Don't let it bother you. Onward and upward!

On 27 November 1961 Lorne Pierce died. But this is not the end of the story. Lorne Pierce was tenacious, devoted to an ideal. He thought of the "Outline" as something that would outlive him. A great Canadian, he was also a pioneer in what needed doing in Canadian literature. He was very generous. When I went away to England, I had asked whether he thought Ryerson could provide $600 for Carl Ballstadt to do some research. Ryerson couldn't afford $600 but, he said generously, $200—and offered to pay it himself. He did send $200 Ryerson money for the purpose, further instalments to be paid later.

He was a benefactor in many ways. I think that much of the progress of publication of Canadian Literature in his time was due to him and books were probably published at a loss—a loss sustained by the Ryerson Press. Of course there was some means of recovery; on his trips across Canada Dr. Pierce used to advertise the textbooks published through Ryerson's Education Department. He was a collector of Canadiana, and his wife was too. What they chose to collect were some of the finest things available to show Canadian culture. Lorne Pierce's books, and his manuscripts, were given to Queen's (notably the Carman material, which had been put into his hands by the will of the poet). He was meticulous, scrupulous, humorous at times. He had a sarcastic note occasionally, but never cutting.

On 4 December 1961, I wrote to Sylvestre, including a tribute to Dr. Pierce and stating that I thought the title page should read first Sylvestre, second Conron, third Klinck. Major and minor authors should be in alphabetical order. On 1 February 1962, Guy replied. He had had a two and a half hour discussion with Dr. Grant, and their understanding was that the *Dictionary* should be mainly critical with no supplement or appendix, a short introduction, and a selected bibliography. Samples of 250, 500, and 750 words should be sent to Guy.

On 14 August Brandy sent Sylvestre a bundle of drafts concerning recent authors and mentioned some ideas for the introduction to the book. By 14 December Brandy and I could report that we were "consolidating information and polishing our sentences." The letter was addressed to Sylvestre, and we asked him how he was getting along, and whether it would be feasible to prepare for a 1963 publication.

Early in 1963, Sylvestre sent seventy-five of his articles to Grant, hoping "in a couple of weeks to have difficulties about 10 authors cleared up." He needed another three or four weeks to polish some of the articles. In mid-February Brandy went to Antigua, and Guy kept on writing letters to us reporting progress. On 8 April 1963, I wrote to Grant. There had been a letter from John Robert Colombo on 20 March. He was evidently serving then in an interim position as editor. We reported that the manuscript would be ready by 1 May and that I would be leaving for Britain on the 18th.

An important issue had now come up. Sylvestre's seventy-five articles and other portions were written in French, and I had been asked whether I approved. Now it happened that I knew—I don't know whether the others knew, but Flemington did—that Pierce thought there should be a translation into English. However, I took the liberty of saying this about the language:

> I have no correspondence regarding the language in which Guy Sylvestre's articles were to be written. Any such arrangement must have been made between Dr. Pierce and Guy. For quite a number of reasons I am not alarmed by the prospect of a book two thirds in English and one third in French. I can believe that Dr. Pierce would have approved of this logical outcome of these efforts in an Anthology and in the Outline, to put the English and French writers together. He might have been happy to see Ryerson still adventurous and far-sighted in such matters. I think that biculturalism has advanced decidedly since the Outline was first published. Most students and many general readers can now cope with French, especially if they are using a reference book to look up French authors, whose titles in any event are going to be in French. Guy's articles are deliberately set in the easiest kind of French. I believe that the English/French text would actually increase the circulation of the book. It might even achieve wholesome notoriety, inspire curiosity and be bought and

paid for outside this Province. It should sell in Quebec as well as it will elsewhere, because most French users of a reference book can read easy English as ours is....Brandy and I do not see the necessity for a thumb-nail history of English-Canadian literature as an introduction to the authors. We propose a chronological table.

On 20 March Colombo had written to Brandy to report that "Grant wants English and French separate—that is, an edition of two columns proposed earlier." Brandy wrote to Grant: "We are proposing a short introduction and a table of historical and literary landmarks and a list of general reference works." We did not agree with the two-volume scheme. Brandy, on 23 April, proposed the bilingual title *Canadian Writers/Ecrivains Canadiens*, which Guy approved, although he also suggested a subtitle, *Un dictionnaire bio-bibliographique français*, and a paragraph in French for the foreword.

In January 1964, we were finally ready to sign the contract and on the 22nd did so. We were in the Ryerson spring lists, and there were some corrections; we were hoping to see final proof during June and July. On 18 August I wrote to Flemington recommending an index, especially on a conventional alphabetical plan. The book was published in 1963 in handsome style and contained the features that we had particularly wished to have: an introduction written partly by Brandy and myself, and a paragraph in French by Guy, and acknowledgement at the beginning and the end of the introduction to the late Lorne Pierce. The chronological table was included and proved to be very, very useful for a great many students. There was a bibliography and an index, and of course Guy's articles were in French and ours were in English.

Three years later, on 29 August, 1967, Mr. Flemington, now editor, wrote to me saying: "Our latest printing of <u>Canadian Writers</u> is getting down below 100 copies, and we may want to reprint before the year is out. I am wondering...whether you would like to let me have any necessary corrections?" On April 29th, 1967, he announced that Guy was opposed to a quick revision, and I was ready to agree.

Over a period of twelve years a very successful book resulted from Lorne Pierce's heroic efforts, his initial contribution—the *Outline*—itself and his labours to have a revision made. It came out in a different form, and through the collaboration of a great many people.

Nevertheless, I was sorry that I could not somehow have produced a book, as he wanted it, during his lifetime.

Along with all the primary research I was engaged in, I had always been committed to the principle that students of literature must read literary works, but as a teacher of Canadian literature I was frequently confronted with the fact that copies of required books were simply unavailable. The scarcity was particularly felt with regard to eighteenth and nineteenth century works. It became part of my program, therefore, to use every means to bring books and students together. The New Canadian Library series, edited by Malcolm Ross, and published by McClelland and Stewart, was a notable aid to all of us. It was my duty and pleasure to respond to requests for the editing and the writing of introductions to *The History of Emily Montague* (1961), *Roughing It in the Bush* (1962), *Wacousta* (1967), *"Tiger" Dunlop's Upper Canada* (1967), and *Antoinette de Mirecourt* (1973).

I believe that I was first aware of Frances Brooke and *The History of Emily Montague* (1769) when I bought a second-hand copy of the book for 25 cents. Perhaps I was attracted by the name of an Ottawa publisher—Graphic Publishers—and by the fact of an appendix by F.P. Grove; the date was 1931. I was fascinated by the readability of this epistolary novel, its age, and the introduction and notes by Lawrence J. Burpee. The appendix itself opened a world I had always wanted to learn about—Lower Canada, and especially Quebec City, in its earliest days of British residence there.

One morning at breakfast after research for the *Literary History* had started Desmond Pacey and I had an entertaining exchange of information with Malcolm Ross. Desmond had published an article on *Emily Montague* in the *Dalhousie Review* in July 1946, entitled "The First Canadian Novel," but Malcolm complained that he had never heard of it. McClelland and Stewart were due for an eye-opener. It was not difficult to make a convert of Malcolm Ross or enlist his support. Earlier, at the Kingston Writers' Conference organized by Frank Scott and attended by Ross and Jack McClelland, publisher of McClelland and Stewart, there had been a resolution passed that Canadian texts in reprint should be made available to students. Malcolm wrote on 13 January 1960, that he would like "to see this title [*Emily Montague*] adopted," but that he needed a "plug" from me for the project to turn over to McClelland. A week later Malcolm had my submission, giving details under the following headings: "intrinsic merit, exceptional quality"; "no difficulty about the novel being or not being Canadian"; "one of the earliest North American novels"; "an early novel even in terms of the novel of England"; "permanently valuable picture of Lower Canadian scenery and society"; "an important historical document"; and on to "amazing modernity."

The question of length was certain to arise. I frankly estimated 130,000 words for the text, and 2500 more words for introduction and notes. McClelland wanted to cut that down to 90,000. My reply of 3 March 1960 was so vital to the whole concept of the New Canadian Library series that I feel obliged to quote it in full:

> Please forgive me if my answer labors the obvious. Any book can be cut down. Emily Montague is entirely epistolary, including a total of 228 letters. I could simply omit one quarter of these; I have not sold myself on the alternative of cutting up individual letters. Would one retain the numbering of the letters and run in dots to emphasize omissions? Re-numbering would yield eventual complications for scholarly readers.
>
> The results of cutting, as I see them now, would be a shifting of emphasis. There would have to be an arbitrary choice between characters to be fully represented and others to be largely omitted (like leaving Fortinbras, Laertes, Rosencrantz and Guildenstern out of Hamlet). Or, there would have to be an arbitrary excision of this or that planned and subtle comment upon the relationship of lovers as people of fine feeling. Any modern decision may shift the nice balance of 18th century sentimentalism which this book enjoys as a unit.
>
> You will see that I must invite you to define the nature of the series of books which you are editing. Do you wish to bring these Canadian novels once and for all before the public, or do you wish to present a tentative school-book edition designed to leave mature readers unsatisfied until someone else does the job fully? This volume should not be the weak sister in the series.
>
> I do not wish to state categorically that cutting is impossible. I believe that a policy of editing in keeping with the highest purposes of your series might yield some savings; yet the editorial job, of course, would be immensely increased if everything in the book had to be

weighed and considered for removal without loss. If this were a padded romantic novel, the cutting process might be easy and the results salutary; but this is an 18th century effort to describe with some precision the whole anatomy of sentiment. It is an exhibition of the range and variety of language for that purpose—a sententious linguistic achievement, rather than a matter of possibly expendable incidents and descriptions. In fact, the descriptions of society and natural scenery in Emily Montague are also vital, being of exceptional interest to Canadian readers. The sentiment and the description are generally both included, as one might expect, in any one of the personal letters which constitute the book. See, for example, the first fifty pages.

I do not wish to stall, but I need your help in answering your own question. I believe that Canadian literature needs this book, and I hope that we can find a way to publish it.

On 7 March 1960, Malcolm agreed that my "points were well taken" and that he had "a very uneasy feeling about such a drastic cut." He recommended to McClelland that an effort be made "to print the book in full next year." It is to McClelland's credit that he agreed to printing the complete book, along with the introduction and so forth. The problem, of course, was cost. I was to be less successful with the later reprinting of Richardson's *Wacousta*, which I discussed in an earlier chapter, yet both these books sold well.

The next problem concerned the edition to be chosen for reprinting. My 16 March suggestion was this: "I shall, of course, regard the old original edition in our library as the authoritative text; but for actual printing purposes we can use the pages of the Graphic text, after I have checked and corrected them, if corrections should be necessary." I stated on page 4 of the McClelland book that: "*The History of Emily Montague*, in four volumes, was first printed in 1769 for J. Dodsley in Pall Mall, London. Another edition, that of 1784, may be regarded as a slightly corrected version; it has been accepted here as the standard text."

McClelland and Stewart's editor for this book was Claire Pratt, daughter of Ned and Vi Pratt. She carried the book expertly through to publication in October 1961, after wrestling with the problem of the edition and of a picture of Frances Brooke for the cover. Carl Ballstadt was then studying at the University of London. I appealed to him to look for such a portrait. His search was successful, and eventually an engraving appeared on the cover.

Before I leave my report of this fascinating book, I wish to pay tribute to Clara Thomas of York University for generously letting me know that much new material of Brooke's *Old Maid* period was available in Britain. Although I was unable to make use of this information, Lorraine McMullen of the University of Ottawa, a persistent and able scholar, has discovered a great deal more by research in Britain. Her biography of Mrs. Brooke is a unique contribution to English and Canadian literary history.

My second book for the NCL series was an edition of Susanna Moodie's *Roughing It in the Bush* (1962). My experience with *The History of Emily Montague* (1961) had alerted me to textual problems, but it had also made me unwilling to battle to print another long book. In my introduction I took the precaution of outlining the history of its preparation and subsequent editions, but I confess my share of guilt in allowing the book to go out without insisting upon having "abridged" clearly shown on the title-page—as indeed it has been in recent reprints.

No decision was made at this early date to regard these books as definitive scholarly texts. If they were so regarded, the lack of rival editions laid this higher, but unannounced, value upon them. In this case, I was attempting to give the NAC a readable book about one woman's life in Upper Canada and to give students whatever an enterprising publisher would offer them, subject to more exact knowledge of the original issues in the library. Now young textual critics in their pride rail against those who laid the foundations for their more esoteric studies by making the texts available in the first place.

For *Roughing It in the Bush* I had no great difficulty in obtaining information. There was source material for my introduction in the book itself, which was evidently autobiographical, and, happily, Mrs. Moodie had been given more notices over the years than most pioneers had enjoyed. Also, Robert McDougall had published an excellent introduction to Moodie's *Life in the Clearings Versus the Bush* (1853) (reprinted in 1959). McDougall was fortunate in being able to spend very little time on editorial matters. Once more, I had to use much of the space allowed for my introduction for apologies and explanations for cutting down the book to the publisher's specifications.

When Ross proposed publication of Mrs. Moodie and Mrs. Traill, I had replied:

> I should like very much to have a hand in bringing out Roughing It in the Bush. If you read my review of Robert McDougall's Life in the Clearings in Canadian Literature (the magazine), you will know that I am interested in the book, not merely as a piece of history (which it is, up to a point), but chiefly as a turning point in our literary history (fiction), and as a work of intrinsic merit. I oppose the notion that Mrs. Moodie is here only a typical Upper Canadian exiled gentlewoman. I think that her book is far too individualistic for that; it is personally biased, "fictionized," and artful. It may be more than that; it may be exactly what we need to show how colonial documentary writings shaped themselves into creative works. And, what is also important, Roughing It may show precisely how that process happened under the special circumstances and conditions which we call Canadian. Briefly then, I think the book had not only Canadian ancestry, but Canadian progeny. I sometimes think of it in connection with Glengarry School Days, but I must not assume any kind of relationship without some more study.
>
> Carl Ballstadt, an M.A. graduate of mine is now busy abroad, preparing for admission examinations to the University of London. He plans to write a doctoral thesis on the life, apprenticeship to literature, literary relationships, and critical theories of Susanna Moodie. He will gather material in Britain during the next two years, but I doubt that much of it will be digested in time to help the writer of the Introduction to Roughing It.

I was in no hurry, for I had not quite completed my introduction to *Emily Montague*. A year later, that book was published, and Ross then wrote to me on 10 October 1961 saying that the publisher was "anxious to move quickly on Roughing It in the Bush." Almost immediately "length" reared its head: the firm was "anxious to eliminate the mid-nineteenth century introductions." Ross wrote on 16 October 1961: "I have asked Miss Pratt to write you about this." I replied concerning the dropped omission: "That means that I shall have to record the stages of her conversion to Canada in my own introduction—as supplementary evidence of what the woman was like. Since I am still rewriting, I can and shall do that. Many of my wise critical remarks will have to go down the drain because of lack of space! But I can have my fling at Mrs. Moodie in the LHC."

There were even more ominous overtones in Claire's letter of 18 October 1961: "The copy we have to set from is the McClelland and Stewart edition of 1923....In view of the fact that this book runs in the 1923 edition to 500 pages it seems it might be a valid reason to omit [Mrs. Moodie's Introduction]."

My reply of 27 October got down to basic matters: I questioned using a later edition and advocated the use of the original text. I evidently did not see much value in printing *all* the poems, the chapters written by Mrs. Moodie's husband, or the 1871 preface. I would have been willing to sacrifice these items for the sake of using the original 1852 version of the remainder of the text. I specified the need for the printers to set from a genuine copy of this Bentley (London, England) edition in two volumes. Failing this, a 1913 or 1923 edition could be modified if omissions were to be made. "The great bulk of the text," I wrote, "remains unaltered....The New York edition of 1852 or the Canadian of 1871 will not do!" Since the genuine edition was said to be "hard to borrow for printers' use," I offered to work over a bound or unbound copy of McClelland and Stewart's 1923 edition and make it authentic by "my interleaves or errata instructions."

I explained further that I favoured omitting J.W. Dunbar Moodie's selections but was "of two minds" about omitting any of Mrs. Moodie's poems: "The poems are earlier than the sketches and represent her development....If we leave them out, we leave out part of her Bush experience. On the other hand, many of these are very poor as poems. Using them all would probably be merely spatial compensation for the omission of J.W. Dunbar Moodie's writings in the 1913 edition." I admitted that I would need an extra two hundred words in my introduction to give "a very brief discussion of textual variations." On October 13, I had almost completed the draft of my introduction (cut down as agreed). I assumed that McClelland and Stewart had kept the rights for the 1913 edition.

About this time came a demand for reduction of the text. Even reduction of Mrs. Moodie's own sketches was under discussion, and I could see no way but loss of whole chapters. On 8 November 1961, I sent Claire Pratt a list of suggested omissions. These, as I explained in my lengthened introduction, were "Phoebe H–," "A Journey to the Woods," "Our Indian Friends," "Burning the Fallow," "A Trip to Story Lake," "The Whirlwind," and "The Walk to Dummer." I have had to do penance ever since for collusion in this massacre.

In the next decade I also provided introductions for *Belinda, or The Rivals* (1970), *Twenty-Seven Years in Canada West* (1970), and *The Canadian Brothers* (1976) for other publishers. I shall not claim that these books and my Introductions were sufficient for a course in the development of early Canadian sketches and novels, but they enable me to illustrate some of the main lines of that history.

A volume that was, in a different way, a companion to *Roughing It in the Bush* was *Twenty-Seven Years in Canada West*, originally published in 1852 by Susanna Moodie's brother Samuel Strickland. I should never have been asked to edit this volume if Mel Hurtig, the Edmonton publisher, had not supposed that the Strickland book was set on the prairies. Hurtig declared that he was "most anxious" to have me do "the new introduction....of [the] two volume in one edition London 1853."

Since I was heavily engaged in work on John Norton and I was going to be away in England for a time, I recommended Carl Ballstadt instead. Hurtig replied that he would be satisfied with mid-October. I agreed and worked on the introduction until November. The book was published in 1970.

This was a very pleasant operation, largely because there were so many anecdotes about "Tiger" Dunlop in the book. I also came to some independent conclusions about Samuel and his sisters. He had left his adopted Canadian home and returned to England just when books by his sisters Catharine and Susanna were being prepared for publication in 1852 and 1853. Agnes, one of the Old Country sisters, is named as editor on the title-pages of Catherine's and Samuel's books. *Roughing It* was dedicated to her. I guessed that Samuel had carried manuscripts from the Canadian sisters to England for editing during the winter of 1851-52, and that he was persuaded then to "give his colonial experience" in *Twenty-Seven Years*, to be published by the Stricklands' favourite firm, Richard Bentley in London.

I was so impressed by the differences between *Roughing It* and *Twenty-Seven Years* that I had to emphasize it. Susanna had written openly to warn English gentlemen of limited means not to take up farming in remote and unfavorable localities; her first book reported her own discomforts. Samuel wrote of his own success. His book, I said, was a parable: "the story of his own career makes his point, in the controversy about success and failure of gentlemanly emigrants, by total illustration rather than by argument."

The only misfortune that occurred in this operation took me by surprise after I had rejoiced in its publication. Someone told me that copies of the book were selling in Montreal for less than a dollar because there was imperfection in the collation of pages. Mel Hurtig was gracious; he allowed me to substitute a new and much improved partial revision of my introduction and issued a replacement as a "Second Printing, 1972."

Another early Upper Canadian book for which I wrote an introduction was *Belinda, or The Rivals: A Tale of Real Life* by A.S. Holmes, published by the Alcuin Society of Vancouver in 1970. I am indebted for this pleasure—as for a multitude of other favours—to Roy Daniells. I was introduced to the Alcuin Society by a letter from Roy, dated 17 February 1968. He had said on the phone that he had a request to relay to me: "There is a small society here known as the ALCUIN Society, chiefly composed of printers and designers and library people [including Roy], whose object is the reprinting of worth-while Canadiana in a distinctive format of high technical quality. Our librarian, Basil Stuart-Stubbs, is a leading member." I was invited to write an introduction to the Society's fourth publication, Catharine Parr Traill's *Canadian Settler's Guide*. I was interested in her but countered by proposing Holmes' *Belinda* to Roy and Stuart-Stubbs.

A letter dated 25 February 1969, almost lost me the chance to do *Belinda*. Stuart-Stubbs thought that I was committed to Mrs Traill's book and was therefore scouting my opinion about approaching Marilyn Davis to write about *Belinda*. A former graduate student of mine at Western, she had become an authority on the subject and in 1963 had written a superb M.A. thesis on "*Belinda* and the Sentimental Seduction Tradition."

I had not discovered *Belinda*. That was done by a historian, Fred C. Hamil of Wayne State University. He found a unique copy printed in 1843 in Detroit and held in the Burton Collection in the Detroit Public Library. Hamil described his discovery in an article entitled "A Pioneer Novelist of Kent County" in *Ontario History* in 1947. He identified the author, "A.S.H.," as Abraham S. Holmes, son of the

Reverend Ninian Holmes and a citizen of Chatham, on the Thames in Canada West. Hamil had given a substantial historical and social account of the region, together with extracts from the novel, but he had said it was "a very bad novel, even though, as the author takes pains to impress upon the reader, it is a true narrative of events which had actually happened." He deplored "the trivialities, the bombastic language and the romantic dressing up of the kernels of truths." And he gave clues to the identity of Belinda and her family. It had not taken me long to decide that, although *Belinda* was described as "a tale of real life," it was also something else. Marilyn Davis made a careful study of records about people in the area of Raleigh Township in the 1830s and 40s; in addition, when she saw the copy in the Detroit Public Library, she found in it a slip which gave information about the identities of the characters in the novel. That slip had disappeared when I made my next trip to Detroit to arrange to get working copies of the book. Fortunately, Miss Davis had a copy of the missing material.

She was fascinated by the fact that the seducer in the story was a woman. Her zealous investigation into the sentimental seduction novel of the early part of the century in the United States led her to the conclusion that a woman seducing men was so uncommon in that tradition as to be almost unique. Holmes had either known the tradition and given it a twist, or he had stumbled on that twist, perhaps because he was telling a story in which he was deeply involved. In fact, on all these points Miss Davis would have given Alcuin an excellent introduction. Her work is admirable in its intensive research, scholarship, interesting local detail, background of literary history, and regard for fictional devices and art. But I did not want to lose a chance to record my own fascination with the art of this novel, for I believed it to show pioneer literary craftsmanship approaching sophisticated narrative art. I was allowed to go on with *Belinda*.

I was especially pleased to develop an observation I had made in the *Literary History*: "Coquetry is one of the lively arts: capturing it in words, as Holmes has done, requires Belinda's or Eve's own skill. Burlesquing it and, at the same time, standing up as a Methodist, took a good deal of doing." In my introduction I tried to enlarge on what I had in mind (because I knew that the story was now in my reader's hands in a beautiful example of the printer's craft). This time I began: "Coquetry becomes in Holmes' hands a literary mode, governing the general plan and every paragraph of the book, just as Belinda, within the scheme, governs her suitors. Nothing is quite what it professes to be. Melodrama and bombast are appropriate means to this end. The readers' response creates still another dimension; while Belinda's victims are deceived, we are not. We adjust to exaggeration, equivocation, <u>double entendre</u> and irony with a growing certainty that this effect is produced, not by chance, but by Holmes' art." At the end I refer to his "literary demonstration of the prostitution of love and truth which language engenders when it is coquettish."

To turn from *Belinda* to Rosanna Leprohon's *Antoinette de Mirecourt* (1864; reprinted in 1973), for which I wrote an introduction for McClelland and Stewart, is to enter a far different world. As I mentioned in an earlier chapter, this novel was written by a woman born in Montreal of Irish parents, who married a French-Canadian doctor, Jean Leprohon, and identified herself with her husband's French-Canadian society and the strict code of morals suggested by the subtitle, "Secret Marrying and Secret Sorrowing." I don't now remember how I became sufficiently interested in Rosanna Eleanor Mullins (Mrs. Leprohon) to undertake publication of *Antoinette de Mirecourt*. Her name turned up frequently as poet and novelist in older books on Canadian writers, but I suppose that one of the first M.A. theses that I supervised at Western made me aware of my ignorance about this prolific contributor to the *Literary Garland*. That thesis, "An Index to the *Literary Garland*," by Mary Markham Brown, provided an impressive list of contributions by "M" or "R.E.M." and identified Mrs. Leprohon in notes from Morgan and other sources. This thesis was published in 1962 by the Bibliographical Society of Canada.

It is even more difficult to remember when I bought a second-hand copy of *The Poetical Works of Mrs. Leprohon*, edited with a good introduction by John Reade in 1881. Reg Watters' *Check List* (1959) gave a long list of Leprohon's novels, and *On Canadian Literature 1806-1960*, compiled by Watters and Bell in 1966, named a promising thesis by Brother Adrian (Henri Deneau) on "The Life and Works of Mrs. Leprohon" published at Fall River, Massachusetts, in 1948.

J.J. Talman, our librarian at Western Ontario, managed to obtain microfilm copies of *Antoinette* and of Brother Adrian's thesis for my use. Meanwhile, I sent McClelland and Stewart a prospectus on "the Desirability of Reprints of Two Novels" in the NCL series. The second Leprohon novel that I described was *The Manor House of de*

Villerai, which was found by chance about 1964 (at the office of the *Montreal Star*) in an old and rare copy of the *Family Herald and Weekly Star*. I first heard about this discovery through Fred Landon and Ferguson of the *Montreal Star*.

As it happened, Malcolm Ross accepted *Antoinette* for publication. Evidently, because the microfilm produced only cloudy pages, the text had to be reset in type. I could not have written a satisfactory introduction without consulting Brother Adrian's thesis. "My indebtedness…does not extend to quotation, but involves reference to dates and a few other biographical details which Brother Adrian obtained from private sources not accessible to me." I wrote to Brother Adrian on 6 November 1972, acknowledging the extent of my use of his work and adding honestly, "You will undoubtedly recognize many sources which I have found and used independently." I sent him a copy of my introduction for reference, and invited his approval. Unfortunately, there was a delay in his receipt of my letter. On 6 December 1972, he replied generously, but said that my proposed note of acknowledgment was inadequate. What he wanted was a clearer statement. Mr. Baker took pains to adjust this matter, and I wrote a long letter of explanation to Brother Adrian on 27 December 1972. He replied like a scholar and a gentleman.

My activity with regard to Rosanna Leprohon did not end with publication of *Antoinette*. There was still *The Manor House of de Villerai*, which had become something of a classic in French in Quebec, but which had never been published in the original English of its first appearance as a serial in the *Family Herald*, (6 November 1859 to 8 February 1860).

Kathleen O'Donnell, a postgraduate student of mine, became interested in preparing for publication a modern edition of *The Manor House of de Villerai* in English. The subject of the Canadian Irish in Montreal had attracted her, for she was of Irish parentage and had been brought up in Montreal. Her skill and originality in research were made apparent in her M.A. thesis on "Thomas D'Arcy McGee's Irish and Canadian Ballads." But her 1978 proposal to reprint *The Manor House* was not accepted either at McClelland and Stewart or at Macmillan. However, J.R. Sorfleet eventually published this novel as number 34 of the *Journal of Canadian Fiction*.

CHAPTER TEN

Later Research

During the 1960s and 1970s I did a lot of enjoyable "sleuthing," and often Margaret and I were able to attach it to travel for pleasure. Some of the fruits of that research, such as that on Sara Jeanette Duncan, led only to a few speeches and asides, but others were published in books and articles on John Norton, Samuel Hull Wilcocke, and Robert W. Service.

Until the *Literary History of Canada* was published, I needed information to be found in Britain. In 1963, Margaret and I made a quick trip through Europe and spent most of the summer in London. Then I had some time for my favourite pastime, this time with Sara Jeannette Duncan as the subject. As I did not publish anything about her as a result, I will describe my activities here.

I became interested in Duncan largely through friends who had collaborated with me in other projects in the late 1950s and early 1960s. One of these was Claude Bissell, who prepared an edition in 1961 of *The Imperialist*, her "Canadian novel," which had been out of print for many years. Bissell's introduction to the book reads as if he had long wished to tell us about "one of our liveliest writers" and "one of our best novels."

It was appropriate that Bissell's own University of Toronto should have sponsored a thesis on Duncan's early journalism three years later. This thesis by Rae E. Goodwin is a scholarly, voluminous, and exhaustive study on Duncan's contributions to many newspapers and periodicals. The biographical chapter gave new information derived through records and interviews in Duncan's home town of Brantford. For Duncan's later career Rae Goodwin had unusually valuable assistance from Watters, who lent her documents and pictures he had acquired by direct address to English sources. Rae, a veritable "sleuth" like myself, obtained a grant to travel to England, where in 1962 she visited Ashstead, Surrey, near London, and found Duncan's house and grave.

In September 1962, I received a letter from James E. Brown, MP for Brant County, asking me "on behalf of the Brant Historical Society to be the speaker on behalf of the Society at the unveiling of a plaque being erected in Brantford in memory of Sara Jeannette Duncan." He explained that the plaque was being "placed by the Archaeological and Historic Sites Board of Ontario on premises adjoining 96 West Street, Brantford, Ontario, the birthplace of Sara Jeannette Duncan."

I was to be the last speaker, after the local and provincial dignitaries (including University of Toronto history professor J.M.S. Careless) had their say. Being short on biographical information about Duncan's early life, I decided to stress her literary work. For this my chief resources were *The Imperialist* (1904) and *A Social Departure* (1890). At this late stage in the proceedings, I decided also to attempt some humour, in keeping, of course, with Duncan's "lighter vein."

There I was, in what I still think was a "funeral home," surrounded by a semi-circle of IODE ladies wearing enormous hats. I am not sure whether the response I got to my opening remarks was rapt attention or disapproving silence; I said that "this ceremony will be incomplete in one respect: Sara Jeannette Duncan is not here to report it in her shrewd, observant, and sympathetic-critical fashion." Perhaps I should not have let myself be carried away. I continued: "If she is watching us from somewhere...one can only guess what words she is conjuring up to describe us....Her novels show that she delighted in ceremonies, for example, in English or Anglo-Indian society. In *The Imperialist* I find almost every other kind of ceremonial, but no reference to setting up a plaque." After I attempted to identify Duncan's distinctive literary achievement—the unsmiling eyes were now staring—I concluded grandly, saying that "literature and art are the surest of memorials. Memorials die like us, but Sara Jeannette Duncan's written memories of Dr. Drummond, and her family, and her town have become permanent possessions of her country."

James Brown became my genial informant about Brantford sites related to Duncan's life. The most memorable and pathetic was an alleged portrait of her that had been sent to Canada by Duncan's sister Mrs. Waterous on the author's death. When Margaret and I found that portrait, courtesy of Brown and Miss King, the librarian, it was indeed in the Public Library of Brantford, stacked in a cupboard in the basement near the furnace. It was huge; the face was incredible, and the body was all wrong, despite the fact that it was supposedly painted by Sargent.

In England, Margaret and I retraced some of Rae Goodwin's steps, especially in Surrey. At "Birdshill Cottage," a few miles from Esher, Margaret and I were invited to supper with Mrs. Cotes and her daughter, Mary. Both of them were gracious and eager to help us although, as Reg Watters had discovered, they knew almost nothing about the first wife of Everard Cotes and were not curious about her.

In the house there were many books which had belonged to Duncan, among them a full set and scattered volumes of her novels. The Coteses named Mrs. Sandford Ross of "Tichfield," Combe, Oxford, as the best source for information. We told them what we knew about Duncan, and that was possibly the first time they realized that she was a distinguished Canadian writer.

I wrote to Mrs. Ross at Oxford, and she suggested that we visit her. We drove up to a beautiful cottage within sight of a wall of Blenheim Place and were received by a charming woman who spoke at length about her visit to India with Duncan—her "Aunt Redney." I suggested that she had a story well worth publication. She decided to think about it and see what she could produce. At the same time she expressed her worry about the condition of S.J.D.'s gravestone at St. Giles Church.

On our first attempt to find the memorial, we had to wait until the verger came out from a long service, and then he was unable to find it. On a second attempt we glimpsed it under a holly bush near a path close to the front door of the church. Some years later, after Mrs. Ross had paid to clean up the memorial and the plot, we saw the inscription Everard Cotes had placed on the stone: "This leaf was blown far."

When Mrs. Ross finally published her story, "Sara Jeannette Duncan" in *Canadian Literature* in 1966, she left out what had happened on the morning of Duncan's burial. That day, there was a loud hammering in the room where Mrs. Cotes lay. Her husband explained that he was having her body sealed in a leaden casket "because Canada might want her back someday."

Upon our return to Canada, one of my graduate students, Thomas McGuffin, began to examine material for a thesis on Sara Jeannette Duncan. Dr. John Cotes took an interest in the project and wrote: "I have been meaning to arrange that her unpublished papers should be sent out to Canada where they should surely belong, but have not yet done so." The generosity of the doctor and his mother and sister was clear when they acceded to a request, made by J.J. Talman, that Western be permitted to give Duncan's papers a safe and permanent location. The family offered the manuscripts on loan, not as outright donations. There was to be no publication without Mrs. Cotes' consent, and copyright and royalties were vested in her. The intention was simply to make the manuscripts available for study by students of Canadian literature. The attached list of titles named twelve plays by Duncan, which Dr. Cotes described: "Some of them are duplicates under different titles and pseudonyms: others are genuine collaborative ventures with different co-authors: these were introduced, so my Father told me, to try and crispen up the plots." Over the years, these plays have been studied and recognized as products of the period when Duncan was interested in the theatre, which began when she and her husband returned to London from India at the beginning of the First World War and ended when they moved from Chelsea to Ashstead.

Mrs. Cotes also sent our library a number of novels. On 4 March 1968 she wrote to me in response to my inquiry regarding three novels I believed had been written by S.J.D.—*Hilda*, *Out of the City*, and *The Gold Cure*. She said, "with regard to the first two, I do not possess copies of them, nor have I heard them mentioned," and continued: "I enquired of Mrs. Ross, and she had not heard of them either. I asked her whether she thought it likely that either had been published under the name of 'Jane Wintergreen'—which was the nom de plume for 'Two in a flat.' She said she thought if very unlikely, because 'Two in a flat' was not a success, so the name was unlikely to be used again....With regard to 'The Gold Cure' I have been able to send you a copy which I am very pleased to give to the University Library....I do not know of any diaries left by S.J. Duncan."

My inquiries regarding Sara Jeanette Duncan coincided with my research on John Norton. By the mid 1960s I had given several papers on Norton—before Section II of the Royal Society, the Institute of Iroquoian Studies at McMaster University, and the Etobicoke Historical Society in Toronto. Margaret and I drove through Ohio and Kentucky and made our first trip to Chattanooga and other parts of Norton's Cherokee country. The same year I also acquired new research material in London and Edinburgh. I prize both the *Journal of Major John Norton* (1970) and the *Literary History of Canada* because they were achieved in faith against all difficulties, the *Norton* over six years and the *History* over eight or nine, perhaps more, years. Together they required my efforts through at least fifteen to twenty years of my life. Norton's *Journal*, however, is still my favourite, for it gave me a roving commission to perform my minor triumphs in research and discovery.

This, then, is the story of a journal of about 1,000 manuscript pages, which I found through a bibliography; of its editing and publication; and of collaboration with James J. Talman, Maurice Zaslow (who arranged for publication by the Champlain Society of Canada), and others.

My story begins with my early interest in the Indians of southwestern Ontario. I always hoped to find the history of the Indians that Joseph Brant may have written; certainly he had mentioned, in a letter to the Reverend Samuel Kirkland on the 8 March, 1791, his wish to have had the "leisure to have visited the distant nations and collected matter to proceed upon my history."

An opportunity came, obliquely, when Donald Kerr of Middlesex College showed me Bernard Crick and Miriam Alman's *A Guide to Manuscripts Relating to America in Great Britain and Ireland* (1961). They listed only titles of historical interest, but by good luck Norton's journal was included because of its subtitle: *Journal of a Voyage of a Thousand miles down the Country of the Cherokees: Through the States of Kentucky and Tennessee: and an Account of the Five Nations, Etc. from an Early Period to the Conclusion of the Late War Between Great Britain and America.*

The only way to secure a microfilm copy was to write directly to the owner of the original, the Duke of Northumberland. Talman did so in January 1963, and the duke gave permission to have the British Museum's film copied. He also invited me to see the original manuscript and, best of all, said: "I will also be prepared to consider the suggestion for publication after Professor Klinck has studied it."

Later, I wrote directly to the duke, telling him that I expected to be in England in 1965. Meantime, Talman found an excellent source of information, an article published in the *Ontario Historical Society Papers and Records* in 1945 on "John Norton" by J.E. McMurray. Three years earlier, Murray had received a phone call from Mary Hoggan, who had what were unmistakably original letters to and from Norton. She was prepared to give them to Murray, and after he died, the papers had reached the Historical Society's vault in the old Normal School in Toronto. George Spragg rescued them and placed them in the Ontario Archives. There was a "small incomplete journal," a little book of thirty-five pages that looked like the beginning of a diary. Murray had made a fair copy of the original. It needed only one more piece of good luck to find the original, hidden in the Regional Collection of the University of Western Ontario Library. Its contents matched with the first pages of the microfilm of the journal in England. Talman soon dug up other sources: the Newberry Library of Chicago had valuable letters in the Ayer Collection, and the New York State Library had a most useful manuscript reporting Norton's visit to Cambridge and the outline of a speech he gave there in 1805.

When the microfilm arrived I read the whole of it and was faced by a huge list of references to be explained. I secured the services of Diane Shillington to turn it into a typescript.

My trip to England began on 10 January 1965, and extended until the 31st of March. The duke invited me to Alnwick on 12 March. My wife, Dick Ruland, formerly of Windsor, Ontario, and I drove down, and I marched alone to the castle. I was met by a Mr. Graham, evidently an official of the household, who was friendly but wary enough to make our conversation a gentle kind of interrogation. After a few minutes he said, "You're all right. Come in." On our way to the library we met the duchess, who gave me a cheery greeting. Mr. Graham left me in the truly magnificent library where, however, I was soon joined by another duchess, the Duchess of Buccleuch, mother of the Duchess of Northumberland, who took me on a tour of the castle. The duke was absent in the south. Mr. Graham found one letter by John Norton for me and allowed me to see a half dozen other letters contributing supplementary information. The Norton *Journal* was in two volumes, and was written by "A.W." as a fair copy for the printers.

Preparation of the manuscript took five years, and it took two more years for it to be published. Establishing the authenticity of the manuscript began with Murray's findings and checking the so-called diary against the *Journal*. There was supplementary information in various letters, establishing the manuscript's authenticity. Later at Alnwick I studied the original books, for the manuscript was in two volumes. I looked at the paper on which the journal was written and at watermarks. In volume I the paper bore the name of C. Brenchley 1816, and there was a lion and crown or Britannia and crown. In

Volume II the name was of J. Whatman, the date 1812, and Britannia with crown. This was very good paper (I might add, official paper, such as was used also in Upper Canada records). The other thing that has to be mentioned about the manuscript is that, if you kept in mind that little diary from the University of Western Ontario, and compared it with the handwriting of the Alnwick *Journal*, you would believe, as we did, that, although the *Journal* was composed by Norton, it was not written in his hand. Evidently the amanuensis who prepared a fair copy for the printer and who signed himself "A.W." in the introductory note, was someone else. As it turned out after considerable research in Edinburgh, I decided that the "A.W." was probably Adam Wilson. Adam Wilson's wife, I discovered one way or another through a good deal of digging in Edinburgh and elsewhere, was probably a cousin of Norton's mother.

From the Wilson letters, which had turned up in various ways, we confirmed this connection between Adam Wilson and Norton. Wilson was what was called in Scotland a "writer," one who made official documents. I think he was also sometimes called a Clerk of Session— legal documents. The handwriting of the Norton *Journal* suggests someone who wrote very well in the sense of good, legible, official handwriting.

I also turned to genealogical sources and found records of the Wilson family in Edinburgh, and through a Miss Baxendine I established the connection between Wilson and Norton. Margaret and I also did some searching in Western Ontario, making repeated trips by car to places associated with Norton. On the Grand River, near a little place called York, where there is an old bridge across the Grand, we saw, high above us, farm buildings, one of which was an old barn and had the name Hill House across it. This confirmed other information to the effect that Norton had owned this farm. It had been sold—we knew this from the records—to a Mr. Bain; and a relative of Mr. Bain now had a new house not many yards away. This Mr. Bain had quite a bit to say about his family's relationship to the farm. He also showed us a silver masonic medal that bore the inscription "To brother Norton Captain and Leader of the Five Nations from Lodge No. 40 at Quebec AYM as a token of remembrance, AL 1814," from the ancient Masonic Lodge of Quebec City. The date 1814 checks with the information available to me at that time, that Norton had been in Quebec in 1814 at the request of Governor General Prevost, who wanted to consult him—this was during the War of 1812—about Indian support for the British army in Upper Canada.

I also found a record of that visit in a letter written by Thomas Scott, the paymaster of a regiment in Quebec to his brother Sir Walter Scott, the famous novelist. I made a very satisfactory discovery in this connection. I found Thomas Scott's letter in collections of Walter Scott's letters, both in J.G. Lockhart's *Memoirs of the Life of Sir Walter Scott* (1845) and David Douglas' *Familiar Letters of Sir Walter Scott* (1894), where it is incorrectly dated 1815. The letter starts: "Yesterday morning Captain Norton, the Chief of the Five Nations, left. I had the pleasure to be his intimate acquaintance, and he is a man who makes you almost wish to be an Indian chief. What do you think of a man speaking the languages of about twelve Indian nations, English, French, German and Spanish, all well, being in possession of all modern literature, having read with delight your Lady of the Lake and translated the same, together with the Scriptures into Mohawk...," and so the letter goes on. I would be delighted someday to find that Mohawk translation of "The Lady of the Lake" (I am intrigued by the thought of the similarities and the differences between the old Scottish dress and customs and the Indian dress and customs). Walter Scott replied, telling his brother about the novel called *Waverly*, which ends: "I beg my compliments to the hero who is afraid of Jeffrey's scalping knife." That reference has to be explained. Thomas had remarked that this Indian chief had written a book, a journal of his travels, but it had not yet been published. "He is afraid," says Thomas Scott, "that the *Edinburgh Review* will be hard on his book. I promised to write to you to have it reviewed in the *Quarterly*." The reference then to Jeffrey is to the editor of the *Edinburgh Review*. All this is beside the main point concerning Norton, yet it is a very interesting footnote to literary history.

I also read about Brant and went through historical and military records of the time, particularly the records of Niagara by Cruikshank and Stone's *Life of Brant*. Brant had found Norton working and trading among the Indians, roughly west and south of Detroit and Toledo. He was impressed by him and gave him a position in the Mohawk community on the Grand River in the late 1790s. Norton was, in effect, Brant's secretary until Brant died in 1807. Just what was Norton's position on the Mohawk settlement? One could not find out from the *Journal*; one had to find out in other ways through the Brant material and through Norton's letter. It is clear that Norton was a successor to Brant, with Brant's blessing. And his duties were not those of an old chief, that is, a hereditary chief. Like Brant, Norton was diplomatic and military leader of the Mohawks of that area. Norton's Indian name was Teyoninhokarawen.

Another area for research was old newspapers. There weren't many in the early years. Right after the War of 1812 there was some growth among them. I read what I could and checked references. There was a note concerning Norton's marriage to a part Indian girl called Catherine. She was very young, and he was about fifty. They were married by the Rev. Mr. Robert Addison, the Church of England missionary at Niagara, in 1813. Among other information that appeared in the newspapers was the tale of Norton's last years in Canada, which was made into a scandal by his enemies. The story, briefly, was this. Catherine was indiscreet in her relationship with a young Indian man, and when Norton ordered them off his land, the young Indian demanded a duel. It must have been one of the last duels in Upper Canada. During the duel the young man tackled Norton physically; in that encounter a pistol went off and Norton was accused by almost everyone of having deliberately shot the young man. His relatives and friends made things very bad for Norton, and the gossip that they circulated was quickly picked up by Lieutenant Governor Gore and by Norton's enemy William Claus, who passed his version on in certain records. The truth of the matter, however, I found in Norton's letter to Colonel Harvey, who was something of a patron, and in an article in the *Niagara Gleaner* of 20 September 1823:

> The King versus Colonel Norton—tried for murder—found guilty of manslaughter only and fined twenty-five pounds which was instantly paid and he discharged. His conduct in the affair (a duel with another Chief) was truly honorable and he would no doubt have been acquitted altogether if he had not from feelings of delicacy withheld his best defence.

I take that last clause to mean that Norton had delicately refused to smear the reputation of his wife. At the same time he left her with a portion of his pension and went far to the west: to Arkansas, to relatives who by this time had left the Eastern Cherokee region and had gone beyond the Mississippi.

Margaret and I always liked to go to Niagara-on-the-Lake; there we found no memorial to Norton except at Butler's Burying Ground on the edge of the town. There Norton and a few Indians had had a very bloody battle against the American forces in the War of 1812, and his name is on a memorial. But it was not on the one at Queenston Heights, where it should be. There is a memorial for Brock, who was killed in the early part of the battle. There is a memorial for Shaeffe, the general who succeeded Brock, but nothing for Norton, who with his Indians held the Americans at a point somewhere west of the present park until Shaeffe and the army came along in force.

We also went to the Mohawk reservation at Oshweken, all that is left of the lands promised to the Six Nations by Governor Haldimand when they first left the United States and settled at the Grand River. They were to have all the land six miles on each side of the Grand from its source (which by the way was even farther north than my own home of Elmira, near the Grand) and all the way down to Lake Erie. The story about the ways in which that land on the river was sold off, largely to speculators and largely with the blessing of the colonial government, had been fully worked out by Professor Charles Johnston of McMaster. Norton actually protested against giving up the Indian land and had some disagreement with Brant in this matter. Also Norton had been sent in 1803 and 1804 to England by Brant himself in order to petition the British government for a deed to those lands that Haldimand had promised.

In our searches around southwestern Ontario, we went to the Mohawk Chapel just outside of Brantford. As we went through the door and looked to the right, to our surprise we saw the name of John Norton. On the right a large window had this notice on it: "Installed with the gracious approval of Her Majesty Queen Elizabeth II to commemorate the special association of the Chapel of the Mohawks with the Royal Family on May 27th, 1962, being the 250th Anniversary of the gift of a Bible to Her Majesty's Chapel of the Mohawks by Queen Anne in 1712. This window portrays the distribution of the Gospels in Mohawk in 1806." When he was in England in 1806, Norton had been asked by the newly formed British and Foreign Bible Society to translate the Gospel of St. John into Mohawk. This he did and his friends in England then sent him home with about five hundred copies for distribution. I don't know who added this quotation to the bottom of the window: "Let us strictly adhere to what our Lord has transmitted to us in the Holy Scriptures, that thereby the unbelievers may know the love we bear the commandments of God." The source for that quotation is indicated; "Preface to St. John's Gospel—Captain John Norton."

There was much more that I was able to find in various sources (particularly the letters) concerning Norton's career. Most of it, but not all, was found in southwestern Ontario. The documents that Dr. Talman had produced were very valuable, especially for my introduction, which was largely biographical. The Cambridge speech which was in the New York State Library was also very useful, although it was not in Norton's original words. Someone who had heard him speak recorded what he said about himself and the Mohawk Indians.

In my searches abroad, I first of all found all I could about Adam Wilson, the copyist. In London, at the Public Record Office, I sought military information in the Muster Rolls and the Army Lists. I could check to see when Norton came to Canada and what his military career was before he became a trader in the old North West. Indeed I went back farther, following up the story that Norton told in the *Journal* to the effect that his father had been rescued from a burning building about 1760 in the Cherokee country (when the South Carolinians had invaded the Cherokee territory). I examined the records of the Carolinian regiments engaged in that campaign, looking for someone of the name of Norton who could have been the young boy rescued by a British officer—a Cherokee Indian who could perhaps have taken the name of Norton. It was an interesting bit of research, displaying the extraordinary possibilities of finding records of a man who had been in the British Army.

Margaret and I returned to Alnwick in 1968. In addition, we visited Syon House in September. In the south, near London, in Brentford, Syon House is a huge building across the river from Kew Gardens. I had been informed by the duke that he had a portrait of Norton that was hanging in one of the public rooms in Syon House, and he was quite prepared to make arrangements to have a reproduction of it in color made for me for use in the book published by the Champlain Society. He told me that the portrait was painted by Thomas Phillips during the time that Norton was in London and probably under the favour of the Second Duke of Northumberland. This Second Duke had been the Commander of the British Forces at New York at the time of Bunker Hill, and in fact during the time when the Mohawk Indians under Joseph Brant had been supporting the British forces against the Americans. The Second Duke and Brant had been good friends. This was background for Norton's acceptance by the Duke of Northumberland when he was over there on visits in 1803 and 1804 and again in 1816. And that is one of the reasons why the *Journal* rested for 150 years in the Library of the Duke of Northumberland. The Second Duke died shortly after the manuscript was sent to him. It was sent to him, no doubt, by the Rev. Mr. Owen, for whom the *Journal* was first made.

Norton put on Indian dress for the occasion of the painting, and now the portrait hangs above a door near a portrait of Joseph Brant by Gilbert Stuart. Canadian visitors have frequently missed the significance of this portrait in spite of the fact that there is a longer paragraph about it than about any other of the pictures of famous people in that room.

Also at Syon House, Margaret and I tried to find a portrait of Catherine, the Indian wife, who went over to Britain with Norton in 1816. It was said that the Duchess of Northumberland had the portrait painted. We couldn't find it. The duke doesn't know where it is. But the curator of the artworks at Syon House told us that it may have been sold. We were disappointed. We tried to find the portrait of Catherine wherever we could look. We tried Sotheby's and we looked for other portraits of Norton that had been mentioned, but without result. In any event, the frontispiece is a remarkable and spectacular thing.

In England also, I worked in the British Museum Library for sources regarding the English Quakers because when Norton was on his way to England the first time, he met in New York William Allen, a Quaker, who suggested that he look up Robert Barclay. Barclay was one of the owners of Barclay's Brewery and very wealthy—wealthy enough to have a home in London and to build a country house at what he called Bury Hill. He was prominent enough to be a friend of the philanthropists and parliamentarians known to history as the Clapham Sect, which included people like Macaulay, Wilberforce, and others. These became friends and supporters of Norton in his efforts to win the deed for the Indian lands on the Grand River. But they also enlisted him in missionary projects—made a missionary convert out of him. They were also the people behind the British and Foreign Bible Society, founded, I think, a year or two before Norton arrived in London. So I had to read up on all these Quakers and the parliamentarians, and Wilberforce, and the British and Foreign Bible Society.

The principal man sponsoring the British and Foreign Bible Society was the Rev. John Owen. I was fortunate in finding his book called *The History of the Origin and First Ten Years of the British and Foreign Bible Society*, published in London in 1816. Norton's story is told in this book, as it is also in the Rev. George Browne's book, *The History of the British and Foreign Bible Society from its Institution in 1804 to the Close of its Jubilee in 1854* (1859). Norton was right on the ground in 1804, and when they asked him to translate the Gospel of St. John into Mohawk, he did it, working day and night to get it done before submitting it to a committee of the Society. The committee raised some doubts: they didn't know Mohawk; and they were assessing the first translation of the Bible into a foreign tongue produced by the British and Foreign Bible Society. The story of that committee meeting is also told in a book by E.C. Woodley, *The Bible in Canada* (1953). He tells the story of Norton's submission of his Mohawk translation of the Gospel of St. John to the committee; and somewhere I picked up this information, that after Owen's book came out, the *Quarterly Review* in June 1827 made some sarcastic remarks about Norton's doubtful qualifications for the job and about the test applied by the Society's committee. Apparently what happened was that, not knowing how good the translation was, the committee said to Norton, "Can you turn it into English?" He did, and it was accepted. What was not accepted was his introduction to the Gospel of St. John, because the Society had a rule that no commentary to the Bible story and the Gospels would be printed, only the biblical text. So the quotation that stands under the window in the Mohawk Chapel is from the discarded introduction to the Gospel by Norton. A few copies were made; and somebody in Brantford must have got hold of such a copy in order to have the words put under the window.

The research to this point involved the finding of supplementary biographical material. That would seem to have been almost enough. But I undertook also to work on the Cherokees. I should explain that Major John Norton's *Journal* included not only the trip to the Cherokee country to see the land of his father, but secondly there were many pages on the history of the Iroquois, the history of the Mohawks (presumably the kind of thing that Brant had planned and had never done), and thirdly Norton's record of his experiences in the War of 1812. Dr. Talman and I had distributed the material this way: I would do the Cherokees; he would do the second and third parts on the Mohawks and on the War of 1812.

Finding out about the Cherokees was in itself a major enterprise, because I started out with no information at all about this Indian nation, and I was confused until I discovered that in Norton's time almost all of them the Cherokees were in the east, just where Tennessee and Florida and Georgia come close together. This territory of the Cherokees in the east is now rather small because of political and military circumstances. When the settlers from the Atlantic seaboard, from the Carolinas and inland Tennessee, wanted more land they wanted to push the Indians out. There was war from about 1760 into the 1790s and then an interim of peace.

At the time Norton was there, there was discussion among the Cherokee chiefs concerning whether they should stay in the east with difficulty or do what the American government wanted, move to the other side of the Mississippi. As we know, the catchword is the "Trail of Tears"; thousands of the Cherokees were escorted by a military force and made to go on a long trek to Arkansas or Oklahoma. Consequently, there were the East Cherokees and the West Cherokees. Norton's knowledge was about the Cherokees still in the east, who, by the way, were related in certain respects to the Six Nations of the north, both the Six Nations and the Cherokees being Iroquoian in origin. I had to learn all this. I found that, because of those historical situations and because of the treatment of the Cherokees themselves by the United States, their story was not told. They were a downtrodden people; they were not the winners. And it is the winners who write the history. It was not an easy matter to make notes for references in the first part of the Norton *Journal*.

I started with geography. Norton had made his voyage to the Cherokee country in 1809 and 1810 by canoe. As he went down the Ohio River, he made a note of the various pioneer settlements he passed. His descriptions have certain value, for some of the great cities along the Ohio now were rather minor in his day. I had to check all this. And then he got to the Cherokee country. There were places, rivers, all sorts of things about which I knew nothing. So geography was the first consideration. I looked for maps in books and got myself thoroughly confused. On a trip to Washington, I went to the map room of the Library of Congress and obtained some early maps of the Cherokee country, that is to say, the Tennessee Valley. Also I picked up some material from the Tennessee Valley Authority, which one might guess had changed the look of the whole country by their dams. The Tennessee Valley Authority maps didn't help much in locating places that Norton had visited. Margaret and I made several trips down to Chattanooga. We got a little information from the library of the University of Tennessee. At Chattanooga and in Georgia, we visited some of the places that remained, such as Fort Laudoun, where, evidently, Norton's father had been rescued from burning around 1760. It has been restored. The Hiwasse River, where most of Norton's friends lived, gave us some idea of the country. Then I turned to what I could find in historical books. I think I did rather well in producing enough to help me.

What emerges from all this is the fact that Norton gave what was almost an ethnological, and certainly a very detailed, account of the Cherokee people about a hundred years before the official ethnological reports began to appear. He described in detail the Cherokees he met—and this is the wonderful thing about the *Journal*—among them some who had signed the treaties. Also I saw the number of English names among the Cherokees. I noticed Meigs' report of the innumerable marriages of the Cherokees with white people, many of whom remained in the Cherokee culture. What I received from this reading was an enlarged view of methods of white settlement and the acquisition of Indian lands in the east. Also I learned something of the character of Norton. He didn't get himself involved in the dispute about whether the Cherokees should move to the west, though he was interested in the pressures being put on his own people of the Six Nations by colonial authorities in Upper Canada. I suppose he had to be careful because he was thought by the military to be a spy. They didn't know why he was there. I know now why he was there. He was there to write descriptions for the use of the British and Foreign Bible Society, and perhaps the British Army, so that they might have knowledge of the United States of the time, and particularly of the Indian situation along the eastern part of the United States. He remained neutral politically.

It is interesting, however, to notice that the year after Norton left (that is to say, in 1811) Tecumseh went down from Detroit and tried to enlist the southern Indians in a war against the United States, to be carried on all along that border of the Ohio and Mississippi and the old North West. He was refused help by some of the tribes down there. But Tecumseh was an active agitator; Norton was a historian, shall we say?

I've been talking about the Cherokees and the kind of information that could be obtained in this case through church records, keeping in mind that Norton's *Journal* was in many respects a missionary document. It is worth saying that his interest was largely in the Moravians. There was a Rev. Mr. Gambold and his wife whom Norton talked to many times while he was there. They lived at Spring Place, Georgia, and he obtained a good deal of missionary information concerning them. I found in various ways that Norton, back in Upper Canada, had been a lay person helping the Rev. Mr. Addison even by way of perhaps conducting baptisms and doing other things of that sort, in addition to taking some part in further translation from the Gospels.

When we came to making a final copy for the printer, we found various difficulties, since neither Jim Talman nor I is an authority on the Mohawk language, and we had no particular resource at the time. We had to do the best we could from Norton's own text. For example, a river in the Cherokee section is spelled three ways at least—Kanegshaugue, Conasauga, or even Gausgi. We adopted the policy of saying that Norton was an authority who heard these sounds and knew the languages; we would accept his spellings and even his variety of spellings. They have some meaning that way. With regard to people's names there were often problems. The manuscript is not very clear on these points. The t's often look like k's, and t's and k's turn up often with reference to the Mohawks. Also, it was very difficult to determine whether a final letter was u or n. In addition to this, of course, there were the problems with regard to Cherokee names. For example, one of Norton's best friends among the Cherokees had the odd name of "Turtle-at-home," which was, I suppose, a translation of Selukuki(gh) Wohhellengh.

The time for publication came, and, on 4 September 1969, I had the pleasure of writing to the Duke of Northumberland and saying that "our edition of the John Norton's Journal is now going into the hands of the printer for publication by the Champlain Society." That does not mean that it was very quickly printed or published. It came out in 1972, because the book went out almost solely to members of the Champlain Society and to libraries, the general public did not, could not, respond. I had tried as early as 1966 to make some of the facts known, by giving a paper at the annual meeting of the Royal Society of Canada called "New Light on John Norton." A distinguished Fellow of the Society, who was also distinguished for writing about the War of 1812, got up and protested that Norton could not possibly have been a commissioned captain in the British Army; and he went on to say that Norton was an impostor, a white man pretending to be an Indian. It almost appeared that the old opposition to Norton had carried on for 150 years.

I repeated the exact details of the document in the National Archives of Canada. This document was the certificate of Norton's commission as a Captain of the Confederate Indians: and the commission was given by General Shaeffe. We compared the dates and Professor C.P. Stacey, the military authority, got up and said, "Oh, that's right. He was commissioned on the field of battle."

It had taken quite some time to make people believe that Norton was not an impostor. I firmly believe, from all the evidence, that he had a Cherokee father: the proof lies in the acceptance of Norton in 1809 and 1810 in the Cherokee country by the chiefs there, and in his finding of relatives there and later among the western Cherokees. I also believe his mother was Scottish. But the notion that he was an impostor has come down all the way through the Indian agencies and those who opposed Norton because he was an upright negotiator for the Indians and led them in battle. The Indians weren't very happy about the way in which the Indian agency treated them after the War of 1812.

The greatest surprise of my work on Norton's *Journal* should not have been a surprise to me. It came in a letter from a professor of Anthropology at the State University of New York at Albany. Professor F. Fenton was a distinguished student of, particularly, Cherokee-Iroquois relationships, and at the time he was writing to me, he was going to deliver a paper at a Cherokee-Iroquois conference somewhere in the west of the United States. His paper shows his point of view. "I have always preferred," he says, "direct forms of testimony and eye-witness accounts over historical reconstructions by comparisons [this was a method ethnologists had used]." By nature a historian, Fenton had become aware as a graduate student that historical inferences from age and area distribution might be helpful in discovering problems, but as explanations they had had their day, and "inference to diffusion without ethno-historical information was unsatisfactory." He mentioned some of the unsatisfactory comparisons that had been made between the Cherokees of the south and the Iroquois of the north. Then most of the rest of his paper was given over to John Norton's *Journal*, "which only became available," he says, "to us recently. Norton establishes the eighteenth century connections of the Cherokee and Iroquois and even speculates on the common origin of their languages and cultures."

I take this to mean that, long before the ethnologists had begun working out the Cherokee-Iroquois relationship, Norton had expressed the common origin of the Cherokee and Iroquois. Not only that: Norton had discussed the question with some of the old men of the Cherokees that Cherokee was an Iroquoian language. They couldn't quite work it all out, but they discussed it. This is in Norton's *Journal*.

On the first question, that Cherokee and Iroquois are one language family, Norton had said:

> Some old Cherokees say that the Nottowegui or Five Nations, and their Ancestors, as also the Ancient Cherokees spoke a similar language; but, separating, it, gradually varied until it finally became unintelligible to each other. None could tell from what cause their ancient wars originated, but since their commencement, they became still more removed from each other.

Fenton thinks that that couldn't have been stated very much better by anybody, and I would like to quote from his final statement: "Ethnology has never developed a successful method of reconstructing cultural history from parallel traits, nor have ethnologists found a satisfactory way of handling oral tradition." But Norton had. Norton's approach, Fenton thought, was more satisfactory, and indeed important. "Coming just after the close of the eighteenth century and the end of the Cherokee-Iroquois wars, it clearly demonstrates the presence and absence of certain activities at both ends of the Iroquois chain." What Fenton is saying is that in Norton's *Journal*, through this documented interchange of persons, a great deal of information about the Iroquois-Cherokee relationship has been, perhaps for the first time, presented. "Undoubtedly much of what used to be cited as evidence," says Fenton, "of the south-eastern origin of the Iroquois represents transfers of this period. Other items may be much earlier. Ethnology lacks the precise techniques of linguistics for making the distinction." In other words, Norton's is a very valuable work for this subject. One of the reasons, of course, is that Norton was an Iroquois, a Mohawk, living among the Mohawks as an Indian, and therefore acquainted with the culture, language, entertainment, and sports of the Iroquois; and, when he travelled down to the Cherokee country, he went as an observer; he reported many conversations, finding out a great deal as an eyewitness and through conversation about both ends of the Cherokee-Iroquois chain.

I came to the other two men on whom I wrote in the 1970s from very different routes, but I found that they and the research I did on them had much in common nevertheless. My work on Samuel Hull Wilcocke prepared me for similar work later on Robert W. Service. Each was a self-revealing writer, creating a public image of himself and, in the absence of any private records, leaving us only what he chose to print. For each one I became involved in a study of what I regarded as biographical data offered by the writer or attributable, by implication, to himself. These showed uncommon relationships between a man and his publications.

I suppose that my interest in Wilcocke and his journal *The Scribbler* dates back to the late fifties and my explorations in the then neglected field of early Lower Canadian journalism in English, which I had to explore for my chapter on "The Canadas 1812-1841" to be published in the then forthcoming *Literary History of Canada* (1965). I did not make full use of my discoveries until the 1970s when, in the summer of 1973, John Moss, editor of the *Journal of Canadian Fiction*, kindly devoted a special issue to honour me on my retirement and included in it my rather lengthy article on Samuel Hull Wilcocke. My supplementary article on "The World of *The Scribbler*" was published by the same journal in a different format in 1975.

The lack of general interest in Wilcocke as a journalist may be explained by the disappearance of all but a few copies of *The Scribbler*, perhaps shortly after it was discontinued in 1828. Wilcocke occupied a small place in Canadian history as a reporter for the North West Company regarding trials held in connection with the Selkirk controversy and, especially, for his "Narrative of Circumstances Attending on the Death of the Late Benjamin Frobisher, A Partner in the North West Company 1819." Colquhoun mentioned *The Scribbler*, "copies of which," he said, "there is reason to believe are still extant."

Dr. W. Stewart Wallace's admirable article on Wilcocke, "The Literature Relating to the Selkirk Controversy," set forth nearly all the directions in which I had to go. Some of those directions in Wallace's article were in England, where Wilcocke was born, in Reigate, Surrey, and where he had published a number of books before coming to Canada. Wallace mentioned some of these: *Britannia, A Poem* (1797), *A New and Complete Dictionary of the English and Dutch Languages* (1798), and *A History of the Vice-Royalty of Buenos Aires* (1820 and 1822). Dr. Wallace's summing up led me where I wanted to go. He wrote:

> Though a man of indifferent character, Wilcocke was one of the best educated men in Canada of his time. He had a wide knowledge both of the classics and modern languages, and his English was marked by a verve and vigor that has real distinction.

Once more history led me to literature. Here, surely, was an early literary man worthy of further investigation. In England I followed several clues in Wallace's note. Reigate yielded no record of Wilcocke's birth, but the English-Dutch connection was confirmed through Wallace's identification of Wilcocke's father as "Samuel Wilcocke MD, afterwards minister of the English at Middleburg in Zealand." In the light of the son's facility with Dutch and the nature of his erudition and scholarship, I assumed that he had a continental education and that he probably returned from Holland to England with his father and his father's family in 1794, when he was thirty years of age. It did not take him long to become a writer in English. I turned to the *Monthly Mirror*—a likely vehicle for reviews. I was making considerable use of these early English journals, which were appearing not so very many years before the literary journals were coming out in America. I turned to the *Monthly Mirror* and found the first printing of *Britannia* in 1796, later published in London in 1797. This poem proposed to be Runic and Celtic, a kind of epic based on old English books, old English history and it was unquestionably written by someone who admired Ossian. Ossian turns up repeatedly in these studies.

I soon found publications, probably brought over from the continent. He published these in English; translations from Dr. J.G. Zimmerman's *On Solitude* and *Essay on National Pride* and Tissot's *The Life of J.G. Zimmerman*.

With evidence from *The Scribbler*, when I obtained a copy of the various issues, I was later able to make a reasonable picture of Wilcocke during his career in business in Liverpool. Not only did he translate three volumes by a Dutch rear-admiral, but he wrote, evidently on short order, a large and strongly documented book on *The Vice-Royalty of Buenos Aires* in 1807. He also helped to establish a botanic garden and a catalogue of the Athenaeum Library. He was a "Manager and Master of the Ceremonies to the Assemblies"—these were social affairs, dances, balls, and so on. He wrote a play called *The Slip*, partly from Middleton, Beaumont and Fletcher, and he prepared scholarly remarks upon the plays of Phillip Massinger, a Carolinian playwright.

This is only a little of what I dug out of the pages of *The Scribbler*—the ten volumes of that periodical from 1822 to 1827. It soon became apparent that not all of Wilcocke's blue-covered books, which became fearful things to many people in Montreal, had remained extant. Appeals to other libraries brought little success. Finally, in response to a request sent to him by J.J. Talman, the National Archivist, Dr. Kaye Lamb, was kind enough to make a collection of copies from every conceivable source, and a microfilm was made of everything that he gathered, everything that was extant. The collection was fairly complete to the end of Volume 6, with odds and ends from volumes 8 to 10. According to our usual procedure, we had copy-flow made. I read through this collection many times in order to make careful notes on Wilcocke's autobiographical outpourings and on the great variety of subjects that interested or infuriated him.

The coarseness and often scurrility of some of his journalism matched or surpassed what I had read in the newspapers of "Tiger" Dunlop in London or in the partisan publications during an election in Liverpool in Wilcocke's time. *The Scribbler* may indeed have been patterned on English models. It was nevertheless a fascinating exercise for a biographer to attempt identification of the fanciful nicknames that Wilcocke was pleased to give to his enemy, the North West Company (the Rat-Catching Company) and to local celebrities. I consulted all sorts of official lists and directories to find the real names of Peter Mogul Legrand, Esq., Harry M'Harry, Esq., Baron Grunt, Major Henpeck, Count Joseph Stairwell, Captain Hornblow, Auld Granny McRope, The Honorable Tory Loverule, Tom Allspice of Castle Folly, Tom Tan, also called Lord goddamhim, and Spasm who was David Chocholm, a rival editor, and many more. Contributors were given pen-names such as Solomon Snear—and Wilcocke himself issued many aliases for his own writings in *The Scribbler*.

The masthead of the journal gave the name of the editor as Lewis Luke MacCulloh, and his beloved partner was not only known by her real name, Anne Lewis, but also as Althea and, usually, as the Louisa of the "Letters from Penang." And, to solve the greatest puzzle, what was the life story of Mrs. Anne Lewis, before she left England and after she left Montreal? Wilcocke asserted that her rank and social status exceeded that of any lady in Montreal, except the wife of the governor and also that she had belonged to brilliant circles of rank and fashion in her own land.

A puzzle which cost me much wasted effort appeared in the Index of the *Literary and Historical Society of Quebec* (1824). On page 211 there was a reference to "Memoirs and Other Manuscripts of Samuel Hull Wilcocke in the possession of the Society" in a padlocked box in the basement of Morrin College in Quebec City. When I visited the college, I was told that such contents had been sent to the Provincial Archives. I was received very kindly there in the summer of 1961 by M. J. Antoine Pelletier, the librarian. He did some digging for me, but there was no luck. He suggested further search at the Librairie Saint-Sulpice, Montreal, and the National Archives in Ottawa.

While I was in Montreal on this errand, I even visited the Archives of the Superior Court, which was in a very old building with a place in the lowest basement once used to hold prisoners. There was no record of criminal charges against Wilcocke, but I had gone to the last extreme in research when I walked on the trodden-down stones of the deepest cells of the old Montreal Courthouse. I had to satisfy myself with the padlocked box of Morrin College. It was as much of a fantasy as the iron box which Wilcocke was alleged to have raided for certain papers and documents "tending," as he said, "to expose certain facts, motives and conduct which some members of the North West Company were interested in concealing." Forgery, it appears, was the charge they used against him. For the story of his imprisonment and escape to the United States, as well as the touching accounts of Louisa's faithfulness to him, one may turn to my digest made from the pages of *The Scribbler* or, if one is lucky, to the microfilm pages in certain university libraries.

In my two articles, I have tried to give a guide to the contents of *The Scribbler*. In addition to the personal record, there is an owlish view of the political, social, bedroom, and street life of Montreal, probably not duplicated in such detail elsewhere; and the man who wrote the gossip appears also as an exile, a constructive critic, a poet, a lover, a hater, and a scholar who could even offer early Montreal classical studies of the plays of Phillip Massinger!

I am indebted for occasional letters about Wilcocke from a fellow enthusiast, Mary Lu MacDonald of Halifax, who has acquired the admirable habit of reading through early Montreal and Quebec periodicals and newspapers. She first gained my gratitude by proving that George Longmore, not Levi Adams, was the author of "The Charivari" and therefore also of *The Tales of Chivalry and Romance*. Dr. MacDonald's M.A. thesis for Carleton was on "The Literary Life of English and French Montreal from 1817 to 1830 As Seen through the Periodicals of the Time." As additional facts about Wilcocke emerged, she sent them to me for my files. I do not feel that I have preempted or completed the subject of Wilcocke and his *Scribbler*. I believe that many new facts may emerge and that a definitive book will be written about one of our most talented and early writers. Meanwhile I shall leave a carton full of notes for the man or woman who is to write it.

I did write a biography of Robert W. Service. It was published by McGraw-Hill Ryerson of Toronto and Dodd, Mead of New York in 1976, thirteen years after I began preparing it. The year 1963 opened with a request dated 4 February from E.T. Williams of Balliol College, Oxford, editor of the *Dictionary of National Biography* to "undertake to contribute to the forthcoming Supplement a notice of the life of Robert Service." I replied on 11 February, stating that "it should be possible for me to secure information about Service on both sides of the Atlantic; I expect to travel in France and England during the summer." So my course was set for the year 1963. Between my submission of copy to Mr. Williams and the end of the year, a great deal happened.

I consulted Peter Revell, who had visited the Services on the Riviera; he gave me the addresses of Mrs. Germaine Service, Robert Service's widow, and of Mrs. Iris Davies, the poet's daughter, in Monaco. Since Margaret and I would be driving to the Riviera at the end of May, I wrote to Mrs. Davies and requested an appointment. On 1 June we visited Mr. and Mrs. Davies, their daughters, and Mrs. Service. We were welcomed, charmingly entertained in their home, and generously provided with more information and authentic impressions of the poet than could have been obtained anywhere else.

By July I was back in London, ready to write the *DNB* article, which I would submit to the view of the Service family before sending it to Mr. Williams. I sent it to them in late November, explaining the restraints of the *DNB* pattern and my wish to be told about any errors. Mrs. Service replied, two days after Christmas: "The account you made about my husband R.W. SERVICE is very accurate and very good considering the limit of words you were forced to." It was the beginning of friendship and a correspondence, maintained, especially at Christmas, to the present time.

Early in 1964, when Mr. Williams wished to learn about any portrait of Robert W. Service, his widow was hopeful but not possessed of information about any such painting. She made a supposition:

> In 1915 we had in Brittany in our house, a Canadian couple, both artists living in Paris. He wanted so much to make a portrait of my husband. Also they were very good friends. He refused at once. As far as I know he would not have lost his precious time (as he called it) to sit for a painter....He never refused to let people take photos of him when he was asked.

(I was later to find that this couple was Frank Armington and his wife, both from Ontario and their pictures are in my book on Service.)

I am tempted to record at length the contents of many letters which proceeded from Monaco or Lancieux in Brittany. I now feel unhappy about leaving out of the book one piece of information that, I should have realized, explained a great deal about Robert Service's thoughts and emotions. I was properly reminded by a reviewer that I had made no mention of the death of the Service's daughter Doris—a twin with Iris—at the age of nine months. I confess that Mrs. Service had told me this in 1963. I thought when I was writing that this was too personal and confidential.

The belief that I could write a book on Robert Service evidently had not then taken shape in my mind. But I was back in England in the winter of 1965. I had confided to Miss Francess Halpenny of the University of Toronto Press my plan to visit the office of Ernest Benn, the British publishers of Robert Service, and I did so in June 1965. On my return to Canada I wrote to Kenneth Day, director of Ernest Benn Ltd. (in Fleet Street) proposing a "book which I should like to prepare on the life and work of Robert W. Service." I supplied a tentative outline and explained that I would base my chapters upon the autobiographies *Ploughman of the Moon* (1945) and *Harper of Heaven* (1948) and upon the novels and collections of poems. I had assumed that the autobiographies would probably not be reissued and that some of the other works would not be reprinted. It was quite clear that I wanted the copyright holders to give me permission to use their literary property in a book that would proceed from their firms. I stated that my approach would be "critical and literary in the sense of giving this writer his due...serious treatment...in the context of his times...displays of Service's own wit and humour."

John R. Denton, the managing editor, replied:

> We have been very interested to hear of your projected book on Robert Service and we should of course be very willing for you to quote from any of his books that we publish. As you know, we only control the rights of the British Commonwealth excluding Canada, and you will obviously have to get permission from the Ryerson Press and Dodd Mead as well.
>
> We have given careful consideration to the possibility of our publishing the book ourselves. Although it would be of interest to us, we do not feel that there would be a sufficient demand in this country to make it practical for us to be the original publishers. If the Ryerson would like to publish the book we would certainly be very willing to consider taking a few hundred copies from them.

Margaret and I made plans to go ahead during August and September of 1968 and to include a visit to Lancieux in Brittany, where the Davies and Mrs. Service spent their summer months. I wrote to Mrs. Service on 24 January 1968, proposing this visit and opening the subject of writing a book:

> Ever since my wife and I spent a very pleasant afternoon with you in Monaco, I had hoped that some day I might be able to write a book on Robert W. Service. I have now reached the point of believing that I could do so during the next year or two. I would not do this, of course, without your permission, or without permission from your publishers in various countries to use a limited number of appropriate quotations from the poet's works. It would also

be necessary for me to refer to a great deal of biographical material from The Harper of Heaven and Ploughman of the Moon, because these are almost the only sources for many facts about Mr. Service. May I ask the privilege of having a conversation with you on this subject?

Mrs. Service replied that there was little, if anything, that she could add to the story told in the two books. Fortunately, she would be in Lancieux during August and September. We looked forward to our trip to Finistère and the Service's "Dream Haven," described in *Harper of Heaven* as "a little red roofed house that stood on a sea-jutting rock." It had formerly been a Coast Guard post. There Service had died in 1958, and he had been buried nearby. Mrs. Service still lived there.

On 7 August 1968, Margaret and I drove from St. Malo to Lancieux on a very wet day. Mrs. Davies was her father's executor, and she not only seconded her mother's talk about Robert W. Service but was also prepared to be realistic about the business affairs, which kept the family living in luxury. Some of the books were in limbo, but problems of copyright needed clear and equitable solutions. I admired her quiet reasonableness and took heart from it for my project. The letter which she wrote to me on 12 December 1968 pointed toward a solution—through Dodd Mead of New York and Mr. Shulman, the family's lawyer.

From 1969 through 1972 I struggled with problems over the copyright and the relationship of Dodd Mead and McGraw-Hill Ryerson formerly Ryerson Press. As well I was having my own struggle with illness beginning late in 1969. On 25 January 1972, I wrote to Mr. Dodd, and he replied on 9 February 1972 that "we would indeed be interested in seeing your work on Robert Service."

About this time McGraw-Hill Ryerson offered about 30 per cent of outstanding shares of the company

> to foster a Canadian identity in McGraw-Hill Ryerson Limited by providing the Canadian public with an opportunity to participate in the growth and development of the book publishing industry in Canada through equity ownership in its Canadian subsidiary.

Probably in response to this "Canadian" policy, and probably in response to a query from Mr. Dodd, McGraw-Hill Ryerson reaffirmed their continuing interest in my biography in a letter of 2 August 1972 from Toivo Kiil, editor of the Trade Division. Evidently he had established some connection with Dodd, Mead. Instead of pleasing me, the letter was distinctly upsetting. Mr. Kiil said,

> Just a brief note to re-affirm our continuing interest in your biography of Robert W. Service.
> When I last spoke with you in the winter, you thought perhaps a rough draft of the ms. would be ready by some time this summer. Is it still realistic for me to expect some sample of the ms. in the next few weeks? We are busy setting up our fall 1973 schedule and would soon have to know whether we can consider the Service biography as a possible addition to our list.
> Mr. Platt at Dodd, Mead suggests as an alternative to the biography, an amalgamation of the two Service autobiographical volumes. My personal opinion is that an original work on Service would be much more welcome than anything pasted up, and therefore encourage you, if I may, toward the completion of it at your earliest opportunity. I will keep Dodd, Mead "at bay" as long as I can in the matter of alternatives, in case they are anxious to market a volume on Service.

The "paste-up" idea turned out to be a red herring. On 11 August 1972 Mr. Kiil gave qualified approval to my outline. "The structure of the original, critical book is fine, although the outline itself is too sketchy to give an idea of the level of intimacy on which you intend to write the book." He also said that "the outline and description suggest too brief and academic a book for the retail market." "However," he concluded, "our prime concern is to have some indication of your interest and willingness to enter into a contractual arrangement for the larger [and more popular] biography. This seems to be the consensus among people at Dodd, Mead and our firm."

He qualified his view of the book as "a definitive biography" by adding "as is possible." "The work should not be turgid, however. We are interested in having something that brings out the humanity and personality of Service, his private life, speculations on 'why' along with the details and facts about his life."

I did not hide from Mr. Kiil certain important details. On 8 September I informed him that "there is apparently no collection of 'papers' of R.W. Service as a writer....The revealing details about Service...are almost wholly in his poems and novels, and, especially, in the two autobiographies." I explained further that "it is definitively his [Service's] words that a biography must yield." Therefore, I stressed again "the virtual impossibility of operating almost wholly in paraphrase, i.e. language at one remove from Service's own words."

The solution as I saw it was "to make many lively pastiches [quotations from Service in the setting of my own discourse]." Then I outlined the necessity for including in the contract a general understanding regarding copyright such as I had previously achieved with the consent of Mr. Dodd, Mrs. Iris Davies, and Mr. John Shulman. Evidently my objections were overcome, or postponed, for on 27 September 1972 Kiil had received authorization from his executive editorial committee "for discussing the Service biography in specifics and detail."

On 3 October 1972, I asked Mr. Kiil for assurance "that we would not be stalled, after much effort, with a completed manuscript rendered too expensive to print because of reprint costs [Dodd, Mead?], and/or perhaps restricted by costs and legal barriers to a limited area for sales, e.g., not saleable outside of Canada. To put it another way, I do not know whether you have in mind a wholly McGraw-Hill Ryerson imprint or a joint imprint with Dodd, Mead." I offered a sample chapter by January 1973.

Jonathan Dodd wrote to me directly on 20 March 1973 to ask "how the work is progressing," and I informed him on 30 March that "the prospects for steady progress on the work have improved because I reached my 65th birthday last week, and I am looking forward to the relative freedom of retirement."

Taking this opportunity to unburden myself of confusion with regard to the Service book, I informed Mr. Dodd that:

> I have been unsettled by correspondence initiated by McGraw-Hill Ryerson of Toronto, a publishing house which, I suppose, inherited the Canadian copyright of certain works by Robert W. Service. I should be more worried about the ethics of mentioning this fact to you if I

had not been, through most of the year 1972, under the impression that some sort of joint agreement about publishing a book on Service was in effect between your firm and McGraw-Hill Ryerson. I have taken the position that I can afford to enter into a project for a book on Service only with a publisher who controls copyright on the chief autobiographical volumes which Service wrote.

A letter from Kiil on 5 June 1973 suggests that I had slowed up in progress on a key chapter required as a sample of my work on Service. On 27 June he sent his best wishes and asked that a copy of this sample be sent to him as well as to Dodd, Mead. My submission of 24 July was mailed to Dodd, but not immediately to Kiil because I was "in some doubt of the involvement of McGraw-Hill Ryerson in my project."

Two copies of a [revised] table of contents went to Dodd on 1 August 1973. He was on holiday, and in turn, I informed his secretary that I was going abroad in early September and was hoping "to find some new material on Service in the British Museum." I had additional information about Glasgow, the Yukon, and the Paris of *The Pretender* when I returned home.

A letter from Mr. Dodd on 30 October 1973, was most encouraging:

> Your first chapter has been read, and we are enthusiastic to the extent that we would like to see one or two more chapters if they are presently available. At that point we will be in a better position to discuss contract terms, etc.
>
> I am taking the liberty of sending a copy of Chapter I and the table of contents to Mr. Kiil at McGraw-Hill Ryerson. We would hope that they too would share our enthusiasm and would be interested in co-publishing the biography.

I responded on 29 November sending Mr. Dodd Chapter 5 and a prospectus for Chapter 2. I also sent copies of the letter and enclosures to Mr. Kiil. Submission of chapters in this manner was carried on until 28 March, when I wrote to Mr. Dodd's secretary about the lack of any notice of receipt.

Mr. Dodd, evidently a very likeable and certainly a gracious man, apologized by telegram, and letter, for what he called his "lack of courtesy." He was also sending (25 April 1974) "the five chapters to [his] uncle, Edward H. Dodd, who is a great Service fan."

I promised to send Chapters 6, 7, and 9 about the 1st of June. Actually I did so on 21 May. I still had to complete Chapter 8 and "a general polish of the whole book." I kept Mr. Kiil informed as I proceeded toward completion of the manuscript. On 22 February 1975, I dictated a telegram to Jonathan Dodd:

> I have verbal offer from McGraw-Hill Ryerson, Scarborough, Toronto, to publish Robert Service manuscript. If interested in co-production, please get in touch with Mr. Kiil of Toronto firm immediately. You have complete manuscript. Personally most eager to have co-production. Kind regards.

A contract was forthcoming from McGraw-Hill with the date of July 1975. I was particularly interested in the "Addendum" which stated that "McGraw-Hill Ryerson will pay all fees for permission to reproduce excerpts from copyright works, up to a maximum of $1000." And "Carl F. Klinck agrees that if it is necessary to delete some excerpts in order to keep fees within the above-mentioned maximum, he will either cut or paraphrase a sufficient number of excerpts."

Co-publication with Dodd, Mead was in prospect on 12 February 1976 (when I was recuperating satisfactorily from a gall-bladder operation). About the same time Mr. Brass sent Mrs. Service her royalty charge and, I believe, a copy of the manuscript, which was now being put through the press, together with the photographs which she had graciously provided and which were so skillfully handled by Robin Brass.

Mrs. Service's reply of 29 March 1976 was in two parts: a most welcome list of corrections of ten of my errors and a letter. I readily made the corrections on the galleys that were coming in. But I read the letter with the sad realization that even a better study than mine must fail to capture the essential man whom his wife and family knew and loved. Mrs. Service confessed that she wished to underline "many others which I might have [fought] towards the truthfulness of my husband's biography but I feel it necessary," she explained, "to conform above all to this will, that nothing should be changed of what he had written. As you probably know, he initially wrote his biography to prevent anybody from doing it, in a way that he might not approve of."

Of course she was right. My book was a literary commentary, not a substitute for the admirable autobiographies *Ploughman of the Moon* and *Harper of Heaven*. But these were unfortunately rare. In cold fact, I thought that I was engaged in reviving public interest in them, for they are more readable and full of the writer's character than my brief references to events. If only details and not "character" were considered, my book could stand as a record of many facts, dates, references, and identities that might be of value to a reader, but which Robert Service had obviously obscured and left to my pedantry.

I owe unbounded gratitude to Mrs. Service and to Mrs. Davies for helping me to do what, perhaps in their hearts, they could not wholly approve. They co-operated fully with never a hint of criticism. My file is valuable for the many sheets of my *Information Requested* which they accepted and faithfully filled in with detailed information, much of which might have gone unrecorded and been lost. I wrote nothing except in good will and admiration for the lady who, in my first interview with her, inspired the tone of my appreciation and approach to her husband's work.

In September 1976, my book was ready. On the 17th, Mr. Brass sent a first copy and added:

> We are also sending copies to Mrs. Service and are returning her photographs. Dodd, Mead's edition has been shipped to them but it will be at least a month or so before they publish, as shipping takes several weeks and they have to jacket their stock.

On 18 October 1976, Mrs. Service sent her congratulations "on a fine piece of work, the choice of the photographs, the dust cover and the precise in research you have made to realize it."

The book was received by reviewers with some favour and more misunderstanding. Frank Watt of Toronto was one who understood. In his review for the *Canadian Forum* he said that Service had not found an ideal biographer in me, but he softened his criticism by praising, as I would have done, the poet's own autobiographies, besides which "the finest academic study is likely to pale." He thought that my biography took on "a quite inappropriate appearance of formal abstraction and college-tie inhibition, an embarrassed uncomfortableness as if unsure what to do with the unrepentantly lowbrow company it finds itself in." He had not met Mrs. Service!

He recognized my method of "extracting the autobiographical elements from Service's novels and poetry in which the personal exists, as Professor Klinck puts it, in a masked or 'subliminal' form. How close to reality this mining brings us we can only speculate. Perhaps it is sufficient that Professor Klinck's interpretations are sensible and persuasive, and that they are certainly one way of establishing an interest for writing of Service which would otherwise have little to offer modern readers."

In the absence of documentary "papers" for a definite biography—my problem from the beginning—I can readily agree with Professor Watt that "there is no doubt still room for a book on Robert Service...which places the man and his work in the context of popular culture." It remains for me to show, without apology, how I attempted my research in the absence of supplementary "paper" documents. The notes in my book suggest only the end-results of the procedure.

For several reasons it was an exercise in clarification. Service had fought shy of dates in his autobiographies. Reviewers usually quoted one another with regard to obvious dates and facts. There were few articles as useful as the "profile" of Service, published by Geoffrey T. Hellman in the *New Yorker* (30 March and 7 April 1946). Gleaning was called for, and then verification, if possible, of some of the stories told by Service or about him.

The notes at the back of my book indicate that my sources were bibliographical records acquired chiefly in the British Museum and other libraries, together with much correspondence and some travel—to Monte Carlo, Paris, Brittany, and the Glasgow region. Of course I was familiar with Vancouver, and I had visited Edmonton and Whitehorse.

I was particularly happy to identify, from maps and directories, the "long Grey Town" of the poet's childhood: it was Kilwinning, where there were neighboring coalpits, iron works, Eglinton Castle, and the ruins of the Monastery of St. Winning. On the spot, Margaret and I confirmed my guesswork. I am happy to say that Mrs. Davies unveiled a plaque to her father, situated on the post office, on 24 September 1976. Perhaps Margaret and I were the first in many years to scrutinize the family memorials erected behind the abbey by Robert. Correspondence provided further details.

There was a real puzzle in Preston, Lancashire, where Robert, it was said, had been born at 4 Christian Road. When we spoke to the person living in a house bearing that number, I experienced real doubts about what we were seeing. We were told that the houses had been re-numbered (perhaps from the upper part of the street): number 4 may have been at the lower end. An appeal by letter to the clerk of the City of Preston brought me confirmation from the Lancashire District Librarian that "No. 4 Christian Road is now numbered No. 9."

There was also official clarity regarding the home of the Services in Glasgow. Again the observation on the spot was confusing, and the clerk of the City, the assistant principal archivist, and our good friend, Mrs. Marie Barbier of Edinburgh, were helpful. The area around Byers Road had also been changed since Robert's youth. Roclea Terrace may have been only one side of Roxborough Street. Robert's attendance at Hillhead School and his matriculation at Glasgow University were well documented. There was doubtful assistance in Preston where one of the residents expressed the opinion that, if we wanted to study "a real poet," we should look at a nearby house associated with Francis Thompson.

Service's employment in the Canadian Imperial Bank of Commerce was very well stated in a letter of 27 November 1973 from Mr. G.C. Northwood, manager of the Personnel Data Systems of the Bank. I also became indebted to Mr. L.E. Bartz of the Glenbow Alberta Institute, Mr. J. Russell Harper, and Mrs. E. Berry of Winnipeg for information about Frank and Caroline Armington. I had been fortunate in finding local copies of the *New York Times Film Reviews* (1913-31) to provide information about the Hollywood films.

For all that is good in my book I am indebted to Mrs. Germaine Service and Mrs. Iris Davies. The faults are my own. I read all the books of fiction, verse and autobiography that Service published, and used them, even the intriguing bad novel *The Pretender*, as the substance of my "subliminal" method. I do not apologize for it. I believe that Service's works taught me the method, for *he* is surely *in* most of his books. My effort is an unconventional experiment in biography. I do not claim that the result is definitive.

CHAPTER ELEVEN

The 1970s and Retirement

During the first half of the 1970s, I was coping with illness, both before and after my retirement. In December 1970 and January 1971 I had operations for partial removal of a pituitary tumor and of the infected bone in my forehead. For a year I walked around without structural support in that area, but eventually a "roof repair" was achieved. Because my birthday came before the 30th of June, I had to retire in 1973, a year earlier than I would have liked, but my friends were concerned about my health. Probably they were right, for I suffered a stroke in April 1975. One result was my enrolment in a medical study plan involving quarterly examinations and many pills—all of which have kept me alive and, in fact, in moderately good health for many additional years.

Besides the books and articles mentioned in the last two chapters, after I retired I also saw a third edition of the *Canadian Anthology* come out, revised and enlarged (1974). In the year of publication of the second edition of the *Literary History* (1976), my *Wilfred Campbell, Selected Poems* appeared, and it was followed by a reprint of my *Wilfred Campbell* (1977) and a booklet *Jean Baptiste* (1978).

I agreed to do journal reviews of only a few books by authors who were well known to me: Elizabeth Waterston's *The Seats of the Mighty;* William F.E. Morley's *A Bibliographical Study of Major John Richardson*; Carl Ballstadt's *The Search for English-Canadian Literature*, and Volume 4 of the *Dictionary of Canadian Biography*, edited by Francess Halpenny.

My association with graduate students did not cease entirely, for in the summer sessions of 1974, 1976, and 1977 I conducted seminars on "Autobiography in Selected English-Canadian Fiction and Poetry."

I also maintained membership in various "learned societies" during most of the decade, but I attended only a few of the annual meetings, the exception being the Association of Canadian and Quebec Literatures. There I collaborated with Sandra Djwa on the report of a "Committee on Major Research Projects in English-Canadian Literature Recommending Areas for Future Research." I also attended several of the Canadian literature colloquia sponsored by the University of Ottawa, and through friends I was invited to give special lectures from time to time. "Greeting the Unknowns with a Cheer," delivered at the Colloquium on Canadian Bibliography of the Bibliographical Society of Canada in 1973, gave me great pleasure. I also spoke on "Tiger" Dunlop before the History Section of the Ontario Medical Association meeting in London in 1975 and before the distinguished Harvey Club of London in 1979. There were several other pleasant events at which I had very little to say.

As my career in research was ending, a few of my mistakes were corrected. As I recorded earlier, Mary Lu MacDonald made some interesting discoveries, particularly regarding George Longmore's authorship of "The Charivari." This evidence also knocked out my theory that Levi Adams had written *Tales of Chivalry and Romance*, which now also belonged to Longmore. On the other hand, though I was not daunted by the efforts of junior textual critics to discredit the editing of the novels of the early Canadian period that I had done for the NCL, I still worry about Edward Lane's dates and wish some younger researcher could verify the facts.

Retirement brought me many honours. The Department of English at Western sponsored a Conference on Canadian Literature in my name in October 1972, and the special summer issue of the 1973 *Journal of Canadian Fiction* was dedicated to me. The front cover displayed a pen-and-ink portrait that had been sketched by an artist-friend, Silvia Clarke, a few years before. Most of the contents were, appropriately, articles on early Canadian writings. John Moss's preface, Clara Thomas's "Carl Klinck: Indefatigable Canadian," and Desmond Pacey's "Conclusion" showed deep understanding of the cause to which I was devoted.

In December 1973, I received the news of my appointment as an Officer of the Order of Canada; and in the spring Margaret was with me in Rideau Hall when my medal was placed around my neck by Governor-General Jules Léger. I found all this attention deeply moving. There was more to come. At its annual meeting in 1978, the

Royal Society of Canada gave me the coveted Lorne Pierce Medal for Literature. The citation contained many kind words.

But the bell had tolled, or would soon toll, for many of my friends: Des Pacey had died in 1975; Henry Wells in 1978; Roy Daniells on Good Friday, and Reg Watters just before Christmas, in 1979. When I received commendations, these men were always in my mind, for the praise belonged at least as much to them. It has been one of my life's great gifts to work and correspond with each of them. The last letters of Henry and Roy were particularly full of thoughts brought by age and declining health. On 13 October 1976 Henry wrote his last letter to me—and probably his longest. I think that it carried a blessing from my master! "We have gone far. We have, happily, had long careers as writers and teachers. My first articles appeared well over fifty years ago. You have been busy almost as long in the good cause. I cannot think of you as I would of a student of mine. You are not. But in a serious sense you have been through all these years my closest companion. Your humanist spirit is very rare and precious to me."

There was in 1977 a Christmas greeting card signed by Henry, but after that letters came only from Katharine. Henry died in New York on 22 March 1978. A few lines in Katharine's letter of 3 December 1978 tell the story of her husband's career: "It is true that Henry led a most fortunate life, free to follow his own intellectual interests without professional or financial pressures. The justification is not only his own unique publications but the example he set for such scholars as yourself."

The bulk of Roy Daniells' letters makes it impossible, as Henry's do, to give an adequate representation of the correspondence of the later years. In 1972 he was made a Companion of the Order of Canada, and in the following months and years his letters were often concerned with the proposals for the revision of the *Literary History*.

He suggested that "the perfect instance of a search for identity is furnished by Hans Anderson":

> The ugly duckling never does know who he is as he experiences the horrors of a frozen landscape (Canadian novels) or the hazards of being assaulted by all and sundry (Canadian poetry). He find[s] it out when the sun shines through the green leaves on the calm waters, when he meets the magnificent transcendental birds, when he sees

his reflection in that context and discovers he is not a duckling after all but a Swan. Heaven speed the day when the collective ego of Canada makes the same discovery.

Almost every letter contained extracts from his store of doggerel and jokes printable and unprintable, in and out of context. A good example came in 1973: "Do you think I should add anything to my parts of LHC? They have as it stands the unflawed beauty of, say, an Edwardian chamberpot without chip or stain." He was deeply disturbed by the course of the project, but he usually found a good-humoured way to express his opinions. Criticisms of the drafts of chapters submitted by contributors were normally circulated among the editors, but Roy addressed his objections and suggestions to me in the hope that I might be a diplomatic representative of demands for higher quality in the second edition.

In 1973 he gave valuable help in choosing contributors, and in early 1974 he made candid and incisive suggestions designed to improve the substance and style of many chapters. On 26 March 1974, he apologized for his "tone of exasperation," which was not "directed" at me. He now hoped for the saving grace of a new explanatory introduction to the *LHC*, so that "the second volume would, in time to come, be remembered more for its introduction than for any other single contribution." "I am not for a moment," he added, "being facetious. Or hyperbolical."

In subtle ways Roy, like Henry, made meanings clear to me. In 1975 and early 1976 he was in Rome, where he was very ill and endured many other inconveniences. He sent me some verses describing the "calcereous" water spoiling his tea, but responsible for the many statues in Rome.

> Is this, said I, this what they drank,
> Heroes of every range and rank
> These saints, whom martyrdom had tested,
> Is this the liquid they ingested?
> These maidens without bodices
> Whom men mistook for goddesses,
> These Cupid children, kings with crown,
> Is this the stuff they swallowed down?
> No wonder, then, that deep inside
> It soon took form; they calcified.

On 3 December 1977, after the editorship of the *Literary History* had been passed on to William New, Roy described a dinner which he and Laurenda attended at "Bill New's place, where were gathered his <u>LHC</u> committee & the Djwas and the Akriggs...there was a sense of exhilaration....Halpenny & Kreisel were in top form and one realized afresh what superbly <u>humane</u> people they are."

The weight of years and heart trouble were beginning to tell upon Roy. Thoughts of death raised questions about immortality. There is a hint of this concern as it involved Christian doctrine in a letter of 1974. I had always thought of him as a humanist and a religious man, probably because he had chosen to study Milton. I was not aware of his upbringing in an English Plymouth Brethren family until his own story was broadcast by the CBC in late 1979 or early 1980.

But his letter of 8 June 1978 indicated a concern with eternal punishment more terrifying than listeners to his post-mortem broadcast would hear: "For myself, my experience of the Bible and of the church has, over many decades, been so dreadful that I would like to escape....Yet good friends continue to suggest that I ought to love the Christ of the New Testament, who, according to the gospels, will hurl my two daughters and my wife into eternal flames because they cannot credit the string of improbabilities the gospels propose."

My "comments," for which he had asked, emphasized the mercy of God in Christ and ended with a question for him to answer, "May we expect to find our loved ones by our sides in the hereafter?" He had "some thoughts on the subject": "My own father and mother I love very dearly indeed (I use the present tense deliberately) but I have never expected to 'meet them in heaven.'...I know I <u>possess</u> my father and mother in a deeper sense than my memory of them or of a biological identity with them genetically....Having been, they are."

As his speculation continued, he resorted at last to Bunyan and expressed in "a familiar allegory of a man named Thoughtful" his awakening from a dream to find his friends about him:

> Then, looking with fresh vision upon them, I saw as it were the countenances of Thoughtful and of Watchful and in the faces of my wife and daughters the likeness of angels. Thus all was fulfilled and the promise of Watchful concerning the river already in adumbration, it being in truth the river of life's revival and of renewal without end.

Deeply impressed by intimations of mortality, Margaret and I were determined to travel as long as we could walk, drive, or fly.

Our venture abroad in 1937 was our first, but certainly not our last. Between 1970 and 1975 we crossed the Atlantic four times, and always to England. In 1970, from February to May of my sabbatical year, the highlights were our first visit to Spain (Algericas); our trip through France; our week in Switzerland, when I lectured at the request of Canadian External Affairs; and two weeks at Wytham Abbey near Oxford. In 1974 we drove through France to live in a villa at El Capistrano near Malaga. In 1975 we attended a conference (at Leeds) of the British Association of Canadian Studies. The sunshine of the Costa del Sol and the amenities of El Capistrano drew us again in the winters of 1976, 1977, 1979, 1980, and 1981. We drove around England and Scotland in 1977; and in September 1978 exchanged houses and cars with a Wiltshire family coming to Canada.

Because one of my reasons for writing so extensively on my past research is to provide future direction to future scholars who might want to undertake further work, I am recording some of the interesting discoveries in Canadian literary history that have not yet added up to a definite certainty.

My principal model in the writing of literary history and the cause of my despair at my lack of success has been Van Wyck Brooks, especially his *The World of Washington Irving*. Thereby hangs a tale, or rather several tales. I found to my sorrow that not everyone shared my interest in this satiric social criticism, which marked the early years of literary, and especially journalistic, activity in the first quarter of the nineteenth century in the United States and Canada. For me, the prime example was Washington Irving's *Salmagundi*, a series of twenty issues of a collection of essays and poems which appeared occasionally in New York between 24 January 1807 and 25 January 1808. Washington Irving had collaborators in offering miscellany, in the form of his older brother William and William's brother-in-law, James K. Paulding. The subtitle of *Salmagundi* was "The Whim-Whams and Opinions of Launcelot Langstaff, Esq., and Others." I do not know whether the existence of this early work was news to the audience I addressed at Duke University at a conference on "The Influence of the United States on Canadian Development." There I repeated Salmagundi names, which were certainly not unknown, even in the Maritimes and Lower Canada before 1825, such as: Launcelot Longstaff, Esq., who wrote from his "Elbow-Chair," Christopher

Cockloft of Cockloft Hall, "a pre-revolutionary Tory," and Jeremy Cockloft the younger, a "travelmonger" in New York and its environs. I was surprised to find several of these pseudonyms used by early writers sojourning in Canada. I shall give three examples.

Three or four years after *Salmagundi* first appeared in New York, Jeremy Cockloft the Elder appeared as author of a little booklet entitled *Cursory Observations Made in Quebec Province of Lower Canada, in the year 1811*. The book was published in Bermuda by Edmund Ward, a Canadian-born publisher, who may also have been the author hiding under the pseudonym of Cockloft. Also in 1811, a remarkable tribute to the Salmagundians was paid by John Lambert, an English or Scottish author and traveller, in his *Travels through Lower Canada, and the United States of North America in the Years 1806, 1807 and 1808*. Lambert had collected *Salmagundi* papers in New York while he was travelling there, and somehow got them all and published them in England in 1811. In 1824, in Montreal, George Longmore, calling himself "Launcelot Longstaff," published "The Charivari, or Canadian Poetics."

My file presents a rather full record of vain attempts to identify the author who hid behind the pseudonym of "Jeremy Cockloft the Elder." William Toye of Oxford University Press in Canada had brought *Cursory Observations* to my attention by his publication of it in 1960 as a booklet. Later, I learned from him that this "Cockloft" had also published an epic poem entitled *Britannia*. In return, I suggested that Cockloft might have been a pseudonym. Apparently he had taken the name at face value and had not attributed it in any way to *Salmagundi*.

I went in search of *Britannia* or, rather, I asked Donald Hair, then in England, to look for the poem in the British Museum. He sent me an elaborate reply about a *Britannia* dated 1823. That was a different *Britannia*. I had also found the irrelevant *Britannia* published by Samuel Hull Wilcocke in 1816. Bill Toye happily explained that L.D. Gurrin, Archivist of the Bermuda Historical Monuments Trust in Hamilton, Bermuda, had told him of a copy of *Britannia, a Poem* in Mr. Gurrin's archives. The pamphlet was signed, as *Cursory Observations* had been, by Jeremy Cockloft the Elder, Esq., M.A. P.C. Bermuda.

I tried Bermuda. Mrs. Hugh Skiffington, head of the Bermuda Library, sent me photocopies of the poem and recommended that I write to Annette Wolfe in Montreal. She suggested Sister Jean de

Chantal of Mount St. Agnes Academy in Hamilton, Bermuda, author of *Biography of a Colonial Town*, and Henry C. Wilkinson, author of *Bermuda in the Old Empire....1684-1784*, published in 1950. Dr. Wilkinson provided the name "Tuzo, an agent for the Patriotic Company of Bermuda," who went to Quebec in 1811, on a business trip, which threw me off completely. I asked Tuzo Wilson, whether he knew of any Tuzos in Bermuda. He poopooed the idea, and someone else who knew something about this area, said, "Oh, it couldn't have been Tuzo who wrote the *Cursory Observations*."

In all this correspondence, there was no identification of Cockloft that could be confirmed. The occasion for the poem appeared to have been related to trade between Canada and Bermuda. I gave up, with the feeling that the best guess would name Edmund Ward, the publisher of *Cursory Observations* and Government Printer at Bermuda from 1809 to 1816. He was also the author of "Seven Years' Residence in Bermuda," published in the *Bermuda Historical Quarterly* (1948-49), and I managed to get photocopies of the so-called "Ward Papers"—autobiographical accounts by Ward himself, but never anything to identify him as the Cockloft author of *Cursory Observations*. In his article, Ward described another possible candidate for authorship of *Cursory Observations*. He did not do so in so many words, but he was interested in Francis Forbes as a young professional gentleman who "wrote very prettily...in an easy and flowing style." Forbes later became a chief justice in Newfoundland and a poet and prominent justice in New South Wales. So I looked up articles on Sir Francis Forbes (he became Sir Francis in New South Wales). Henry Wilkinson's article on him in *The Bermuda Historical Quarterly* in 1949 states that he was called to the bar in Lincoln's Inn in 1810—in other words, he was in England when Lambert made his comments on American literature and in particular on *Salmagundi*. Forbes was appointed attorney general of Bermuda in 1811; so he came to Bermuda from England. Did he travel back home by way of Quebec? I tried the Mitchell Library in Sydney, NSW, where I understood Sir Francis' papers had been deposited, but they were not yet available.

Ward? Forbes? John Lambert? Why do I always think of John Lambert when I read the *Cursory Observations*? It's a matter of style and detail and eyewitness information. Yet, when I think of attributing *Cursory Observations* to John Lambert, Forbes sticks in my mind, and when I mention John Lambert, I always think "Whoever *he* was!" His identity is the most elusive of my puzzles, although I can supply considerable detail about what he did. Some of this detail was printed in "The Influence of the United States on Canadian Development."

One looks in vain in biographies, in bibliographies, in the *Dictionary of National Biography* for details concerning Lambert's life. There are virtually no details apart from his book of travels. Another problem was that no one had traced his lineage, and the problem is multiplied because Lambert is a common name in different countries, even in France.

Moreover no one had traced the fortunes of his uncle John Campbell, with whom he had come to Lower Canada to raise hemp. And no one had investigated his earlier education or followed clues in *Travels*. An 1814 first edition of *Travels* was rarely mentioned. Finally, no one seems to have recorded that he was the editor in England of Washington Irving's *Salmagundi*.

How can one identify a John Campbell who had a nephew John Lambert? Scotland is full of John Campbells. England is full of John Lamberts. *Travels* lets us know that Captain John Campbell embarked on the brig *Hope*, Matthew Henry, master, at Greenock, and sailed for Quebec with seventeen women and children. They arrived in Quebec on 30 October 1806, according to a notice in the *Quebec Gazette*. Lambert accompanied Campbell to Becancour, in Lower Canada, where he was to raise hemp, since there was danger of Britain's supply of hemp for the navy being cut off during the Napoleonic Wars.

I spent some time at the Public Record Office in London searching for documents relating to the actions on this matter by the British Board of Trade. The *Gazette*, quoting the *Mercury* of Quebec, published on 7 May 1807 a long letter by Lambert in defence of Campbell's suit to bring back certain indentured servants who owed him a great deal of money. Through Colonial Office records, now in the National Archives of Canada, I collected information about the fortunes of hemp growers in Canada, and further information existed in the Canada Land Petitions.

I doubt that Lambert was a serious cultivator of hemp, for he left Campbell at the end of a year, having spent a good deal of time in Quebec City and Three Rivers. Lambert appears to have been mainly interested in social life in cities.

The most fascinating prospect for biographical information was

Lambert's reference to his being "a schoolfellow" of John By (later Lieutenant-Colonel By), who was born in England in 1781, educated at the Royal Military Academy at Woolwich, commissioned in the Royal Artillery, transferred to the Engineers, and a resident of Quebec from 1802 to 1811. Lambert reported the "unexpected pleasure of meeting in Canada a school fellow, Captain By of the Engineers, after an absence of ten years." I assumed that school fellows would be of more or less the same age, and that Lambert might have attended Woolwich, as By had done.

I drew a blank in the army lists, and decided to write to the Commandant of the Royal Military Academy at Woolwich, who informed me that no cadet register was kept prior to about 1820—only muster rolls, the earliest of which, 1799, mentioned By, but no John Lambert. If Lambert was in fact a gentleman cadet at Woolwich in 1797 or 1798, there is no record of his being commissioned between 1799 and 1802.

My old reliable Scots Ancestry Research Society of Edinburgh could not identify my John Campbell or John Lambert from a host of others, and I read more about John By without additional satisfaction regarding Lambert. When I consulted a very rare record book of Woolwich Academy at the British Museum I found that the famous watercolourist, Paul Sandby, was chief drawing-master there from 1768 to 1797. I felt that Lambert must have been a cadet there in Sandby's time, for that would explain the watercolours he published in *Travels*.

At a picture gallery in London, I saw the following for sale: Anglo-Canadian Style 1829, 1834 by J.L., *Winter Posting in Lower Canada* (I don't know by whom) and, as I thought, one definitely by Lambert himself, *An Officer of the British Army and a Merchant of Quebec in Their Winter Dress*. I did not have the money to buy them but became convinced that Lambert occupied a modest place with the very many early watercolor artists among travellers and army officers who drew Canadian scenes after study under Paul Sandby. Coburn is another example.

The National Archives of Canada have a microfilm of an 1816 letter addressed to the Earl of Bathurst regarding expenses Lambert had incurred in his uncle's hemp-raising venture. Lambert evidently felt that his uncle might have collected funds on his behalf without passing anything on. Lambert's address at this time was East County

District, Rotherhithe. I tried no end of other Lamberts, with no results. All the other details I discovered relate to Lambert's publications.

In their *Bibliography of Canadiana* Frances M. Staton and Marie Tremaine list the *Travels* as having been printed in London for Richard Phillips in 1810. The two-volume copy of the *Travels* in the Rare Book Room at the University of Western Ontario Library is evidently a second edition, published by C. Cradock and W. Joy in London and described as "Corrected and Improved." This edition included a map and numerous engravings.

What happened to cause the long delay between the two editions requires some explanation. But the *Gentleman's Magazine* (July-December 1810) reported that, on Sunday, 28 July; "About three this morning, a dreadful fire broke out in the printing office of Mr. Guillet, near Salisbury Square, Fleet Street, which completely destroyed the building, as well as the whole of the printing material and stock; and property to a great amount, belong to Sir Richard Phillips, Mr. Stockdale, and other booksellers." There was also a report in *The Morning Chronicle*, on Monday, 30 July, and Lambert himself explained that his first edition "had scarcely been published two months when half of the edition was destroyed." "And," he continued, "ere I could receive whole of the money for the copy-right, my publisher became a bankrupt. Thus the project of a second edition and the emoluments arising from it, are entirely vanished, unless the copyright should perchance be purchased by a more successful publisher; at present it is locked up in the hands of assignees."

I was delighted to add to a Lambert bibliography my discovery of the almost entirely neglected book that he edited and published in London in 1811. It was entitled *Salmagundi, or the Whim-Whams and Opinions of Launcelot Longstaff Esq. and Others*. "Reprinted from the American Edition, with an Introductory Essay and Explanatory Notes," by John Lambert. Lambert thus became the herald in England of this early work of Washington Irving and his associates. But Lambert's interest in *Salmagundi* began, as he himself records in his *Travels*, when he left Montreal on 10 November 1807 and travelled to New York. In Volume 2 of the *Travels* he reports that he found in the great city young men possessing "literary qualifications and talents." The most prominent of these late productions is the *Salmagundi*, published in monthly essays at New York:

Many of the young men, too, whose minds have not been wholly absorbed by pounds, shillings, and pence, have shown that they possess literary qualifications and talents, that would, if their time and fortune permitted, rank them among some of the distinguished authors of Europe. The most prominent of their late productions is the *Salmagundi*, published in the monthly essays at New York. This little work has been deservedly a great favourite with the public, and bids fair to be handed down with honour to posterity. It possesses more of the broad humour of Rabelais and Swift than the elegant morality of Addison and Steele, and is therefore less likely to become a classical work; but as a correct picture of the people of New York, and other parts of the country, though somewhat heightened by caricature, and as a humorous representation of their manners, habits, and customs, it will always be read with interest by a native of the United States.

In his edition of *Salmagundi,* he relates how interested he was in this American production:

The American production which I have now the pleasure to introduce to the notice of the British public, made its appearance during my residence in the United States in 1807. It was published in New York in twenty numbers, one of which came out nearly once a fortnight....Just before my departure from the United States the essays were discontinued and I had an opportunity of procuring a complete copy of the whole. On my return to this country, I published a work entitled *Travels* etc. in which I introduced a few of the Salmagundian essays as a specimen of American literature. The work on which I bestowed considerable care and attention was not, however, to be more fortunate here than its author was in America, where it had scarcely been published two months when one half of the edition was destroyed by a conflagration at the printers. The first essays from the Salmagundi given in that work, having been greatly admired, I have been induced to publish the whole together with an introductory essay and explanatory notes. These last will, I trust, serve to elucidate such passages as are of a local nature, and I hope render my readers better acquainted with American manners than they have hitherto been. Should I have the good fortune to be instrumental to the removal of one single prejudice against the Americans or in any way tend to conciliate the minds of my countrymen in favour of a people whose character has been grossly misrepresented, I shall feel myself amply rewarded for my trouble and consider such a change of sentiment to have risen more from the liberal opinions of my readers than any feeble effort of mine.

For good measure he wrote an introduction as well as a preface. The former dealt with "British anti-American feeling cf. the War of 1812; a brief review of American history; manners, habits and customs; learning and education; and observations on Salmagundi."

Here, indeed, was God's plenty to register Lambert's ideas and literary manner, but only a few insights into the man himself. I wait impatiently to see what the *Dictionary of Canadian Biography* will say, or will not say, about Lambert. Surely a closer study of the man is overdue.

When the English Department of the University of Waterloo invited me to give a paper at its 1979 colloquium in honour of Fred McRae, who was retiring, I was pleased with the title given the event, "Light in Dark Corners." I decided to shed my "light" on Wilcocke, but I also took the opportunity to make it my valedictory address.

I repeated my strong opinions regarding literary research in Canada. Stressing the importance of following up all hints of source material, I faced the difficulty still experienced by scholars with regard to securing unique original documents. With the use of new copying materials, a library is now able to build up a very useful body of early material.

My second exhortation was to work with historians. I found my way to Wilcocke's story through a bibliography by the historian Stewart Wallace. One must pay attention to what the historians have found, whether they followed up a clue or not. Their notes are of great value.

My third bit of advice concerned the need to travel, especially to places where authors have lived and to the local and national libraries of the countries from which they came. Certainly, as my research on

Dunlop, Wilcocke, Norton, and Robert W. Service indicates, we have not exhausted the knowledge of literary traditions and biographical facts to be found in Britain.

As I passed in 1978 the disturbing age of *seventy*, and my career of research and writing seemed to be over, I sank for several years into the doldrums of retirement, until I committed myself to a non-autobiographical study of the preparation of my publications.

Eventually, however, I had to give up the protesting against writing in an autobiographical manner. There appeared a continuity in my work which could be explained only in terms of interests and attitudes affecting my life; unity lay in the inner drive. Many imperfections and awkwardnesses in my chapters resulted from the vagaries of memory distorting the flow of objective discourse—especially when I was recording on tape. This present book became the most difficult task of research and writing I ever attempted. The bulk of items to be sorted out of chaos was enormous, and writing meant putting my mind through a wringer. Without pleasant co-operation, I would never have begun this task or continued on it with vigour over four years.

Afterword

My Thanks:

To Mrs. Pauline Campbell for her patient, kindly, and skillful attention to all my requests for typing.

To Mr. Edward Phelps, Regional Collections Librarian, for conveying my papers to the Library, and to Mrs. Beth Miller, Special Collections Librarian, for cataloging and shelving my numerous boxes and neatly directing the process of assessment and donation.

To Dr. John E. Brent, a friend since school days, for positive action to direct my collection of papers to the University of Western Ontario.

To Dr. George Connell, President, Dr. Robert Lee, Director of Libraries, and Mr. Stuart Finlayson, Comptroller, for official help in completing the arrangements for donation.

To Margaret, my wife, with gratitude for her patience, tolerance, and constant support.

To Miss Wilda Graber, who encouraged me, during my difficult years of adjustment to retirement, to undertake (as a form of therapy) tape recordings of my memories of teaching and research. She also gave assistance in recovering and classifying my "papers," and in making dozens of reels and cassettes. Over nearly a decade, she patiently drew out of me a record of countless memories which I had not known that I possessed. For her unselfish service, devotion, and encouragement, I offer my heartfelt thanks.

To Professor Sandra Djwa, who, also in the first years of my retirement, teased me into believing that my "papers" held information worthy of sorting, organizing, interpreting, and submitting to archives, as well as offering a contribution to my sense of identity. She then gave me timely and excellent advice about a program of recording, typing, and editing chapters designed to explain significant events in my literary life. Through the years she kept up my spirits by very welcome visits (from Vancouver), by thoughtful and cheerful advice, and by constant personal friendship and public sharing in the cause of Canadian literature. I am deeply indebted to her and grateful for being given a new lease on the life of the mind during retirement.

To the Canada Council for a generous grant to cover the expenses of the project. Dr. André Fortier, the President, surprised me by stating that I was awarded more than I requested because, in the experience of the Council, my transcription and typing costs would probably be greater than I had foreseen.

Carl F. Klinck

Selected Bibliography

Books and Parts of Books
Wilfred Campbell: A Study in Late Provincial Victorianism. Toronto: Ryerson, 1943.
Edwin J. Pratt: The Man and His Poetry. Toronto: Ryerson, 1947.
Canadian Anthology (co-editor with R.E. Watters). Toronto: Gage, 1955. Rev. ed. 1966.
Major Richardson's "Kensington Gardens in 1830" (edited, with an introduction). Toronto: Bibliographical Society of Canada, 1957.
William "Tiger" Dunlop: "Blackwoodian Backwoodsman" (edited, with an introduction and notes). Toronto: Ryerson, 1958.
Tecumseh: Fact and Fiction in Early Records (edited, with introductions). Englewood Cliffs, NJ: Prentice-Hall, 1961.
The Poems of Adam Hood Burwell, Pioneer Poet of Upper Canada (edited, with a biographical introduction). *Western Ontario History Nuggets* (mimeographed), no. 30, May 1963.
Canadian Writers / Ecrivains Canadiens (co-editor with Guy Sylvestre and Brandon Conron). Toronto: Ryerson, 1964. Rev. ed. 1966.
Literary History of Canada (general editor). Toronto: University of Toronto Press, 1965. Reprinted 1966, 1967, 1970. Translation by Maurice Lebel, *Histoire Littéraire du Canada, Littérature Canadienne de Langue Anglaise.* Sainte-Foy: Les Presses de l'Université Laval, 1970.
The History of Emily Montague by Frances Brooke (edited, with an introduction). Toronto: McClelland and Stewart, 1961.
Roughing It in the Bush by Susanna Moodie (edited, with an introduction). Toronto: McClelland and Stewart, 1962.
"Annual Bibliography of Commonwealth Literature: Canada." *The*

Journal of Commonwealth Literature 1, no. 1 (September 1965): 27-43.

"Annual Bibliography of Commonwealth Literature: Canada." *The Journal of Commonwealth Literature* 11, no. 2 (December 1966): 39-55.

"Tiger" Dunlop's Upper Canada (edited, with an introduction). Toronto: McClelland and Stewart, 1967.

Wacousta by John Richardson (edited, with an introduction). Toronto: McClelland and Stewart, 1967.

Twenty-Seven Years in Canada West by Samuel Strickland (edited, with an introduction). Edmonton: Hurtig, 1970.

Belinda, or the Rivals by A.S. Holmes (edited, with an introduction). Vancouver: The Alcuin Society, 1970.

The Journal of Major John Norton, 1816 (edited, with introductions and notes, by Carl F. Klinck and James J. Talman). Toronto: Champlain Society, 1970.

"James Lynne Alexander." *Dictionary of Canadian Biography*. Vol. X. Edited by Francess Halpenny. Toronto: University of Toronto Press, 1972, p. 5.

"Salmagundi in Canada: Washington Irving, James K. Paulding, and Some of Their Contemporaries in Canada." *The Influence of the United States on Canadian Development: Eleven Case Studies*. Edited by Richard A. Preston. Durham, NC: Duke University Press, 1972, pp. 226-44.

Antoinette de Mirecourt by Mrs. Rosanna Leprohon (edited, with an introduction). Toronto: New Canadian Library, 1973.

Canadian Anthology (co-editor with R.E. Watters). 3rd ed., revised and enlarged. Toronto: Gage, 1974.

Robert Service, a Biography. Toronto: McGraw-Hill Ryerson, 1976.

Literary History of Canada (general editor). 2d ed. Toronto: University of Toronto Press, 1976.

The Canadian Brothers by John Richardson (edited, with an introduction). Toronto: University of Toronto Press, 1976.

Wilfred Campbell, Selected Poems (edited, with an introduction). Ottawa: Tecumseh Press, 1976.

Wilfred Campbell: A Study in Late Provincial Victorianism. Reprint. Ottawa: Tecumseh Press, 1977.

Jean Baptiste: A Poetic Olio in II Cantos by Levi Adams (edited, with an introduction). Ottawa: Golden Dog Press, 1978.

"John Norton," "Samuel Hull Wilcocke." *Dictionary of Canadian Biography*. Vol. VI. Edited by Francess Halpenny. Toronto: University of Toronto Press, 1987, pp. 550-53, 814-16.

"Wilfred Campbell." Dictionary of Literary Biography: Canadian Writers 1890-1920. Vol. 92. Edited by William H. New. Detroit, New York, London: Gale Research, 1990, p. 35-37.

Articles and Bulletins

"William Wilfred Campbell: Poet of the Lakes." *Canadian Bookman* (August-September 1939): 34-37.

"Salvaging Our Literary Past." *Ontario Library Review* 27 (August 1943): 339-41.

"Bibliography of Wilfred Campbell" [a full record of his books, pamphlets, etc.]. In the Libraries of Queen's University, Columbia University, and Wilfrid Laurier University, bound. 34 pp. 1943.

"Early Creative Literature of Western Ontario." *Ontario History* 45 (Autumn 1953): 155-63.

"Major Richardson's 'Kensington Gardens in 1830.'" *Ontario History* 48 (Summer 1956): 101-7.

"Life in the Army 150 Years Ago" (abridged). *London Free Press*, 29 September 1956.

"Irish Immigrants Tell of London in Garrison Days." *London Free Press*, 4 April 1959.

"Impact of Railways, Oil, Noted in Irish Letters." *London Free Press*, 18 April 1959.

"Some Anonymous Literature of the War of 1812." *Ontario History* 49 (Spring 1957): 49-60.

"John Galt's Canadian Novels." *Ontario History* 49 (Autumn 1957): 187-94.

"Adam Kidd—An Early Canadian Poet." *Queen's Quarterly* 65 (1958): 495-506.

"The Cacique of Ontario." *University of Toronto Quarterly* 39 (October 1959): 21-32.

"The Canadian Chiefs and 'Tiger' Dunlop." *Waterloo Review* (Summer 1959): 43-51.

"The *Chârivari* and Levi Adams." *Dalhousie Review* 40 (July 1960): 34-42.

"A Note on *A Canadian Campaign* by Major John Richardson." *Papers of the Bibliographical Society of Canada* 5 (1966): 93-94.

"New Light on John Norton." *Transactions of the Royal Society of Canada* 4, series 4 (June 1966), section 2, pp. 167-77.

"Canadian Literature: Theses in Preparation." An annual list, mimeographed and sent to English Departments in universities across Canada. Nos. 1-12 (1959-71).

"Post-Graduate Theses in Canadian Literature: English and English-French Comparative." In *Journal of Canadian Fiction* 3 (Summer 1972): 68-73.

"Samuel Hull Wilcocke." *Journal of Canadian Fiction* 2, no. 3 (Summer 1973): 13-21.

"Greeting the Unknown with a Cheer." *Papers of the Bibliographical Society of Canada* 12 (1974): 31-37.

"The World of *The Scribbler.*" *Journal of Canadian Fiction* 4, no. 3 (1975): 123-48.

"The Frogs: An Exercise in Reading Lampman." In *The Lampman Symposium.* Otttawa: University of Ottawa Press, 1976, pp. 29-37.

Report to Committee on Major Research Projects in English-Canadian Literature. Edited with Sandra Djwa. Association of Canadian and Quebec Literatures [London], May 1978.

Index

Adams, Levi, 59, 77, 185, 198
Addison, Rev. Robert, 171, 178
Ahrens, Fred, 18
Alexander, Peter, 54
Allen, William, 174
Alman, Miriam, 167
The American Way of Poetry, 46
Anderson, Patrick, 52
Annals of the Parish, 63
Antionette de Mirecourt, 62, 151, 160-61
Appraisals of Canadian Literature, x, 12
Armington, Frank 186, 195
Australian Literature: A Bibliography, 105, 111
"The Awakening in Canadian Poetry," 46
Ayres, Harry Morgan, 7, 18

Bagley, William C., 8
Bailey, Alfred, 50, 112, 113, 117, 118, 119, 122, 123, 124, 129, 134, 137
Bailey, Jacob, 87, 108
Baker, Ray Palmer, xv-xvi, 34, 46, 49, 108
Baldwin, Charles Sears, 9, 44
Ballstadt, Carl, xvi, 78, 148, 153-54, 155, 157, 197
Barclay, Robert, 174
Barnouw, Adrian J., 7
Bateson, F.W., 54
Beasley, David R., 79
Beattie, Munro, 55, 112, 118, 119, 126
Beattie, William, 64
Belinda, or The Rivals: A Tale of Real Life, xvi, 63, 157, 158-60
Bell, Inglis, 160
Benét, William Rose, 45, 46, 105
Bentley, D.M.R., xvii
Berger, Carl, 137
The Bible in Canada, 175
Bibliographical Society of Canada Papers, 78
A Bibliographical Study of Major John Richardson, 75, 197
Birney, Earle, 52, 92, 112, 124

Bissell, Claude, 50, 51, 111, 113, 115, 118, 119, 120, 124, 126, 127, 134, 135, 136, 137, 163
Blackwood, George William 65, 67
Blackwood's, 60, 64-5, 67
Blennerhasset, Margaret, 59
Bliss Carman: A Study in Canadian Poetry, 12
Bohne, Harald, 135
The Book of Canadian Poetry, xvii, 46, 89, 90, 104-5
The Book of Roberts, 12
Bouchette, Joseph, 83, 84
Bowering, George, xvii
Brant, Joseph, 167, 170, 172
"Bras d'Or," 22-23
Brass, Robin, 192, 193
Brebner, J.B., 36, 48
Briggs, William, 64
British Columbia: A Centennial Anthology, 115
Brock, General Isaac, 172
Brook Farm: A Guided Research Series, 71
Brooke, Frances, 68-69, 87, 107, 108, 151-54
Brooke, Rupert, 24
Brown, E.K., xi, 46, 47, 49-50
Brown, George, xx, 103-4, 107, 111, 132
Brown, James E., 164
Brown, Mary Markham, xvi, 61, 126, 160
Browne, Rev. George, 175
Buckingham, James Silk, 67
Burpee, Lawrence J., 151
Burwell, Adam Hood, 79-80
By, John, 205-6

Cambridge History of English Literature, 12
Cameron, George Frederick, 89, 108
Campbell, Major Basil, 30-32
Campbell, Faith, 32
Campbell, Oscar, 35
Campbell, Pauline, xxii, 126, 134
Campbell, William Wilfred, x, xiii, xiv, 15, 17, 29-39, 69
"Canada's Best Known Poet, E.J. Pratt," 46
"The Canadian Authors Meet," xii, xiii
The Canadian Brothers (also called *The Prophecy Fulfilled*), 76, 78-91, 157
"A Canadian Campaign by a British Officer," 75, 78
Canadian Literature, 101
"Canadian Literature: Theses in Preparation," 56
Canadian Magazine, 59
Canadian Poetry, xvii
Canadian Poets, 12, 24, 45
Canadian Review, 59, 80
Canadian Review and Literary Historical Journal, 80
Canadian Settler's Guide, 158
Canadian Writers/Ecrivains Canadiens, xi, 141-50
Cappon, James, 12, 15-16
Careless, J.M.S., 164
Carlyle, Jane (Walsh), 66
Carlyle, Thomas, 66, 67
Carman, Bliss, 15, 38, 45, 89-90, 123, 148
Carr, Bill, 57

Casselmann, Alexander Clark, 68, 74
Chandler, Frank W., 8
Chapman, John E., 136
Charles G.D. Roberts and the Influences of His Time, 12
Check List of Canadian Literature and Background Materials 1628-1960, xi, xviii, 50, 88, 93, 101, 104, 106, 110, 111, 113, 114-15, 120-21
The Chequered Shade, 124
Chisholme, David, 59-60
Chittick, V.L.O., 118
Chocholm, David, 183
Christie, Dr. A.J., 59-60
Clark, Harry Hayden, 91
Clarke, Silvia, 198
Claus, William, 171
Clausen, Rev. Dr. Fred, 39, 40
Cogswell, Fred, 118, 119
Colden, Cadwallader, 69
Collected Poems (E.J. Pratt), 45
Collins, W.E., 23, 46, 49, 143
Colombo, John Robert, 149, 150
Conron, A. Brandon, xii, 44, 146-7
Connor, Ralph, 3, 24
Corbett, Joan, 55
Corbett, Paul, 46
Cotes, Everard, 165
Cotes, Dr. John, 165
Cotes, Mary, 165-66
Crawford, Isabella V., 89, 108, 116
The Creative Reader, 87, 92
Creative Writing in Canada: A Short History of English-Canadian Literature, 105, 108
Creighton, Donald G., xx, 50, 104, 111, 113
Crick, Bernard, 167
Cross, Michael S., 135
Cruikshank, Ernest A., 170
Cursory Observations Made in Quebec Province of Lower Canada, in the year 1811, xii, 203
Curwood, James Oliver, 3
Cushman, H.B., 73

Daniells, Laurenda, 201
Daniells, Roy, xii, xiii, xiv, xx, 50, 51, 101, 105, 111, 112, 113, 116, 118, 123, 125, 127, 129, 130, 131, 134, 137, 139-40
Davey, Frank, xvi
Davies, Iris, 185, 190, 193, 194, 195
Davies, Robertson, xiv
Davis, Marilyn, 158, 159
Dawson, Moses, 72
Day, Kenneth, 186
Deacon, Rev. Job, 81, 82
Deacon, William Arthur, 36
de Chantal, Sister Jean, 203-4
Deeper into the Forest, 124
DeMille, James, 92, 115
Deneau, Henri (Brother Adrian), 160
Denton, John, R., 187
Dictionary of Canadian Biography, 83, 209
Djwa, Sandra, 198, 201
Dodd, Jonathan, 190-92
Doherty, Eleanor, 21
Douglas, A. Vibert, 121, 135

Douglas, David, 170
Drake, Benjamin, 72
The Dread Voyage and Other Poems, 37
Duncan, Sara Jeanette, 92, 115, 116, 163-66
Dunlop, William "Tiger," xvi, xvii-xviii, 53, 54, 59, 60-61, 63, 64-68, 87, 92, 157, 183, 209

"Early Theatres in Waterloo County," 45
Ecarté, or Life in Paris, 74, 76
Edgar, Sir James David, 12
Edgar, Pelham, ix, x, xiii, 11-14, 17, 29-30, 45, 47, 49
Egoff, Sheila A., 135
Eight Years in Canada, 74
Elliott, Brian, 51
Elliott, Gordon, 102

Fairchild, Hoxie N., 11, 68
Fenton, F., 179, 180
Feuillerat, René, 7
Finch, Robert, 52
Fiske, John, 39
Fleck, PAul, xvi
Flemington, Frank, 147, 149
Forbes, Francis, x, 204
Fosdick, Harry Emerson, 6
Fowke, Edith, 122
Fox, Sherwood, 41
Frascati's, or Scenes in Paris, 79
French, Donald G., x, 105
French, William, xvi
Froates, Willis C., 9, 21, 39
Frye, Northrop, xii, xiii, xiv, xvii, xviii-xix, 38, 50, 56, 101, 103, 109, 110-1, 112, 114, 118, 119, 122, 124, 127, 129, 131, 133, 134
The Fugitives, 83-85

Galloway, David, 118, 119
Galt, John, xvi, 53, 59, 60, 63, 64, 67, 87
Garvin, John W., x, 12, 45
Glengarry School Days, 155
The Gold Cure, 166
The Golden Dog, 24
Goldsmith, Oliver, 79, 89
Goodwin, Rae E., 163-65
Gore, Lieutenant-Governor, 171
Goudge, Thomas, 135
Graber, Wilda, xxii
Grant, Anne McVicar, 68, 69
Grant, Douglas, 130, 146-7, 148, 149, 150
Grant, John Webster, 135
Greenwood, Thomas, 142, 143, 144
Grove, Frederick Philip, 23, 151
Gurrin, L.D., 203
Guthrie, Norman, 12
Gutteridge, Don, xvii

Hair, Donald, xvi, 203
Hakluyt, Richard, 87
Haldimand, Gov. Sir Frederick, 172
Haliburton, Thomas Chandler, x, 87
Halpenny, Francess, 103, 111, 121, 122, 125, 126, 133, 138, 186, 197
Hambleton, Ronald, 52
Hamil, Fred C., 158
Hammond, M.O., 33

Hampden, John, 54
Harmon, Eleanor, 103
Harper, J. Russell, 195
Harper of Heaven, 187, 188, 193
Harrison, General W.H., 71
Hawley, William Fitz, 61, 83
Headwaters of Canadian Literature, x, 12
Heavysege, Charles, 89
Hellman, Geoffrey T., 194
Highways of Canadian Literature, xiii, 15, 24, 105
Hilda, Out of the City, 166
Hill, H.P., 79
Hirtle, R.J.E., 41
The History of the British and Foreign Bible Society from its institution in 1804 to the close of its Jubilee in 1854, 175
History of Christ Cathedral (1832-1932), 79
The History of Emily Montague, 68, 151-53, 155
A History of English-Canadian Literature to the Confederation, xv, 34, 46
History of the Choctaw, Chicasaw and Natchez Indians, 73
The History of the Origin and First Ten Years of the British and Foreign Bible Society, 175
Hogg, James, 65, 67
Holmes, Abraham S., 63, 158-59
Hopwood, Victor, 118
The House of Blackwood 1804-1954: The History of a Publishing Firm, 64
Howe, Joseph, 87, 89
The Huron Chief, 80, 81, 82
Hurtig, Mel, 157, 158

The Imperialist, 163, 164
In the Days of the Canada Company, 1825-1850, 63, 64
"The Indians," 69
Irving, John, 51, 111, 118, 119, 135
Irving, Washington, 202, 205, 207

Jack Brag in Spain, 75
Jameson, Anna, 87
Jamieson, Jean, 133, 134, 135, 136, 138
Jeanneret, Marsh, xx, 103-4, 107, 112, 114, 120, 121
Jeffares, D. Norman (Derry), 51, 133
Jefferis, J.D., 40
The Jesuit Relations, 69
Jewitt, Arthur, xvi, 42
John Richardson, 74
Johnson, A. H., 111, 135
Johnson, Thomas, 105-6
Johnston, Charles, 172
Jones, Joseph, 55, 56
Journal of Canadian Fiction, 181, 198

Kenner, Hugh, 44
Kensington Gardens in 1830, 54, 75
Kerr, Donald, 167
Kidd, Adam, 54, 61, 68, 79, 80-

83, 141, 169
Kiil, Toivo, 189-90, 191, 192
Kilbourn, William, 121, 127, 128, 135
King, William Lyon Mackenzie, 30, 31
Kirby, William, x, 24
Kirkland, Rev Samuel, 167
Klein, A.M., 52, 143
Klinck, Adam, 1, 26
Klinck, Albert, 26
Klinck, Anna, 1-4
Klinck, Carl, <u>Works</u>
  "Adam Kidd: An Early Canadian Poet," 54, 83
  "The Cacique of Ontario," 69
  Canadian Anthology, xi-xvii, 50, 62, 87-102, 104, 110, 141, 142, 197
  "The Canadian Chiefs and 'Tiger' Dunlop," 54
  "The *Chârivari* and Levi Adams" 54, 77, 185, 198
  "Early Creative Literature of Western Ontario," 63, 144
  Edwin J. Pratt, The Man and His Poetry, xvi, 45, 48
  "Formative Influences on the '1860 Group' of Poets," xiv
  "John Galt's Canadian Novels," 54, 64
  Journal of Major John Norton, 74, 166-67
  "Life in the Army 150 Years Ago," 75
  "Light in Dark Corners," 209
  "The Literary Reputation of John Galt," 55
  "Recollections of the American War of 1812-1814," 68
  Robert W. Service, xi, 185-193
  "Salvaging Our Literary Past," xv-xvi
  "Some Anonymous Literature of the War of 1812," 54, 55, 76
  Statistical Sketches of Upper Canada for the Use of Emigrants, 66, 68
  A Survey of Commonwealth Studies in Canadian Universities, 55
  Tecumseh: Fact and Fiction in Early Records, xi, xviii, 70-74
  William "Tiger" Dunlop: Blackwoodian Backwoodsman", xi, xvii, 54, 68, 110
  William Wilfred Campbell: A Study in Late Provincial Victorianism, xi, xv, 46, 110, 197
  "William Wilfred Campbell: Poet of the Lakes," xv, 34, 46
  "The World of the *Scribbler*," 181
Klinck, David, xviii, 38-39, 43
Klinck, George, 26
Klinck, Jack, 3, 4
Klinck, John, 1
Klinck, Karl, 25, 26
Klinck, Margaret (Witzel), xv, xviii, 17-18, 21-22, 24-27,

43, 44, 47, 53, 55, 126, 127, 139, 163, 164-65, 167, 168, 174, 177, 187-88, 194-95, 198
Klinck, Nicholas, 1, 26
Knopf, Alfred, 45
Knox, Canon Raymond Collyer, 6
Krapp, George Philip, 18
Kreisel, Henry, 138
Kristman, Jakob, 26
Kyte, Cockburn, 30

"The Lady of the Lake," 170
Lafitau, Joseph-François, 70
Lake Lyrics and Other Poems, 35, 69
Lamb, W. Kaye, 80, 183
Lambert, John, xii, 203, 204-5, 206, 207, 209
Lamontagne, Léopold, 132
Lampman, Archibald, 15, 38, 92, 109, 142
Lande, Lawrence, 79, 80
Landon, Frederick, 41, 63, 160
Lane, Edward, 79, 83-85, 198
Lane, Lauriat, Jr., 136
Lawrence, William Witherle, 18, 19
Lawrie Todd, 63
Leacock, Stephen, x
Leavis, F.R., 54
Lebel, Maurice, 113, 121, 131
Lee, H.D.C., 12
Léger, Jules, 198
Legrand, Albert, 132
Leprohon, Dr. J.L., 62, 160
Leprohon, Rosanna, 62, 108, 160-61
Letters from the Mountains, 69

"Letters in Canada," 105
Lewis, Anne, 184
"Lexis and Melos," xvii, 103
"The Life and Works of Mrs. Leprohon," 160
Life in the Clearing versus the Bush, 154-55
Life of Brant, 170
Life of Right Reverend, the Honourable Charles James Stewart, Second Lord Bishop of Quebec, 79, 83
Literary Garland, 59, 61, 62, 80, 160
Literary and Historical Society of Quebec Transactions, 184
The Literary History of Canada, xi, xvi, xvii, xviii-xx, xxi, xxii, 51, 54, 92, 98, 99, 101, 103-40, 141, 159, 197
Literary History of the United States, xv, xviii, 92, 103, 105-6, 111, 116
Literature in the Middle Western Frontier, xiv
"The Literature Relating to the Selkirk Controversy," 80, 181
Livesay, Dorothy, 52
Lizars, Kathleen, 63
Lizars, Robina, 63
Lochhead, Douglas, 78, 138
Lockhart, John Gibson, 65, 67, 170
Logan, J.D., x, 15, 105
Longfellow, Henry Wadsworth, 35
Longmore, George, 77, 185, 198

Longmore, Capt. John, 59
Loomis, Roger Sherman, 19
Lorne, Lord, Duke of Argyll, 34
Lossing, Benjamin J., 72-73
Lovell, John, 61
Lucas, Alec, 118, 119
The Lucubrations of Humphrey Ravelin, Esq., Late Major in the...Regiment of Infantry, 76, 77

McClelland, Jack, 151
McCool, Katherine, 96
MacCulloh, Lewis Luke, 183-84
MacDonald, Mary Lu, 77, 185, 198
MacDonald, Wilson, xiii, 16, 22-23
McDougall, Robert, 50, 51, 111, 112, 118, 120, 154-5
McGee, Thomas D'Arcy, 61, 87
MacGeorge, Rev. Robert Jackson, 66
McGuffin, Thomas, 165
McGugan, Don, 43
MacKay, Sandy, 131
MacKendrick, Louis, xvi-xvii
Mackenzie, William Lyon, 60
Maclise, Daniel, 66
MacLure, Millar, 112, 118, 119, 128-29
MacMechan, Archibald, x, 12, 45
McMullen, Lorraine, 154
McNeill, Alexander, 31-32
McPherson, Hugo, xvii, 118, 119
Macpherson, Jay, 118, 119
McRae, Fred, 209

Maginn, William, 65, 66, 67
Makers of Canadian Literature, 74, 143
The Manor House of de Villerai, 62, 160, 161
Marjorie Pickthall, A Book of Remembrance, 37
Marquis, T.G., 34
Massinger, Phillip, 183, 185
Matheson, Wallace, 71
Matthews, Brandon, 7
Mayo, Henry B., 135
Metford, Jacques, 143, 144
Miller, E. Morris, 50, 105
Millman, Thomas R., 79, 81, 83
Minifie, James N., 57
Mitchum, Peter, 121
Moodie, J.W. Dunbar, 156
Moodie, Susanna, 59, 63, 87, 108, 154-56
Morley, William F.E., 75, 78, 197
Morton, W.L., 113
Moss, John G., 181, 198
Mountain, Archdeacon G.J., 81, 82
Mountain, Bishop Jacob, 80, 82
Mullins, Rosanna Eleanor—*see* Leprohon, Rosanna
Munro, Alice, xvii
Murray, J.E., 167, 168

Neff, Emery, xv, 19, 20, 35, 36
Neville, K.P.R., 41
New, William H., xxi, 136, 137, 138, 201
New Era, 75
The Noble Savage, 11
Northumberland, Second Duke of, 167, 174

Curwood, James Oliver, 3

xvii-xviii, 53, 54, 59, 60-

Norton, Catherine, 174
Norton, John, xvi, xviii, 74, 157, 163, 166-81, 209

Oberlander, Rev. Dr. Frederick J., 6
O'Connor, Rev. Ronald, 82-83
"Ode on the Death of Bliss Carman," 22
O'Donnell, Kathleen, 161
Old Lamps Aglow, 79, 80
On Canadian Literature, 1806-1960, 160
On Canadian Poetry, xvii, 46, 50
Our Canadian Literature: Representative Verse English and French, 45
Outline of Canadian Literature, x, 12, 30, 62, 141, 145-46
Owen, Rev. Mr. John, 174, 175
Oxford Book of Canadian Verse, x

Pacey, Desmond, xii, 50, 105, 107, 108, 109, 111, 112, 115, 116, 117, 118, 119, 122, 124, 130, 131, 134, 136, 137, 151, 198, 199
Page, P.K., 52
Parker, Gilbert, 24
Patterson, Frank A., 7
Paulding, James K., 202
Pelletier, J.J. Antoine, 184
"Persona Grata—The Romantic Puritan," 38
Pickthall, Marjorie, 37-38
Pierce, Lorne, x, xiii, 12, 30, 36-38, 45, 49, 62, 64, 68, 74, 92, 110, 121, 141-8, 149, 150
Pierre and His People, 24
"A Pioneer Novelist of Kent Country," 158
Ploughman of the Moon, 187, 188, 193
The Poems of Adam Hood Burwell, 141
Poems, Chiefly Rural, 69
The Poetical Works of Mrs. Leprohon, 160
The Poetical Works of Wilfred Campbell, 30, 142
Poetry of Archibald Lampman, 12
Ponteach, 78
Potter, Alex O., 5
Pratt, Claire, 47, 153, 155-56
Pratt, E.J., xiii, xvi, xxi, 12, 13, 14, 23, 38, 45, 47-48, 49, 69, 105
Pratt, Viola, 47
"Preface to an Uncollected Anthology," xviii, 133
The Pretender, 195
Priestley, F.E.L., 119, 120
Procter, George, 76

"A Quest for National Identity, Canadian Literature vis-à-vis the Literatures of Great Britain and the United States," 101

Ralph, J.D., 113
Recollections of Literary Characters, 64
Revell, Peter, 185
The Revenge, 78
Reviews and Criticisms, 78

Rhodenizer, V.B., 143
Rich, E.E., 54
Richardson, Major John, xvi, 53, 59, 63, 68, 74-6, 87, 107, 108, 117, 153
Richardson, William, 68. 70
Riddell, William Renwick, 74
Ripley, John, 136
Ritchie, Don, 95, 97, 99
Robbins, John E., 50, 53, 105, 113, 120, 121
Roberts, Charles G.D., 13, 14-17, 89, 109, 122, 123, 142
Roberts, Lloyd, 12
Robertson, Norman, 53
Rogers, Robert, 78
Rogers, W.S., 113
Roper, Gordon, 50, 112, 115, 118, 119
Ross, Malcolm, 77, 112, 118, 119, 120, 136, 137, 151, 153
Roughing it in the Bush, 151, 154-6, 157
Roland, Dick, 168
Rusk, Ralph Leslie xiv, 18, 19, 29, 68

Salmagundi: The Whim-Whams and Opinions of Launcelot Langstaff, Esq., and Others, 202, 204, 207-9
Sandby, Paul, 206
Sangster, Charles, 117
"Sara Jeanette Duncan," 165
Scadding, Henry, 79
Scargill, M.H., 121
Schultz, Gregory, 63, 143
Scott, Duncan Campbell, 32
Scott, F.R., xii, xiii, xiv, 143, 151
Scott, Thomas, 170
Scott, Sir Walter, 170
The Scribbler, 59, 80, 181, 183, 184
Selected Poems of Wilfred Campbell, 142
Service, Doris, 185
Service, Germaine, 185-93, 195
Service, Robert William, xviii, 163, 181, 185-95, 209
Sewell, Elizabeth, 54
Shaeffe, Major General Robert H., 172, 179
Shepard, Odell, 12
Sherman, Francis, 16
Shillington, Diane, 168
Sinclair, David, 79
Smith, A.J.M., xii, xiii, xvii, 46, 49, 52, 63, 89, 95, 104-5, 112, 113, 143
Snowflakes and Sunbeams, 32
A Social Departure, 164
Spenceley, James A., 42
Spettigue, Douglas, xvii
Spiller, Robert E., 120
Spragg, George, 168
Stacey, C.P., 179
Stevenson, Lionel, x, 12, 49, 56
Stewart, Bishop Charles James, 82
Stiling, Frank, 41, 43, 121
Stratford, Philip, 127, 138
Strickland, Samuel, 63, 157
Stuart, Archdeacon G.O., 81, 174
Stuart-Stubbs, Basil, 158
Swinton, William M., 136
Sykes, W.J., 30, 142
Sylvestre, Guy, xi, 144-47, 148-

49, 150

Tait, Michael, 122
Tales of Chivalry and Romance, 77, 185, 198
Talman, James J., xi, 53, 160, 166, 167, 168, 173, 175-6, 178, 183
Tamblyn, William, 24, 42
Tecumseh, 70-4, 177
Tecumseh (Richardson's), 78
Thatcher, B.B., 72
This Canada of Ours and Other Poems, 12
Thomas, Clara, 87, 136, 138, 142, 154, 198
Thompson, Francis, 195
Thomson, James S., 121, 135
Thomson, Katharine, 64
"Tiger" Dunlop's Upper Canada, 151
A Topographical Dictionary of the Province of Lower Canada, 83
Toye, William, 203
Travels through Lower Canada, and the United States of North America in the Years 1806, 1807 and 1808, 203, 205, 206, 207, 208
Traill, Catharine Parr, 63, 154-55, 158
Tredrey, F.D., 64
Twenty-Seven Years in Canada's West, 63, 157

The Unknown or Lays of the Forest, 83
University of Toronto Quarterly, 105

Verner, Robert, 87, 89, 90-91, 94

Wacousta (also called *The Prophet*), 68, 74, 77, 78-9, 151, 153
Wallace, W. S., 80, 181-182, 209
"Wanted—Canadian Criticism," xvii
Ward, Edmund, xii, 203, 204
War of 1812 with Notes and a Life of the Author, 68, 74, 75, 76
Waterston, Elizabeth, 122, 126, 128, 197
Watt, Frank, 111, 118, 119, 121, 193, 194
Watters, Beth, 100-101
Watters, Reg, xii, xiv, xvi-xvii, xviii, 50, 51, 62, 87-102, 104, 105, 106, 107-11, 112, 113, 114, 116, 118, 119, 120-1, 142, 160, 165, 199
Wees, Wilfred, 93, 95
Weiller, Irmgard, 99
Wells, Henry W., xiv, xv, xvi, 19, 20, 36, 37, 45, 46, 47, 48, 51-2, 55, 105, 110, 143, 199
Wells, Katharine, 47, 199
Westbrook the Outlaw, 79
Westmacott, Charles Malloy, 66
Whalley, George, 112, 113
White, Mr., 84
The White Savannahs, 23, 46
The White Stone Canoe: A Legend of the Ottawas, 12

Wilcocke, Samuel Hull, x, xii, 59-60, 80, 163, 181, 182, 183-85, 203, 209
Wiles, Roy, 121, 131
Wilkenson, Henry C., 204
Williams, E.T., 185, 186
Willison, Rev. Nils, 5
Wilson, Adam, 169, 173
Wilson, Jean, 134, 137, 139
Wilson, John, 65
Wilson, Tuzo, 204
Windsor, Kenneth N., 122, 136
Wismer, Sally, 137
Woodcock, George, 112, 135
Woodhouse, A.S.P., xiii, xiv, 50, 52, 105, 106, 113, 114, 120
Woodley, E.C., 175
World Literature in English, 56
The World of Washington Irving, 202
Wright, Ernest Hunter, 7, 18, 19, 68
Wyczynski, Paul, 132

Young, Edward, 78

Zaslow, Maurice, 167

CANADA FIRST

p.12   Sir James David Edgar — 12 Apostles of "CANADA FIRST"
         father of Pelham Edgar

p.15   — Charles G.D. Roberts — CANADA FIRST

IMPERIAL FEDERATION LEAGUE

p.31   William King & Wilfred Campbell
p.32